The New American Vegetable Cookbook

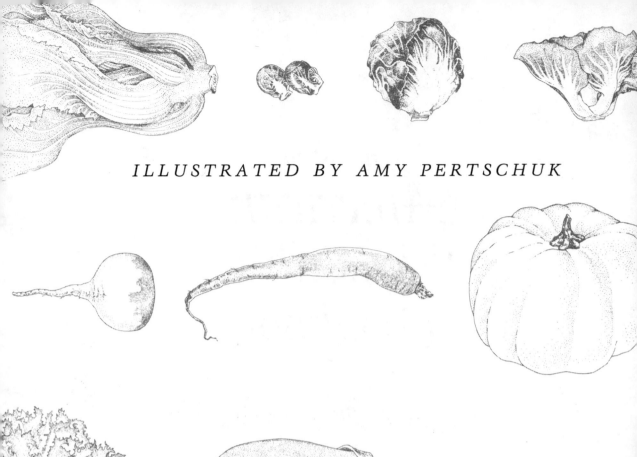

ILLUSTRATED BY AMY PERTSCHUK

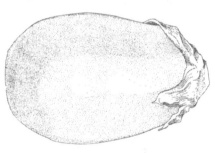

ARIS BOOKS

ADDISON-WESLEY PUBLISHING COMPANY, INC.

Reading, Massachusetts   Menlo Park, California   New York
Don Mills, Ontario   Wokingham, England   Amsterdam   Bonn
Sydney   Singapore   Tokyo   Madrid   San Juan

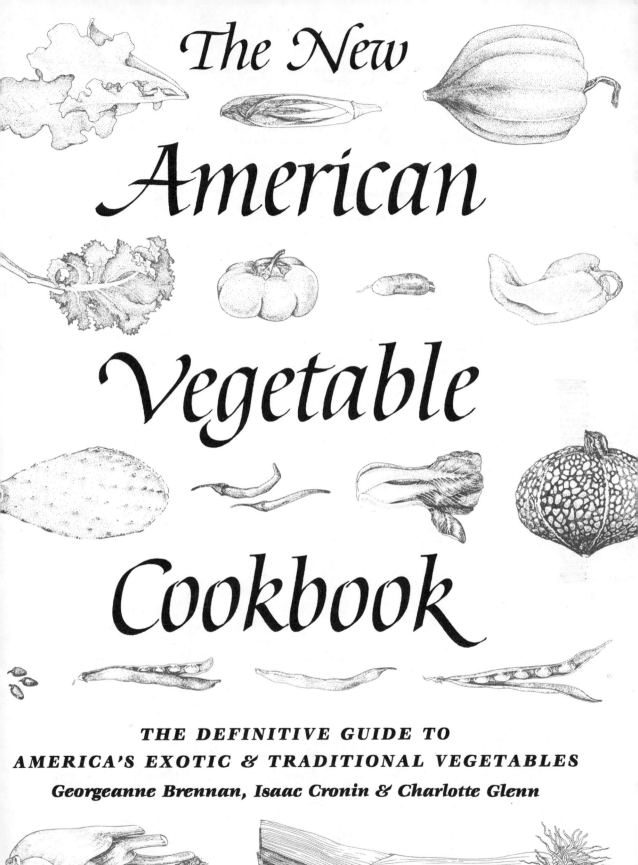

The New
American
Vegetable
Cookbook

THE DEFINITIVE GUIDE TO
AMERICA'S EXOTIC & TRADITIONAL VEGETABLES

Georgeanne Brennan, Isaac Cronin & Charlotte Glenn

Library of Congress Cataloging-in-Publication Data

Brennan, Georgeanne, 1943–
    The new American vegetable cookbook: the definitive guide to
  America's exotic & traditional vegetables/Georgeanne Brennan,
  Isaac Cronin & Charlotte Glenn; illustrated by Amy Partschuk.
      p.   cm.
  Bibliography: p.
  Includes index.
  ISBN 0-201-19182-2
    1. Cookery (Vegetables)   2. Cookery, American.   I. Cronin, Isaac,
  1948–   .   II. Glenn, Charlotte, 1943–   .   III. Title,
  TX801.B695   1988
  841.6′5 – oc 19   88-39467
                                              CIP

(Previously published by
Harris Publishing Co.,
ISBN 0-943186-24-2 and
ISBN 0-943186-25-0, pbk.)

Aris Books Editorial Office
and Test Kitchen
1621 Fifth Street
Berkeley, CA 94710

Book design by Jeanne Jambu and Kajun Graphics
Edited by Carolyn Miller
Typeset by Artype
Calligraphy by John Prestianni

ABCDEFGHIJ-VB-898
First Addison-Wesley printing, October 1988

CONTENTS

ACKNOWLEDGMENTS

*T*he authors would like to thank the many people who made contributions to this book.

A wealth of information was contributed by experts including: Charles Bettencourt of Sunset Produce; Tom Chino of Chino Ranch; Bill Fujimoto of Monterey Foods; Tom Jacobs; David Jeffery of Sharpes Seed Company; Patty Johnson of Berry Hill Herb Farm; Sibella Kraus of Greenleaf Produce; Marie Palazolli; Achille Perini; Warren Roberts of the University of California at Davis; Hans Van Der Meer; Norman Weir of Nature's Bounty; Sandra Leftoff; Mary Anne Pohl.

Our editors, Carolyn Miller and Mimi Luebbermann, supplied invaluable support and guidance. Jeanne Jambu brought visual order and clarity with her elegant graphic design. Amy Pertshuk contributed the stunningly accurate drawings that are an essential part of this book.

And our publisher, John Harris, supplied much of the initial impetus for the book, gave us the liberty to organize the subject in the way we felt appropriate, and provided us a wonderful kitchen in which to test our recipes.

ILLUSTRATED INDEX

Asparagus   **Cabbage Family**

page 39

Chinese Broccoli
page 44

Flat Cabbage
page 46

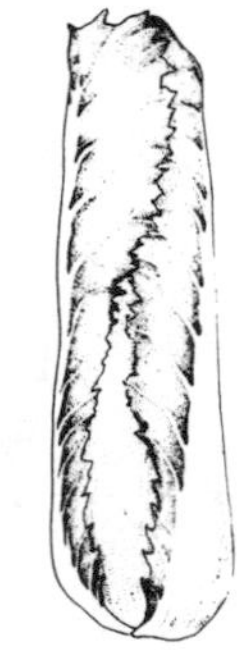

Michili Cabbage
page 46

Flowering White Cabbage
page 46

Nappa Cabbage
page 47

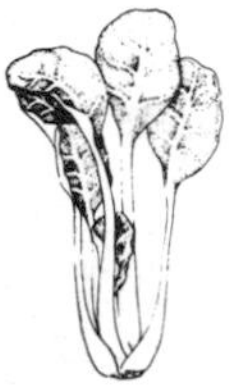

Tai Sai
page 48

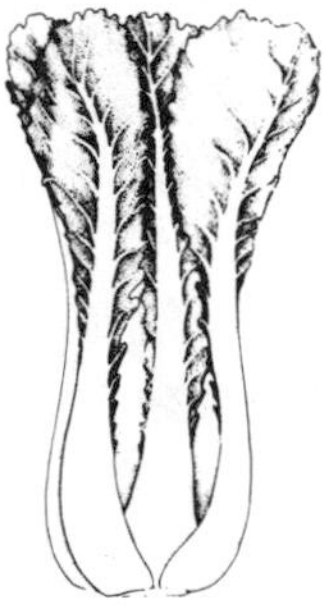

Pak Choy
page 48

Chinese Mustard
page 50

Chinese Mustard Leaf
page 50

Chinese Broad Mustard
page 50

Broccoli
page 52

Brussels Sprout
page 54

Cabbage
page 56

Savoy Cabbage
page 57

Cauliflower
page 59

Cima di Rapa
page 62

Common Cress
page 64

Watercress
page 65

Horseradish
page 67

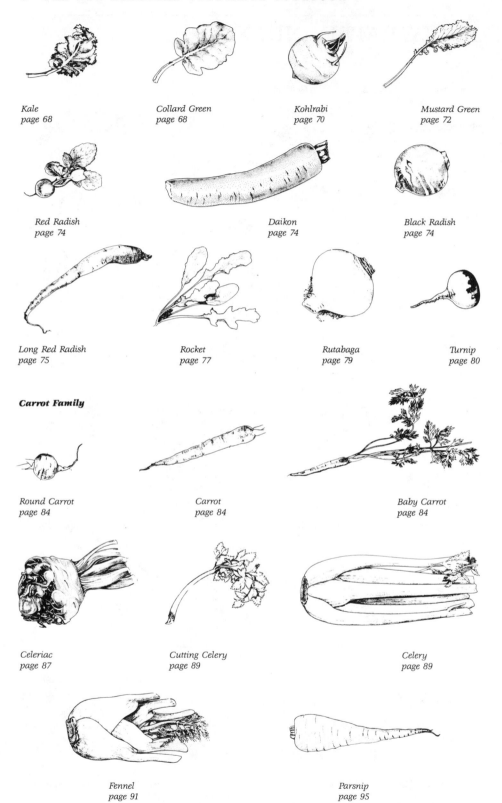

Kale
page 68

Collard Green
page 68

Kohlrabi
page 70

Mustard Green
page 72

Red Radish
page 74

Daikon
page 74

Black Radish
page 74

Long Red Radish
page 75

Rocket
page 77

Rutabaga
page 79

Turnip
page 80

Carrot Family

Round Carrot
page 84

Carrot
page 84

Baby Carrot
page 84

Celeriac
page 87

Cutting Celery
page 89

Celery
page 89

Fennel
page 91

Parsnip
page 95

Corn   **Goosefoot Family**

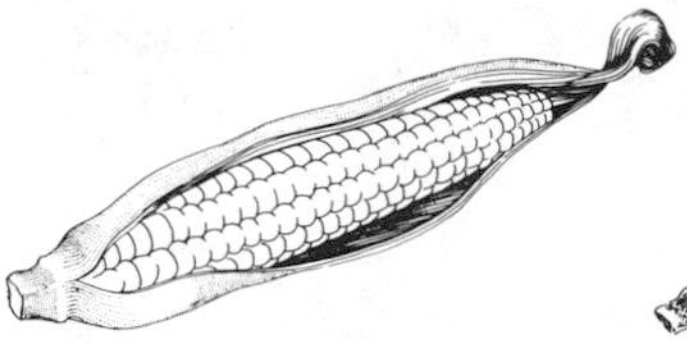

Corn
page 97

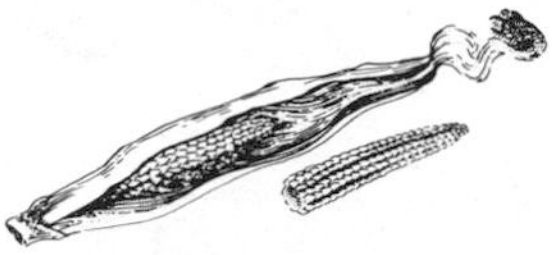

Baby Corn
page 97

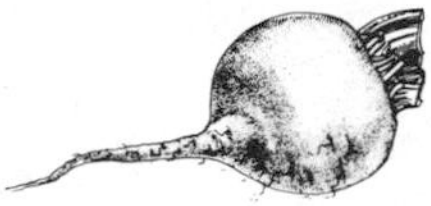

Beet
page 102

Beet Green
page 102

Chard
page 105

Spinach
page 108

Ceylon Spinach
page 112

Chinese Spinach
page 113

New Zealand Spinach
page 114

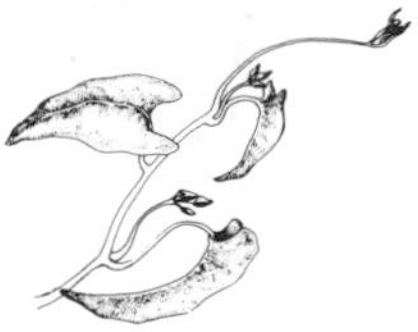

Water Spinach
page 115

Gourd Family

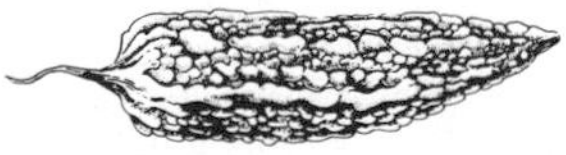

Bitter Melon
page 118

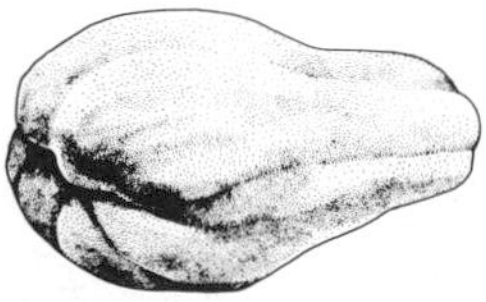

Chayote
page 120

West Indian Gherkin
page 122

Cornichon
page 122

Dill Cucumber
page 122

Lemon Cucumber
page 123

English Cucumber
page 123

Green Market Cucumber
page 123

Crookneck Squash
page 127

Zucchini
page 127

White or Yellow Zucchini
page 127

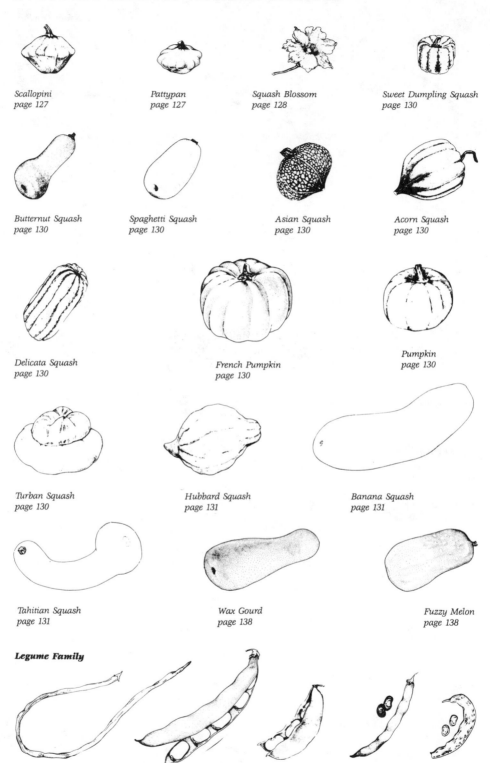

Scallopini
page 127

Pattypan
page 127

Squash Blossom
page 128

Sweet Dumpling Squash
page 130

Butternut Squash
page 130

Spaghetti Squash
page 130

Asian Squash
page 130

Acorn Squash
page 130

Delicata Squash
page 130

French Pumpkin
page 130

Pumpkin
page 130

Turban Squash
page 130

Hubbard Squash
page 131

Banana Squash
page 131

Tahitian Squash
page 131

Wax Gourd
page 138

Fuzzy Melon
page 138

Legume Family

Chinese Long Bean
page 143

Fava Bean
page 146

Lima Bean
page 149

Runner Bean
page 151

Coco Bean
page 152

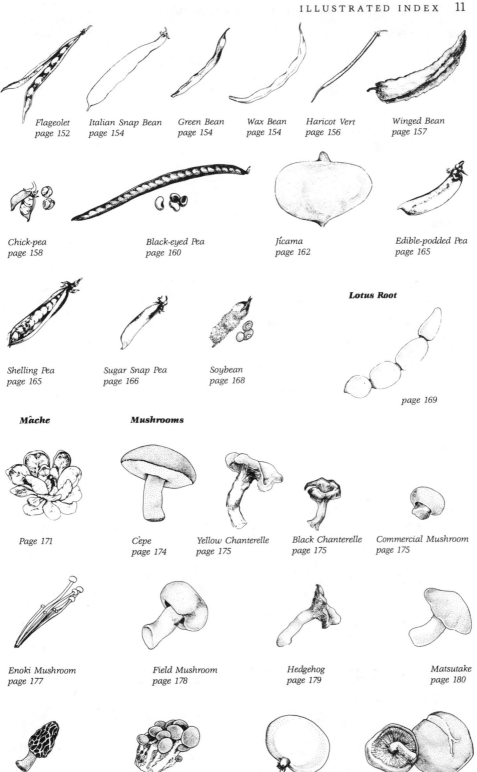

Flageolet
page 152

Italian Snap Bean
page 154

Green Bean
page 154

Wax Bean
page 154

Haricot Vert
page 156

Winged Bean
page 157

Chick-pea
page 158

Black-eyed Pea
page 160

Jícama
page 162

Edible-podded Pea
page 165

Shelling Pea
page 165

Sugar Snap Pea
page 166

Soybean
page 168

Lotus Root

page 169

Mâche

Mushrooms

Page 171

Cèpe
page 174

Yellow Chanterelle
page 175

Black Chanterelle
page 175

Commercial Mushroom
page 175

Enoki Mushroom
page 177

Field Mushroom
page 178

Hedgehog
page 179

Matsutake
page 180

Morel
page 181

Oyster Mushroom
page 182

Puffball Mushroom
page 183

Shiitake
page 184

Nightshade Family

White (Thai)
Eggplant
page 193

Tiny White Pickling (Chinese)
Eggplant
page 193

Long Purple (Japanese)
Eggplant
page 193

Eggplant
page 194

Ground Cherry
Page 198

Bell Pepper
page 200

Bulls's Horn Pepper
page 201

Cubanelle Pepper
page 201

Japanese Green Pepper
page 202

Pimiento Pepper
page 202

Lamuyo Pepper
page 203

Anaheim Pepper
page 204

Ancho Pepper
page 205

Thai Pepper
page 206

Cayenne Pepper
page 206

Jalapeño Pepper
page 207

Paprika Pepper
page 208

Pasilla Pepper
page 209

Pequin Pepper
page 210

Serrano Pepper
Page 210

Russet Potato
page 215

Fingerling Potato
page 215

Red Potato
page 215

Tomatillo
page 220

Tomato
page 222

Sauce Tomato
page 224

Cherry Tomato
page 224

Slicing Tomato
page 225

Yellow Tomato
page 225

Nopales   **Okra**   **Onion Family**

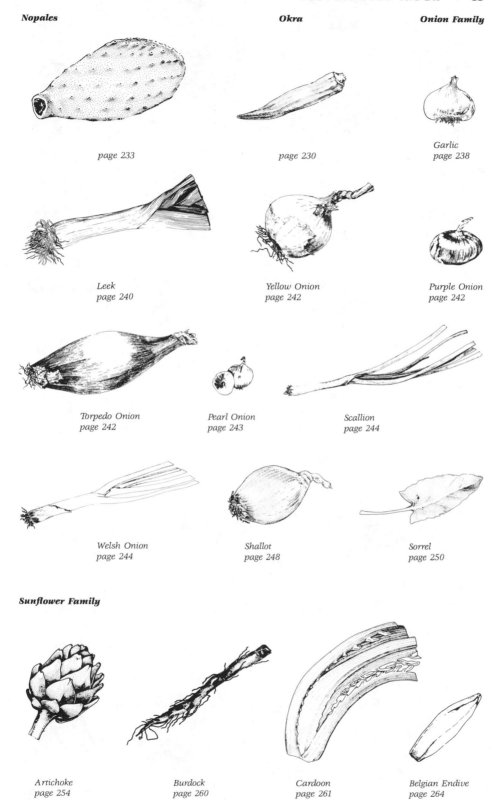

page 233   page 230   Garlic
                                                           page 238

Leek   Yellow Onion   Purple Onion
page 240   page 242   page 242

Torpedo Onion   Pearl Onion   Scallion
page 242   page 243   page 244

Welsh Onion   Shallot   Sorrel
page 244   page 248   page 250

Sunflower Family

Artichoke   Burdock   Cardoon   Belgian Endive
page 254   page 260   page 261   page 264

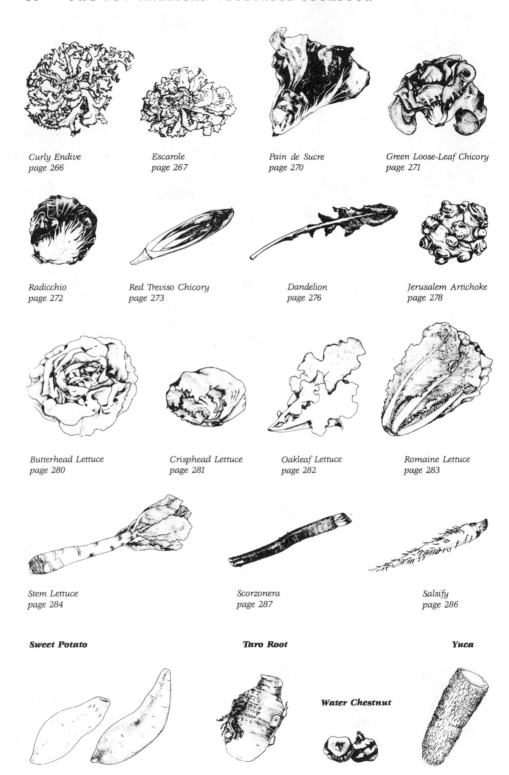

Curly Endive
page 266

Escarole
page 267

Pain de Sucre
page 270

Green Loose-Leaf Chicory
page 271

Radicchio
page 272

Red Treviso Chicory
page 273

Dandelion
page 276

Jerusalem Artichoke
page 278

Butterhead Lettuce
page 280

Crisphead Lettuce
page 281

Oakleaf Lettuce
page 282

Romaine Lettuce
page 283

Stem Lettuce
page 284

Scorzonera
page 287

Salsify
page 286

Sweet Potato

Taro Root

Yuca

Water Chestnut

Sweet Potato
page 288

Yam
page 288

page 291

page 293

page 295

AN ALPHABETICAL LIST OF VEGETABLES

Following is a list of the major categories of vegetables in this book. Specific vegetables within the categories are listed in the general index.

FOREWORD

One spring day in 1982, two schoolteachers from Dixon, California, came to visit me at the Wholesale Produce Market in Los Angeles. They had decided to go into business for themselves and felt that what they planned to do might have an effect on my business, which is the merchandising and wholesaling of unusual produce.

And that is just what happened. Georgeanne Brennan and Charlotte Glenn, in forming Le Marché, one of the country's most reliable sources of top-quality seeds, have had a real impact in the world of fresh produce.

Their timing couldn't have been better. With the fitness and health movement encouraging people to eat "fresh," variety in food is becoming more important all the time. Superior-quality seeds for vegetables such as rocket, *haricots verts*, *radicchio*, *mâche*, and lots of other European, American, and Asian varieties that have been showing up at top restaurants and on the produce stands of markets around the country are now available via mail order—fully guaranteed—from their innovative seed company.

Enter Isaac Cronin, author of several fine cookbooks. Isaac recruited Georgeanne and Charlotte to work with him on a book that he and his publisher wanted to be the definitive guide to America's growing vegetable bounty. *The New American Vegetable Cookbook* is that book. The authors' enthusiasm for fresh vegetables shows up in this storylike guide. They generate the reader's interest in trying new recipes, incorporating both the familiar and unfamiliar. I like it because it is fun to read, full of accurate up-to-date information, and it is never boring. Best of all, it is not over-whelming but can be enjoyed by experts and amateurs alike.

As a merchandiser and wholesaler of unusual fresh produce, I get questions daily on every aspect of produce from growers, retailers, chefs, and consumers in every part of the North American continent. What is it? Where can I buy it? How do I cook it? There is a growing interest in produce and especially in better-quality produce of all types. The buying public is demanding more and more information. *The New American Vegetable Cookbook* is just what they are looking for.

—Frieda Caplan
Frieda's Finest/Produce Specialties
Los Angeles, California

INTRODUCTION

At a time when shoppers are confronted with an ever-increasing number of vegetables in the produce sections of supermarkets, there is a need for a cookbook that not only serves as a guide to the many new vegetables for sale but also inspires the cook to use them successfully. Cooks are confronted with mysteries in the market nearly every week. On your trips to the produce section you have probably often asked yourself: What is this vegetable? What does it taste like? How do I prepare it? We have tried to answer these questions for the entire range of vegetables currently available to American cooks.

Today, with so many new cookbooks to choose from, a title must communicate the content of a book concisely and accurately in order to attract the audience for which it is written. *The New American Vegetable Cookbook* is *new* because it deals with the increasing diversity of vegetables available in our markets from the United States and from all over the world. *The New American Vegetable Cookbook* is *American* because its culinary approach, like our culture in general, is eclectic. New immigration patterns have brought many Asian and Latin American peoples to our country along with their cuisines. At the same time there is a greater appreciation of America's bounty. Regional cuisines have come to the fore, emphasizing fresh, local ingredients and a heightened awareness of seasonal availability.

Although this is a vegetable cookbook, it is not a vegetarian cookbook. Some recipes use meat in a way that reflects the current trend toward the use of less meat in the diet. Now that Americans are becoming aware of the effects of too much fat in the diet, many cooks are using meat as a flavorful accent rather than as a main ingredient. Some of our main-course dishes show this new balance, with vegetables predominating. Most of the salads and a good number of the main-course dishes in this book are vegetarian.

One of the most delightful things about vegetables is their texture. We have tried in our recipes to conserve both the texture and the nutritional qualities of vegetables, so simple and quick cooking techniques are emphasized. These techniques are well suited to the time-conscious lifestyle of many Americans who want to minimize the amount of time they spend in the kitchen without sacrificing the quality of what they eat. Techniques are outlined in the Cooking Methods section.

American cooks are actively interested in where their food comes from as well as how it can be prepared. We have set up the book to facilitate this broader approach to our subject. The main body of the book is organized as an encyclopedia. Listings are organized alphabetically according to the common name of the botanical family (vegetables that are the only culinary member of a family are interspersed alphabetically among the families). Each family is introduced with a brief essay that describes the botanical characteristics common to all members of the family. Historical, horticultural, and culinary information is presented for each vegetable, followed by a box that lists its common names, how it is grown, its seasonal availability, its peak of freshness, and how to prepare it for cooking. The entries include vegetables commonly available fresh in urban produce markets and supermarkets as well as in specialty shops. We have not included legumes that are sold only dried, or herbs, except those that can also be prepared as a vegetable. Recipes and cooking suggestions follow the boxes. To make the book easier to use we have provided an alphabetical list of vegetables (page 15) as well as a general index.

An increasing number of Americans are finding that the best guarantee of quality is to grow part of what they eat. Thus suggestions are provided for the gardener, though this book is not intended as a gardening companion. We have limited gardening information to that which can be used by urban as well as backyard gardeners and to facts of general interest to all cooks.

The third section of the book is a miscellany that includes tips on grilling vegetables, recipes for a summer feast, and information on new trends in vegetables.

Even as we were finishing this project we began to hear of newly available vegetables that had not been included. Such omissions are unavoidable, given the rapidly expanding produce market in America. Still, if we can make the broad range of currently available vegetables more accessible to interested cooks, our purpose in writing this book will have been achieved.

A Cook's
Introduction to
Vegetables

Part I

TIPS FOR BUYING AND HANDLING VEGETABLES

Really Fresh

It is much easier to describe a vegetable when it is not fresh than to tell how it looks at its peak. Bill Fujimoto of Monterey Market in Berkeley, California, describes a fresh vegetable as one that "looks alive, like it was just picked." The most universal signs of freshness are a bright sheen and true, vibrant colors. Purple cabbage, for example, is really purple, not a washed-out shade.

Buying Seasonal Vegetables

Seasonal buying of produce has two distinct advantages:

1. The vegetables are at their peak of flavor, texture, and freshness.

2. You enjoy the lowest prices. Zucchini is cheap in mid-August because it is plentiful, not because it is of poor quality and therefore priced to sell quickly. Vegetables are at their best when they are the most available.

Storing Vegetables

We have always marveled at the organization of some cooks, as exemplified by the Tupperware demonstrator who washes and preps all her vegetables a week prior to using them. She organizes them in sequential fashion in airtight containers, color-coded by day. All this is fine and dandy—except that most cooks don't do this, or want to. But it is also true that while most cooks strive to use very fresh ingredients, most of us do need to store fresh vegetables for several days at a time. The question then arises: What is the best way to store vegetables?

1. Some vegetables are best left out of the refrigerator, as the cold air causes their starches to turn to sugars and their textures to change. The classic example is the potato, but onions, shallots, and garlic also fall into this category. A cool dry shelf in a darkened room with plenty of air circulation makes an ideal spot for storage of these vegetables. Tomatoes that are not fully ripened are best left on a windowsill for further maturation.

2. Almost all other vegetables are best refrigerated. Leafy greens seem to store best when they are washed and dried, then put in plastic bags. See page 284 for information on proper washing and drying of leafy greens.

3. Bulky vegetables such as carrots, beans, celery, and cucumbers may be stored in the refrigerator in plastic bags or covered containers for a few days, then washed when prepping. In all cases, watch out for the drying tendencies that frost-free refrigerators seem to have—food should be covered to protect it from the circulating draft set up inside.

4. A few vegetables do well with their cut stems or tips kept in water. Parsley and cilantro should be arranged upright, much like a bouquet, in a glass of water and kept on the kitchen counter. Change the water daily. Tiny root crops such as radishes, baby carrots, and turnips may be bundled together root tips down and placed in ice water.

Peeling Vegetables

Occasionally it's handy to peel vegetables well ahead of the time you plan to use them. Be aware that some vegetables, notably the roots, tend to discolor as a result of oxidation of the exposed tissues. Have handy an acid water bath made from vinegar or lemon juice and water (proportions are 1 tablespoon acidic liquid to 1 quart water. Some vegetables will ooze fluids if cut ahead of time. Stem lettuce, *nopales*, and salsify are cases in point. It's nothing really to worry about—just make sure the vegetable you're handling is placed in a container.

Crisping and Salting Vegetables

Some vegetables are traditionally crisped in ice water ahead of time. Radishes, kohlrabis, cucumbers, celery, and carrots respond to icing if you want a crispy result. On the other hand, some vegetables, such as eggplants, zucchinis, and cucumbers, have traditionally been salted prior to their use. The salt draws out moisture from the tissues, and as it does, some bitterness seems to come out with the moisture. Older cookbooks mention salting as a prep method more frequently than recent cookbooks. Recent developments in both culture and types of vegetables have resulted in less-bitter types, and there is a new concern regarding salt in the diet.

Cooking Vegetables

A friend of ours told us of how he went to dinner in a chic *nouvelle cuisine* restaurant in New York City and was served a salad with *al dente* beets. When he tried to pick one up with a fork, it skidded across his plate and onto the floor. Our friend was not amused, and he quickly abandoned his salad, which had become altogether too much work.

The traditional American approach to vegetables has been to overcook them mercilessly. The currently fashionable *al dente* school, however, inspired to a great extent by Chinese wok cooking, favors minimal or sometimes undercooking of most vegetables.

The *New York Times* recently devoted considerable space to defining a "properly cooked" vegetable as opposed to a "tender" or "firm" one. Their compromise formulation ruled out the *al dente* tendency but suffered from the weakness of all such broad generalizations: the exceptions probably outnumbered the appropriate applications. There are so many types of vegetables with such varied cooking characteristics, it is best to treat each one individually on a recipe-by-recipe basis, and this is what we have done.

COOKING METHODS

*I*n this section we discuss how to execute a number of techniques for cooking vegetables. We have not included sautéing (essentially the same technique as stir-frying except that it is done in a sauté pan or skillet instead of a wok and usually without a thickener), braising or stewing, baking and blanching (not to be confused with the agricultural technique for lightening the color of vegetables), because most Americans are familiar with these approaches. Individual recipes supply any additional information beyond what is traditionally called for with these techniques.

Deep-frying

Probably the most troublesome of all cooking techniques for the home cook, deep-frying can be mastered with a little attention to details. And the details are worth observing, because the difference between a perfectly prepared deep-fried dish and a total disaster can be just one small operation poorly performed. Deep-frying is usually done in a deep-fryer with a basket or in a wok with a fine mesh scoop to handle the food.

1. Cut foods into uniform-sized pieces so they will cook evenly. Food should be at room temperature when it is deep-fried so it will decrease the temperature of the oil as little as possible when it is added. Food should also be thoroughly dry, as water and oil are an explosive combination.

2. When applying a batter, handle the food as little as possible, because you increase the chance of losing some of the batter with every extra movement.

3. Start with clean, good-quality vegetable oil. If you are reusing oil, be sure to strain out any particles that remain from the last use. Usable oil is golden rather than dark brown. Meat or fish imparts more of an odor to oil than do vegetables like potatoes, and oil used to cook meat or fish should be changed more frequently.

4. Heat oil to the desired temperature, usually in the 350° to 375° range. It's more accurate to use a candy thermometer to determine temperature, rather than tossing a drop of water in and waiting for the sizzle. Oil temperature is important: too cool and the food will absorb too much oil and become soggy; too hot and it will burn on the outside while remaining uncooked in the middle.

5. Fry a small batch of food at a time. A large quantity will lower the temperature of the oil appreciably. Skim off any loose bits of batter or vegetable while you cook.

6. Remove excess oil by placing the fried food on paper towels. It's best to serve deep-fried foods immediately. If this is not possible, a feasible alternative is to quickly re-fry the food just before you serve it. Strain the oil before saving it.

Grilling

Both tools and timing are very important to proper grilling. For tips on grilling specific vegetables, see page 299.

1. Begin with a clean, well-oiled grill.

2. Use a good fuel—mesquite charcoal and hardwoods burn clean and hot, which cannot be said for most commercial charcoal briquets—and make a hot fire, but one without an open flame.

3. Have all foods at room temperature.

4. Preheat the grill for at least 5 minutes.

5. Handle the food as little as possible, using a good set of tongs (spring-loaded commercial tongs are best).

6. Overcooking is the most common mistake in grilling. The best way to avoid it is to systematically experiment and learn the cooking times for individual foods.

7. Serve grilled foods immediately, as both the aroma and the mystique disappear quickly.

Steaming

Steaming is a simple technique that can be done with a broad range of equipment. A steaming basket set in a pot over boiling water, a plate on a metal steamer tray or a bamboo steaming rack in a wok, and a saucepan with a little liquid in the bottom all produce similar results: moist, tender steamed foods. In all cases, the water should be boiling before the food is added to the steamer, and the steamer should be covered while the food cooks. Overcooking is probably the most common mistake—foods cook quite rapidly even though they are not immersed in liquid—and it is important to check frequently, especially if you are new to this technique.

Stir-frying

Classic stir-frying consists of cooking food over high heat in a wok, first in oil, then with the addition of some liquid to make a sauce. Careful preparation is necessary because the total cooking time is usually less than five minutes. All the ingredients must be prepared ahead of time so they can be added to the wok quickly. The amount of oil should be ample, and foods should be stirred almost continuously so they cook evenly. Some advance cooking may be necessary before stir-frying: blanching helps seal in flavor, and sometimes vegetables are steamed before they are stir-fried.

A typical step-by-step procedure:

1. Cut ingredients the proper size (bite-sized in nearly all cases) so they will cook quickly. Slicing vegetables on the diagonal increases their surface area and speeds up cooking.

2. Arrange the ingredients near the wok so they can be added at the right moment.

3. First, cook seasonings such as garlic, ginger, peppers, then remove them from the wok with a slotted spoon so they won't overcook; they will be returned to the wok later.

4. Cook meat and fish, if any, until nearly done, then remove them from the wok with a slotted spoon.

5. Cook vegetables until nearly done, adding the longest-cooking vegetable first. A bit of liquid may be added at this point to keep the vegetables from sticking to the wok. The wok can be covered to shorten cooking time.

6. Return the meat or fish to the wok.

7. Add the previously cooked seasonings and sauce ingredients and, finally, cornstarch dissolved in liquid if called for. Serve the dish as soon as the cornstarch solution has slightly thickened the sauce and become translucent.

SPECIAL INGREDIENTS

Americans are using a broader range of ingredients today and demanding more information about them than ever before. The knowledgeable cook is better able to execute a dish because he or she understands how ingredients are combined and how appropriate substitutions may be made.

Our point of view is that quality is essential. We choose quality over authenticity nearly every time; for us it is usually better to use a first-rate substitute than a mediocre version of the listed ingredient. Fortunately, with the increased demand for quality ingredients most urban cooks can find what they need fairly easily.

This glossary contains descriptions of uncommon ingredients as well as clarifications on our use of widely available foods. Sources for hard-to-find ingredients are listed.

Aji Pon Vinegar: A Japanese vinegar that contains soy sauce. Available at Asian groceries.

Black Beans, Salted: A salted, dried product produced in China. The key ingredient in black bean sauce, it is sold in small plastic bags. Quality does not vary greatly from brand to brand. It keeps indefinitely in the refrigerator in a sealed container. Available in Asian groceries and the special-ingredients section of supermarkets.

Butter: We use unsalted butter in all recipes. It is easy to add salt to a dish and impossible to take it out.

Chicken Stock: Stock for Western recipes can be made by slowly cooking wings and backs along with vegetables such as carrots, celery, and yellow onion, and fresh or dried herbs such as parsley, oregano, and thyme. Stock for Asian recipes can be made from chicken parts, scallions, and ginger slices. The fat should be removed before using.

Coconut Milk: A thick unsweetened liquid made from the pulp of the coconut. It is sold canned in Asian groceries and in the specialty section of some supermarkets.

Cream: Heavy cream, whole cream, and whipping cream are the same thing, and they all contain at least 10 percent butterfat.

Crème Fraîche: A thick cream made by adding buttermilk to heavy cream and letting it mature overnight. It has a nutty, slightly sour flavor, and is perfect for sauces that need to be reduced, since *crème fraîche* does not separate when boiled. It is available in gourmet food shops and in the specialty section of some supermarkets. To make your own, add 2 tablespoons of buttermilk to ½ cup of heavy cream. Cover and store overnight in a warm place with a temperature of 85° to 90°.

Curry Leaves: An herb grown in India and parts of Southeast Asia and imported dried to the United States. It resembles a bay leaf, though the flavor is milder. Available in Asian groceries.

Dried Shrimp: Tiny shrimp sold in clear plastic packages. They are widely used in Asia, West Asia, West Africa, and Brazil. They will keep indefinitely in a sealed container. There is no substitute for them. Available in Asian and Latin groceries.

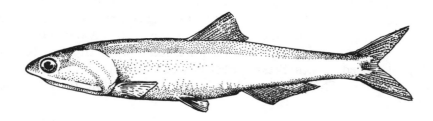

Fish Sauce: Used like soy sauce in much of Southeast Asia. Made from salted anchovies, the end result is a clear, amber, salty liquid. Quality varies greatly, so get the most expensive brand (which is not all that expensive). There is no substitute. Available in Asian groceries and in the specialty section of some supermarkets.

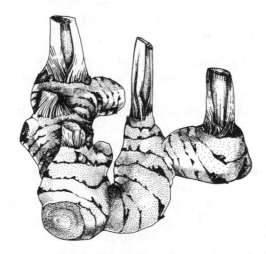

Galangal: Also known as Thai ginger, Laos root, or Java root. A rhizome occasionally available fresh in the United States. It is also sold dried in slices or powdered in some Asian groceries. There is no substitute.

Ginger: A rhizome that is used in its fresh form and is also dried and ground to produce the spice of the same name. Most of our recipes call for fresh ginger. Young ginger is fresh ginger picked before it has reached maturity. Its flavor is milder and its appearance quite marked: the rhizome is white with pink-tipped shoots. Fresh ginger is sold in many supermarkets and Asian groceries. The young variety is usually available only in Asian markets.

Goat Cheese: Domestic cheeses tend to be fresher and less salty than the imported brands. Goat cheese is delicate and should not be overcooked. Feta—sheep's milk cheese—is generally stronger, saltier, less creamy, and not really a substitute. Available in gourmet food shops, cheese shops, and the specialty section of some supermarkets.

Lemon Grass: This grass, which resembles the scallion, is an essential ingredient in many Southeast Asian dishes and is now grown in the United States. It is discarded after cooking. The flavor is citrus and floral. There is no substitute. Available in some Asian groceries and a few produce shops. Dried lemon grass can be used in cooking. It is also used as a tea, and is sold in health food stores.

Oil: In our recipes *oil* indicates a tasteless or nearly tasteless oil such as peanut, safflower, corn, or sunflower. Cold-pressed oils are generally of higher quality and are more expensive. Peanut oil is most common in Asia, though the others also work well in Asian recipes. A number of nut oils are now used for salads, among them hazelnut, walnut, and almond. Their delicate flavors are destroyed by heating.

Olive Oil: Olive oil quality varies greatly and labels are often misleading. In Spain, Italy, and France designations are by level of acidity, the less acid the better. The best rating is *extra virgin*. In other countries *extra virgin* may not indicate low acidity, since there is no government supervision of labeling. Olive oil loses its flavor when heated above 140 °. Therefore, extra-fine oils (top-quality oils from Italy, Spain, and France) should be added to dishes that will not be cooked or after they have been cooked. A less expensive but good-quality oil should be used for cooking. Extra-fine oils are usually available in gourmet food shops.

Oyster Sauce: A salty sauce made from an oyster reduction. An important ingredient in Cantonese cooking. More expensive oyster sauces are generally of higher quality. There is no substitute. Available in Asian groceries and in the specialty section of some supermarkets.

Rice Flour: A finely ground flour milled from rice. It is sold sweetened and unsweetened. Rice flour can be made into a very light batter. Cornstarch may be substituted for it in some recipes. Available in Asian groceries and in the specialty section of some supermarkets.

Sesame Oil: There are two kinds of sesame oil. The cooking oil is cold-pressed from raw sesame seeds and is sold in health food stores. Our recipes call for Asian sesame oil, which is a strong flavoring agent made from toasted sesame seeds. This oil should be added after cooking, as its smoky flavor is destroyed by heat. Available in Asian groceries and in the specialty section of some supermarkets.

Shao Hsing: Dry rice wine made in China. Dry sherry is an acceptable substitute.

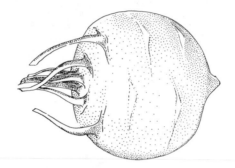

Sichuan Preserved Vegetable: A cabbage family member, probably kohlrabi, dry-pickled with dried ground peppers and salt. It is very salty, and must be rinsed. When boiled with water it makes a delicious broth.

Soy Sauce, Light, Medium, and Dark: The Chinese make both light and dark soy sauce, used similarly to white and red wines. The two are very similar in taste. Light soy sauce is used with most vegetables. Root vegetables and eggplant can be caramelized with dark soy sauce. Japanese soy sauces, though unlabeled, are closer to light than dark. We have labeled them medium. Available in Asian groceries and in the specialty section of some supermarkets.

Turmeric: This orange-colored rhizome is related to ginger. When cooked it produces the distinctive yellow color common to curry powder. Fresh turmeric is increasingly available in the United States, mostly in Asian markets. It has a distinctive sweet barklike flavor. Dried turmeric is a passable substitute, though it has none of the sweetness of the fresh variety.

Vinegars: A few years ago the vinegar selection at most stores was small. There were wine vinegars (red, white, and sherry); cider vinegar; distilled vinegar; and a few odd bottles. Today the choice is staggering. There are wine vinegars of many varietal grapes, fruit vinegars, rice vinegars, and more. A few guidelines: wine vinegar and olive oil make the classic vinaigrette. Asian ingredients mix well with milder vinegars such as rice wine vinegar and distilled vinegar. Fruit vinegars complement some foods, particularly salads with meat. Our choices of vinegars and oils for vinaigrettes are fairly traditional; you may prefer other combinations.

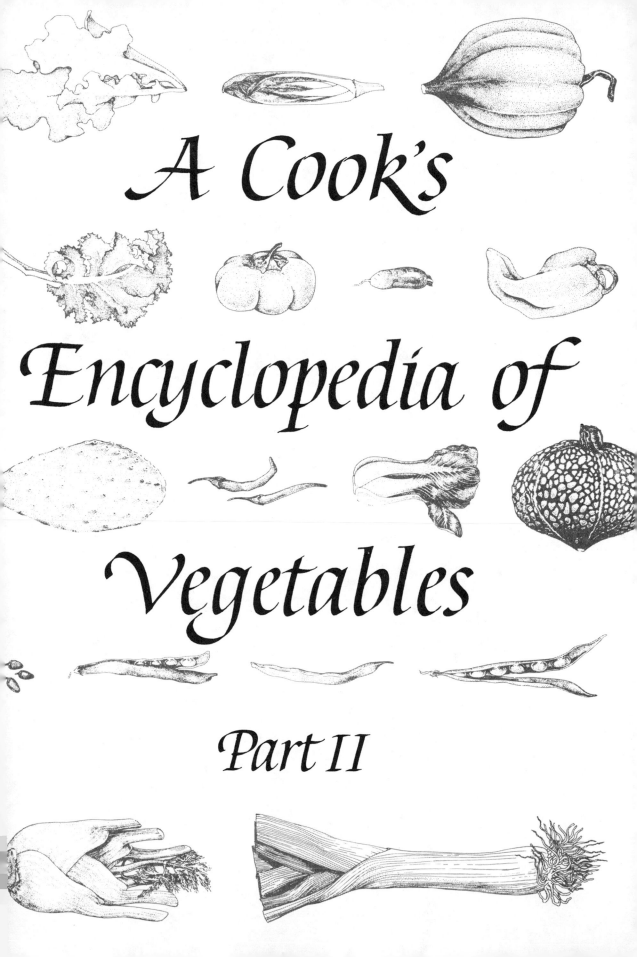

A Cook's

Encyclopedia of

Vegetables

Part II

INTRODUCTION TO THE ENTRIES

This book is organized alphabetically according to botanical families, and within families alphabetically according to members. Vegetables that are the only culinary member of a family are interspersed among the families. An alphabetical listing of all the vegetables can be found on page 15.

Key to the Entries

For each entry we have listed only those categories of information that are appropriate. For example, the lettuces all have the same method of propagation, so *how grown* is given only for the first entry.

Name: Appears at the top of the entry. We have chosen what we feel to be the most widely used common name, followed by the genus and species.

Other names: Other common names.

How grown: How each vegetable is propagated.

Availability: Months when the vegetable is harvested or, in the case of imports, is generally available. This is a kind of national average. Locally grown produce may be available for longer time periods.

Peak of freshness: A description of the vegetable at its culinary height and/or signs of deterioration to avoid.

To prepare: What to do to get a vegetable ready to cook it.

BOTANICAL CLASSIFICATION AND NOMENCLATURE

*T*he classification system we use today was set up by Karl von Linne in 1735 when he published his botanical work, *Systema Naturae.* The Linnaen system, known as *binomial classification,* divides the plants into increasingly specific categories, beginning with phylum, then class, order, family, genus, species, and, if even more specific categorization exists, into subspecies, and cultivars, in the case of domesticated vegetables. Each plant is known by its binomial designation, which includes the genus (always capitalized) and the species.

Take the tomato as an example. All market tomatoes bear the binomial *Lycopersicon lycopersicum,* but there are many tomato cultivars that are distinct types. (A cultivar is a named horticultural variety. It is distinct from the species although it belongs to the species.) A yellow pear tomato is very different from an oxheart tomato; each is a cultivar. The term *variety* is used in this book in place of the more technical *cultivar.*

Tomatoes belong to a family unit, the nightshades or Solanaceae. Genera (from genus) are grouped together into families, usually on the basis of common flower characteristics and geographical distribution. Families in turn are placed into orders, then into classes, and finally into phylla. The plant kingdom is the largest grouping and includes single-celled plants as well as the more complex plants.

The text of this book is organized by plant families in alphabetical order by common name. We have done this because it allows the reader some insight into the natural groupings of vegetables. Vegetables that are the only culinary member of a family are interspersed among the families alphabetically.

While this book is not meant to be a strict taxonomic guide to vegetables, we have tried to be correct and up-to-date. In most cases we have relied upon *Hortus Third: A Concise Dictionary of Plants Cultivated in the United States and Canada* to be our guide. In isolated cases we have relied on other sources for current taxonomical designation.

A BOTANICAL GLOSSARY

ANNUAL: A plant that completes its life cycle within a year. Annuals generally have a tender texture.

BIENNIAL: A plant that takes two years to complete its life cycle. The flowering and seeding generally take place in the second year.

BLANCHING: Covering a plant from sunlight so that it remains white or yellow rather than turning green.

BOLT: The response of a plant to certain conditions (climate, water, etc.): it sends up a flowering stalk, flowers, and turns to seed.

BULB: A flattened underground piece of stem made of of fleshy leaves or scales that overlap each other. The outside scales of bulbs are papery and dry.

CORM: Much like a bulb in shape. A corm is really a flattened underground piece of stem.

CULTIVAR: A named horticultural variety. A Rose Fir is a cultivar of the red potato. In this book, *variety* is used in place of the more technical *cultivar*.

FORCING: The process of encouraging a plant to produce a desired plant part. Forcing may be accomplished by altering climatic conditions and/or nutritional conditions.

GROUP: A division within a species.

GENUS: A definable group of plants that are more or less related. It is the first word of the binomial name for a plant.

GREEN: Used interchangeably with *potherb* or *salad green*.

HERBACEOUS: A tender, leafy plant, as opposed to a woody plant.

HYBRID: A plant resulting from a cross between parents that are genetically unlike, such as two species. Some hybrids occur in the wild, but most are created by plant breeders.

PERENNIAL: A plant with a life cycle of more than two years. The roots and top growth stay in place for several years or more.

POTHERB: A herbaceous plant used for cooking. Traditionally a tender green that was boiled before serving.

RHIZOME: An underground stem that spreads by creeping. Ginger is a rhizome.

SAVOY: A word used to describe any leaf that is bumpy, wavy, or wrinkled. The term is derived from the Savoy cabbage, which has ruffled leaves.

SET: A piece of plant used to produce another plant. An onion set is a small bulb that will develop into a full-sized onion.

SPECIES: A kind of plant that is unique unto itself. It normally reproduces itself true to type. It is the second term in binomial classification.

STRAIN: A general term used to indicate a group of plants, within a variety, that have some distinguishing characteristic in common.

SUBSPECIES: A further refinement of a species, usually a naturally occurring phenomenon and not a cultivar.

TAPROOT: A single plant that extends deep into the soil. Carrots are taproots. Plants with taproots are normally more difficult to transplant than those with spreading roots.

TUBER: A fat underground stem. Potatoes are tubers.

TYPE: Used in a general way to mean a *kind* of vegetable, and in a specific way to mean a prototype vegetable for the marketplace.

VARIETY: A physically distinct plant within a species. Used in this book in place of the more technical *cultivar.*

INTRODUCTION TO THE RECIPES

To present a comprehensive sampling of recipes for many vegetables we discuss would require a very large volume, probably about the size of the Manhattan yellow pages, so we had to set limits. In doing so several criteria were employed.

Our recipes emphasize newer and more esoteric vegetables that many cooks don't purchase simply because they don't know how to prepare them. We have also tried to select recipes that can work equally well with more than one kind of vegetable, as well as recipes that suggest new ways of combining ingredients. And, of course, we have tended to include more recipes for our favorite vegetables.

How To Locate Recipes

Recipes for a given vegetable appear after the entry for that vegetable. Recipes that feature a vegetable as an alternative or as a secondary ingredient are listed in the general index under the name of that vegetable.

Notes on Recipes

Cooking Times: We suggest minimal cooking times for sautés, stir-fries, and grilling recipes in order to allow vegetables to retain their texture and flavor.

Menus: When appropriate, we suggest other dishes and foods to accompany a recipe.

Portion Size: In general we have alloted ¼ pound of vegetables per person as a serving for side dishes, though this varies. The majority of recipes are written for four people. Some dishes with large numbers of ingredients are written for larger quantities.

Salt and Pepper: Our recipes usually call for salt and pepper to taste. Salt, though unhealthy in excess, is an essential ingredient because it brings out the flavor of other seasonings.

VEGETABLES A TO Y

Asparagus

Asparagus officinalis

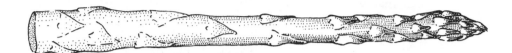

Asparagus is a very popular member of the lily family. Many cooks judge the onset of spring by the beginning of the asparagus season, as the perennial roots lie dormant each winter until the heat of the spring sun warms the soil. Then the shoots begin to grow and the tips push through the soil. In Europe beds of asparagus are blanched by being covered with a mulch that protects the emerging tips from the sun, producing white asparagus.

Asparagus has been the subject of intensive research and hybridization. Tissue culture, a process by which a plant is raised from a single cell, produces a very uniform crop.

Wild asparagus, which usually appears two or three weeks after the beginning of the commercial season, is much sought after by those who have tasted the sweet spears, and many prefer to eat it raw. It is found near cultivated asparagus.

In selecting asparagus you should note that the thicker stalks tend to be more tender than the thin reedy ones. Asparagus should be cooked briefly to preserve its firm texture and sweet flavor. Steaming, stir-frying, and poaching are appropriate techniques. Very tender asparagus is wonderful raw. Asparagus combines well with eggs and egg-based sauces such as mayonnaise and hollandaise.

How grown: By tissue culture or from seed.

Availability: Spring and summer.

Peak of freshness: Plump, firm stalks. The tops should not be broken, and the cut ends should not be woody or too dry. The tips should be closely grouped, not loose.

To prepare: Wash. Cut off the reedy ends.

Stir-fried Asparagus Beef

Asparagus is delicious stir-fried with almost any meat. Chicken and pork are also wonderful cooked in this manner.

Serves 2 as a main course, 4 or more as a side dish

1 teaspoon salted Chinese black beans
1 tablespoon shao hsing or dry sherry
1 tablespoon chopped garlic
2 small dried hot red peppers, chopped (optional)
3 tablespoons oil
½ pound tender beef, cut into strips ¼ inch by ½ inch by 2 inches
1 pound asparagus, cut into 1-inch pieces
½ cup chicken stock
2 tablespoons soy sauce
1 tablespoon chopped fresh cilantro
2 teaspoons cornstarch dissolved in
2 tablespoons water
Cilantro leaves for garnish

Coarsely chop the black beans and soak them in *shao hsing* or sherry for at least 15 minutes.

In a wok or large skillet, sauté the garlic and peppers in the oil over medium heat for 2 minutes. Add the beef and stir-fry for 1 minute. Add the asparagus and cook 30 seconds. Add the chicken stock, black bean–sherry mixture, soy sauce, and cilantro. Cook until the asparagus is tender. Add the cornstarch-water mixture and serve as soon as the sauce thickens, garnished with cilantro.

Asparagus and Prosciutto Baguettes

Asparagus spears make a delicious filling for crusty baguettes, especially in combination with prosciutto and an herbed mayonnaise.

Serves 4 as a main course

*1 dozen very tender asparagus
   spears
16 slices prosciutto or Parma
   ham
8 to 12 large basil leaves
½ cup Basic Mayonnaise,
   page 161
1 baguette cut into 6-inch
   lengths and sliced open*

Steam the asparagus for 1 to 2 minutes, or until a knife just pierces the thickest part. Run under cold water to stop the cooking, then drain on paper towels. Mince the basil leaves and mix into the mayonnaise. Wrap 3 asparagus spears with 4 slices of prosciutto. Repeat to make 4 bundles. Spread each sandwich with 2 tablespoons of mayonnaise and the asparagus and prosciutto.

Asparagus Tips and Baby Leeks with Scrambled Eggs

This is an interesting variation of the classic French dish of wild asparagus and eggs.

Serves 4 as a main course

*1 cup asparagus tips, or tips and
   tender stalks cut into 1¾-inch
   pieces.
12 to 15 baby leeks, 6 to 8 inches
   long
3 tablespoons butter
10 eggs, beaten
4 tablespoons crème fraîche, sour
   cream, or mascarpone*

Steam the asparagus and 4 of the leeks for 2 to 3 minutes, or until a knife just pierces the thickest part of the asparagus. Run under cold water to stop the cooking and drain on paper towels. Chop the remaining leeks finely. Melt 1 tablespoon of the butter in a large sauté pan or skillet and sauté the chopped leeks for 1 minute. Remove the leeks from the pan with a large spoon and set aside. Melt the remaining butter in the pan over medium-low heat. Add the eggs, let them sit for about 1 minute, then stir with a fork. Add the asparagus, chopped leeks and *crème fraîche*, stirring until the eggs are the consistency desired. Garnish each serving with a steamed leek.

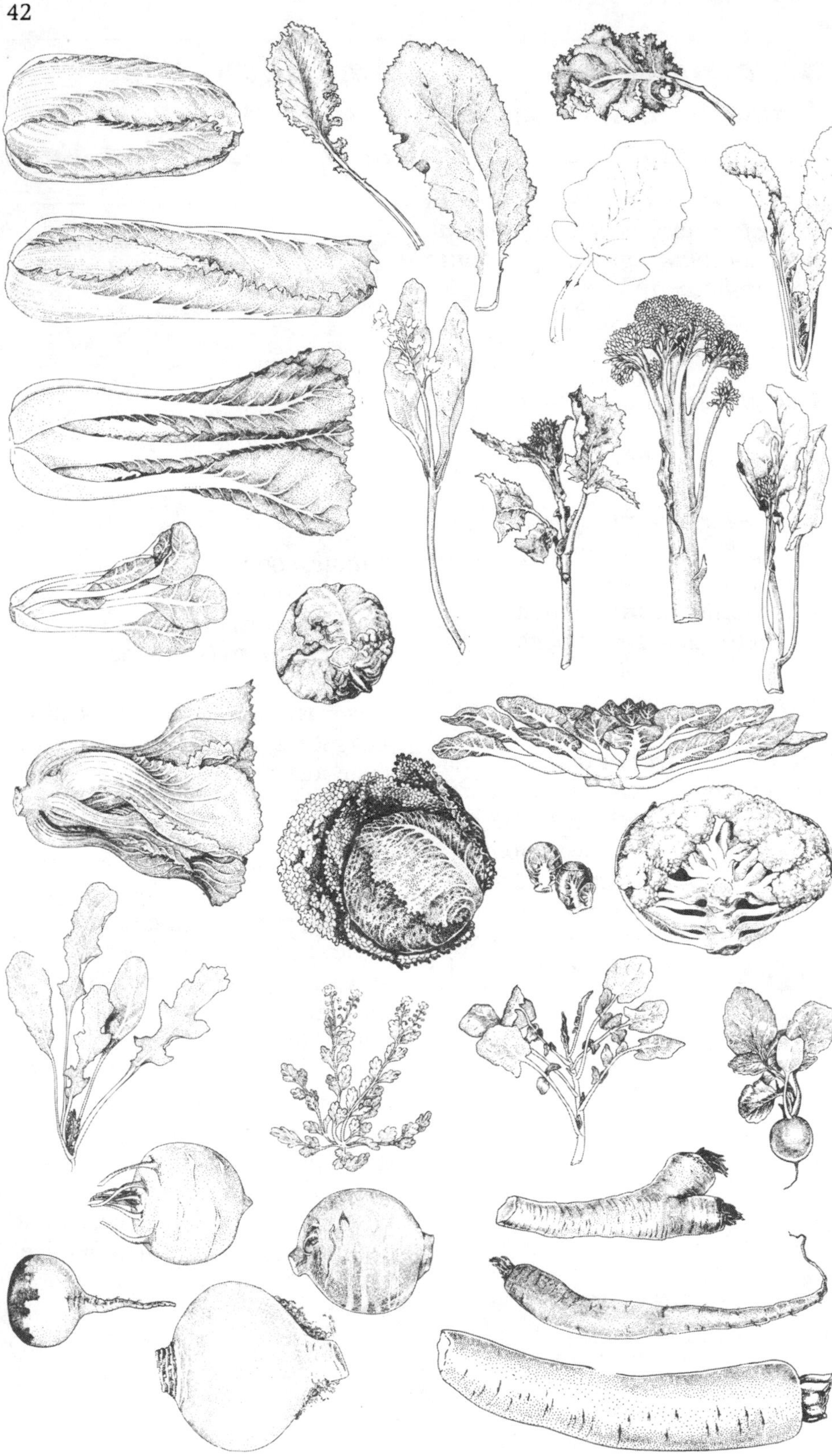

Cabbage Family

Brassicaceae or Cruciferae: Chinese Broccoli, Chinese Cabbage, Chinese Mustard, Broccoli, Brussels Sprout, Cabbage, Cauliflower, Cima di Rapa, Cresses, Horseradish, Kale, Kohlrabi, Mustard Greens, Radish, Rocket, Rutabaga, Turnip

For years botanists have struggled with the organization of the cabbage family, also known as the brassica family, the crucifer family, or the mustard cabbage family. Many members of this large group are ancient plants with unknown origins, but it is presumed that most originated in Asia and Europe. The Chinese have fancied radishes for centuries; there are accounts of sixteenth-century *daikons* weighing up to one hundred pounds. Wild turnips grew in both Europe and China, while broccoli and cauliflower, as well as kohlrabi, kale, European cabbages, and Brussels sprouts were developed from a wild cabbage that grew in the North Atlantic areas of Europe.

The brassicas all have crosslike flowers with four petals that are yellow, white, pink, or lavender. They are generally regarded as cool-weather crops, and most grow quickly. Many of the brassicas, including the mustards, the radishes, and horseradish, contain mustard oil. The hotter the climate, the more mustard oil is produced, and the hotter the vegetable tastes.

We have divided the brassicas into two groups—Asian and Western—according to where they are most commonly grown. All brassicas fall into three general categories: those with edible roots (turnips and *daikons*), those with leafy greens (kales and mustards), and those with heads (Brussels sprouts and cabbages).

As Eastern cultures are integrated into our own we will see more and more varieties of Asian mustards and cabbages. Immigrants bring seeds with them and plant them as soon as they find suitable soil. *Pak choy* for example (commonly called *bok choy*), has been widely available for several years, while today ten or more "choy" relatives are showing up in the market with increasing regularity. Since many of these brassicas are quick to prepare, relatively inexpensive, and versatile, they should be accepted by American cooks.

ASIAN BRASSICAS

Asian brassicas include Chinese broccoli, Chinese cabbages, Chinese mustard greens, and Chinese turnips. These vegetables have been classified under a bewildering variety of names made more complex by linguistic and cultural differences between East and West. The experts do agree that they are interrelated. Over the centuries the brassicas were transported to different regions of Asia, where they hybridized or changed drastically in adapting to new conditions.

In antiquity many of these crops, especially the turnips and mustards, were grown for their oily seeds as well as for their greens. The seeds provided oils and condiments, while the greens were used for potherbs and animal fodder.

CHINESE BROCCOLI

Brassica oleracea Alboglabra Group

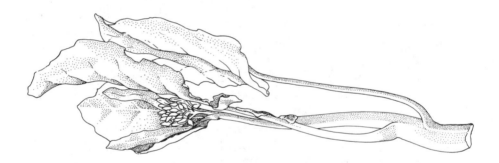

Other names: Chinese kale, *gai laan.*

How grown: From seed.

Availability: Fall through spring.

Peak of freshness: The stems should not be pithy. The flower buds should be just breaking open so you can see the color of the blossoms.

To prepare: Wash; trim stem ends and peel the stems. Discard over-large leaves.

Chinese broccoli is unlike any broccoli grown in Europe or America. It vaguely resembles the flowering turnip or sprouting broccoli in color and structure. Its leaves are gray-green and its thick stems are smooth. The plants are perennial, but are treated as annuals. Most American botanists describe Chinese broccoli as having white flowers, and in most markets the white-flowered type is sold. But there are strains with yellow or even rosy pink flowers.

Chinese broccoli has a sweet flavor like broccoli. It is frequently stir-fried with oyster sauce and beef. It may be used interchangeably with broccoli.

CHINESE CABBAGE

Brassica Rapa

How grown: From seed.

Peak of freshness: The leaves should be firm, never limp. Small heads will be the least bitter. In summer, bitterness may develop due to the heat.

To prepare: Look for soil at leaf bases. Discard any discolored leaves. Wash thoroughly. Trim stem ends, strings, and tough ends.

In China, the cabbage is an extremely important food plant. The heading varieties are more typical of the colder north, while the south, with its subtropical zones, is more suited to the open leafy and flowering cabbages. *Pak choy* is the standard cabbage of the south, but there are many forms of *pak choy*.

Although fifth-century Chinese literature mentions the mustards and turnips, it does not refer to wild or domestic Chinese cabbage, and we have learned little about its origins. We do know that there are several head shapes. These range from open heads that are almost all leaf and stalk, to those that are tightly formed with overlapping leaves. The leaves may be dark green and smooth, or they may be hairy or savoyed. The flavors range from succulent and sweet to almost bitter.

FLAT CABBAGE

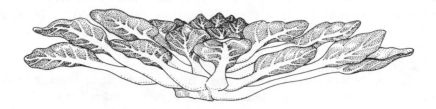

This is an ancient cabbage. It forms an open rosette of leaves that are dark green and spoonlike in shape. The entire head looks flattened, as if snow has weighed down the spreading leaves. This cabbage survives the cold and is sometimes the only fresh green in the marketplaces of North China during poor weather. In the United States it is found only in specialty shops.

It may be used like *pak choy*, though it tends to be a bit stronger in flavor.

FLOWERING WHITE CABBAGE

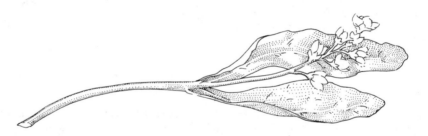

Thought by many to be a strain of *pak choy*, it is grown for its thick-stemmed flowering shoots. It is often confused with Chinese broccoli, but its stems are lighter. The fresh stalks have flowers. The buds should be just opening when cut for the market. It can be cooked like any other green.

MICHILI CABBAGE

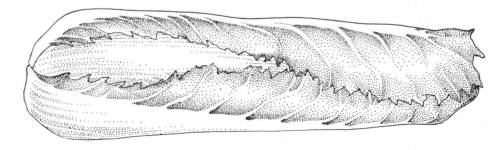

> **Other names:** Chili, tall Chinese cabbage, celery cabbage.
>
> **Availability:** Fall through spring.

Taller and more slender than nappa cabbage, this is also called celery cabbage and resembles the shape of that stalked vegetable more closely. Some *michilis* have pale blonde leaves that flare out from the top of the head, others have leaves that tuck inward. Its taste is a bit stronger than the nappa. The slender heads are easy to slice and are traditionally pickled or stir-fried.

NAPPA CABBAGE

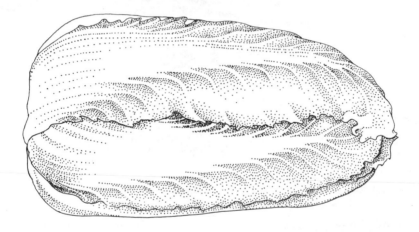

> **Other names:** Celery cabbage, Napa cabbage.
>
> **Availability:** Year round.

Nappas have stout, pale-green, almost translucent heads that are firm and succulent. The leaves of nappas are slightly savoyed and tightly wrapped around a central head. Nappa cabbage is mild and delicious and may be quickly cooked or eaten raw. The nappa is the most common type of Chinese cabbage in the United States, and seed researchers have developed strains that mature year round.

Nappa cabbage can be stir-fried with pork or duck, added to vegetarian stews with tofu, and used in soups and salads. Try substituting it for European cabbage.

WHITE-STEMMED CABBAGE (PAK CHOY)

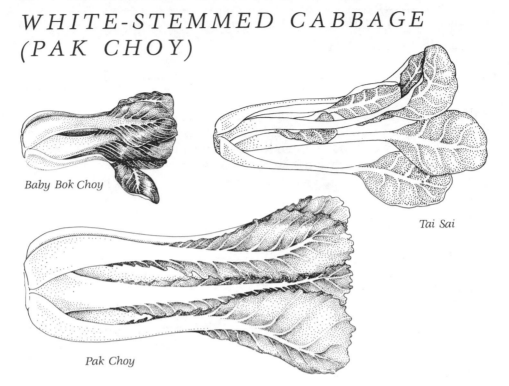

Baby Bok Choy

Tai Sai

Pak Choy

Other names: Bok choy, lei choy, tai sai, baby bok choy, bok choy sum.

Peak of freshness: The stalks should be crisp with fresh-looking leaves.

To prepare: Wash. Trim stem ends and discard discolored leaves.

Availability: Year round.

Pak Choy is the cabbage of South China and grows well under subtropical conditions if not planted in summer. Pak choy is commonly marketed as bok choy. Pak choy is thought to be one of the original parent lines of the michili and nappa cabbages, which crossed with the Chinese turnip in ancient times. The pak choy typically has very green leaves with succulent white mid-ribs starting from a bulbous base. The stalks of the pak choy are generally crisp, with very little bitterness. (Tai sai, though technically a pak choy, has very thin leaf bases and delicate leaves.) Pak choy has spread to many parts of China, and the Shanghai variety has green mid-ribs and leaf bases, rather than white. Baby pak choy is increasingly available and is sometimes marketed as bok choy sum.

Pak choy is usually stir-fried and served with oyster sauce or added to soups with meats such as shredded pork. It can be served in a raw salad with a soy-based dressing like the one in Chinese Greens Salad (page 51).

Michili Cabbage, Pear, and Persimmon Salad

This winter salad with its Middle Eastern dressing could accompany kebabs or roast lamb.

Serves 4 as a first course

½ *head* michili *or nappa cabbage*
2 *small hard apple-type persimmons*
1 *winter pear such as Comice or Bosc or Asian pear*

DRESSING

¼ *cup* tahini (*sesame butter*)
¼ *cup water*
¼ *cup fresh lemon juice*
Salt to taste

Shred the cabbage. Peel and slice the persimmons and pear. Arrange the sliced fruit on top of a bed of cabbage. Mix the dressing and pour it over the salad.

Nappa Cabbage with Cellophane Noodles and Tofu

This hearty winter stew can serve as a main course. Try it with Chinese Greens Salad, page 51.

Serves 2 to 3 as a main course

2 *tablespoons oil*
1 *tablespoon minced garlic*
1 *tablespoon chopped roasted peeled peanuts*
2 *or more cups chicken stock*
¼ *pound baked tofu (available at natural foods stores and Asian groceries), cut into ½-inch cubes*
One *½-pound package cellophane noodles (*sai fun, *available at Asian groceries)*
2 *thin slices smoked ham such as Smithfield, cut into strips ¼ inch wide and 3 inches long*
6 *cups chopped nappa cabbage*
1 *tablespoon cilantro leaves for garnish*

Heat the oil in a wok and stir-fry the garlic and peanuts for 2 minutes. Add the chicken stock, tofu, noodles, and smoked ham and cook over medium heat until the noodles are soft, about 10 minutes. Stir in the cabbage. Add more stock, if necessary, to make a sauce, but not a soup. Serve mounded on rice and garnished with cilantro.

CHINESE MUSTARD

Brassica juncea

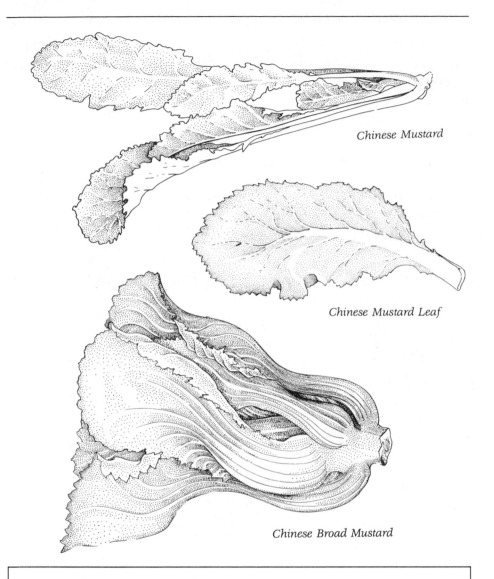

Chinese Mustard

Chinese Mustard Leaf

Chinese Broad Mustard

Other names: Mustard cabbage, Swatow, big-stem mustard.

How grown: From seed.

Availability: Year round.

Peak of freshness: The leaves are stiff, not ragged. The roots are stout.

To prepare: Wash; discard any tough stems. Trim stem ends. Peel fibers from the mid-ribs if necessary.

The Chinese mustards are quite different in appearance from the Western mustards. They are less frilly, with harsh, fuzzy leaves of dark green or red, or variegated with the two colors. The leaves are often strangely contorted in shape. If you are a gardener, you might consider growing a number of these mustards, which are at once exotic and beautiful.

When small, the leaves are both sweet and bitter tasting. Older leaves are strong tasting. Generally Chinese mustards are pickled, sometimes with bean paste, salt, and vinegar. Some are used in soups with pork, especially the Swatow when the leaves are small. In China, the roots are dug in fall and winter for pickling. Chinese mustards are interchangeable with Western mustard greens and kale.

Chinese Greens Salad

This salad features the stems as well as the leaves of Chinese mustard and bok choy. *Young greens are best, but you can make a fine version with older vegetables.*

Serves 2 as a first course

2 cups leaves and stems of
    Chinese mustard and bok choy
1 teaspoon sesame seeds

DRESSING

2 teaspoons light soy sauce
1 tablespoon fresh lemon juice
½ teaspoon sugar

Cut the stems into ¼-inch slices and the leaves into bite-sized pieces.

Toast the sesame seeds until brown in a sauté pan or skillet. Mix the dressing and pour it over the greens. Toss the salad, sprinkle with sesame seeds, and serve.

WESTERN BRASSICAS

Western brassicas include the six distinct vegetables developed over the centuries from a wild leafy cabbage that grew on the northern coast of Europe. They are kohlrabi, cauliflower, broccoli, kale, cabbage, and Brussels sprouts. But the western brassicas also include greens such as the cresses, mustard greens, and rocket, as well as root vegetables: horseradish, radishes, rutabagas, and turnips.

BROCCOLI

Brassica oleracea Botrytis Group

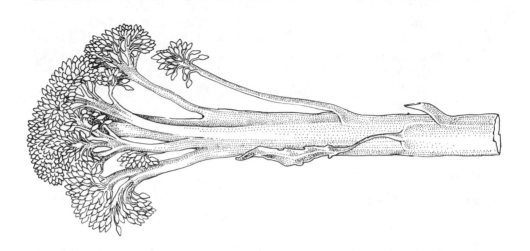

Other names: Green or standard broccoli.

How grown: From seed.

Availability: Usually year round. Fall through spring is the peak time.

Peak of freshness: Tight green heads. Avoid those that have begun to produce tiny yellow flowers and yellow heads. The stalks should be green, without signs of drying along the sides. Some drying at the cut end is inevitable and not a cause for concern.

To prepare: Wash. Trim stem ends. Some people cut off the bottom part of the stem but don't cut off the leaves. Others cut off the leaves and peel the skin from the stem with a sharp paring knife.

One of the vegetables developed from the wild cabbage, broccoli is the result of modifying the inflorescence, or flowering head, of that leafy green. The compact plants produce thick central stalks with grayish-green leaves. The stalks may produce a single head at the top and additional side shoots, or only the single head. In recent years, broccoli has been intensely hybridized because large commercial producers demand quick-maturing uniform plants that are easily harvested.

Broccoli is used extensively in Western and Eastern cuisines. It can be used interchangeably with cauliflower. Broccoli stems may be grated and sautéed in olive oil with garlic and fresh hot peppers. Warm broccoli may be served with a vinaigrette or a mayonnaise.

SPROUTING BROCCOLI

Brassica oleracea Italica Group

How grown: From seed.

Availability: Fall through spring.

Peak of freshness: Small firm florets on crisp green stalks. The florets should show no signs of growing or flowering.

To prepare: Wash. Trim ends.

Nearly unchanged from its primitive state, sprouting broccoli is a popular vegetable in Europe. Its hardy constitution withstands frost and snow, making it easy to grow in northern climates, and it produces steadily after being cut. The plants are somewhat weedy looking, growing to 4 feet. They are not as compact as the green broccoli types and are very leafy, with many small branches topped with small white or purple florets. Sprouting broccoli is just now appearing in American markets and is becoming increasingly popular, in part because of its color. The heads resemble a single tiny floret of cauliflower, an inch or so in diameter. The flavor of sprouting broccoli is much the same as that of standard broccoli and may be used the same way in cooking.

Golden Curried Broccoli Stems

Broccoli stems are usually discarded because people think they are tough or bitter. Fresh broccoli stems are not bitter, however, and slow cooking renders even tough stems tender.

Serves 4 as a side dish

1 tablespoon minced fresh ginger
1 tablespoon minced garlic
2 tablespoons butter
1 tablespoon minced fresh turmeric, or 1 teaspoon ground dried turmeric
½ teaspoon ground cumin
½ teaspoon ground ginger
Stems from about 1½ pounds whole broccoli, peeled and cut crosswise into ¼-inch slices (2 cups sliced)
1 cup chicken stock or water

Slowly cook the ginger and garlic in the butter in a heavy saucepan until the garlic begins to color. Add the spices and cook another minute. Add the broccoli stems and stock or water and simmer covered for 10 to 15 minutes or until the stems are tender. Serve this dish hot or at room temperature.

Double-Oyster Broccoli Stir-fry

The Chinese are fond of using two forms of a single ingredient to create one dish. Here fresh oysters and oyster sauce are combined with broccoli, producing a sharp contrast in textures and tastes.

Serves 2 as a main course, 4 as a side dish

3 tablespoons peanut oil
2 teaspoons minced garlic
2 teaspoons minced fresh ginger
1 tablespoon dark soy sauce
1 tablespoon oyster sauce
½ pound broccoli florets, cut into 4-inch-long thin strips
8 fresh-shucked oysters, or one 10-ounce jar of medium oysters with their liquid
1 tablespoon cornstarch dissolved in
2 tablespoons water
Cilantro leaves for garnish

Heat the peanut oil in a wok or large skillet. Add the garlic and ginger and cook for 30 seconds, stirring constantly. Add the soy sauce, oyster sauce, and broccoli. Stir-fry for 2 to 3 minutes. Add the oysters and cook for 1 minute. Add the cornstarch mixture and cook until the sauce thickens. Garnish with cilantro and serve.

BRUSSELS SPROUT

Brassica oleracea Gemmifera Group

How grown: From seed.

Availability: Fall through spring.

Peak of freshness: Tight green heads, with no sign of yellowing.

Avoid sprouts with loose leaves around the base.

To prepare: Wash. Trim the stems and remove any yellow or discolored leaves.

Often maligned and ridiculed, frequently held in derision by cooks of Mediterranean origin, the Brussels sprout can be an excellent vegetable if not over cooked.

Brussels sprouts were first cultivated around 1700 as one form of domestication of the wild cabbage. It is a tremendously practical vegetable to have in the garden because its production increases with picking: the more sprouts are picked from the tall stalks, the more new sprouts will be produced. Plants that begin bearing sprouts in the fall will continue to produce through early spring.

A tender, fresh Brussels sprout is very much like a baby cabbage and can be treated in a number of ways. Its robust nutlike flavor combines well with assertive meats such as pheasant, duck, or ham. Brussels sprouts make a flavorful winter soup, especially when flavored with bacon or ham, and they are an interesting addition to a stir-fry with hot peppers and scallions.

Brussels Sprouts and Ham Salad with Warm Vinaigrette

Many people who don't usually like Brussels sprouts have eaten this dish with pleasure. It is simple to prepare and attractive.

Serves 4 as a first course

1 pound Brussels sprouts

VINAIGRETTE
¼ cup olive oil
1 teaspoon chopped garlic
1 tablespoon sherry vinegar
½ pound lean ham slices, cut into strips 3 inches long and ¼ inch wide

Butterhead lettuce leaves

Steam the Brussels sprouts until cooked but still very firm, about 6 or 7 minutes. Keep them warm in the steamer with the heat turned off.

Heat 1 tablespoon of the olive oil in a sauté pan or skillet and sauté the garlic over medium heat for 3 minutes. Add the remaining olive oil, vinegar, and ham and sauté for 1 minute, stirring frequently. Layer the lettuce on individual warmed plates. Mound the Brussels sprouts on top of the lettuce. Pour the dressing over the salad and serve.

CABBAGE

Brassica oleracea Capitata Group

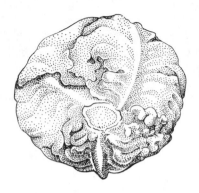

How grown: From seed.	***To prepare:*** Wash. Trim the stem end. Remove any damaged or discolored leaves. Some people remove the core as well.
Availability: Year round.	
Peak of freshness: Firm heads, with no drying of the core.	

The cabbage has been a staple in Northern Europe for centuries. Innumerable varieties have been developed, and in Great Britain you may find a different strain in almost every neighborhood. The British love cabbage. They harvest it all year and use a "cut and come approach" to produce a second growth after the head has been harvested.

In the United States, we are most familiar with large round cabbages, but they may also be flat or conical. Flat cabbages are commonly called drumheads and may be large or small, with savoyed or smooth leaves. The conical types are quite popular in Britain and are found in many home gardens there. Red or purple cabbages are a different strain from green cabbages. They take longer to mature and as a result are occasionally tough.

Cabbages are an important addition to soups and stews, including minestrone and borscht. In Eastern Europe cabbage is served sweet-and-sour style and, of course, stuffed. European cabbage is interchangeable with Chinese cabbage. It may be added to lettuce in many salads. It can be substituted for dandelion greens in Wilted Dandelion Salad (page 277).

SAVOY CABBAGE

Brassica oleracea Capitata Group

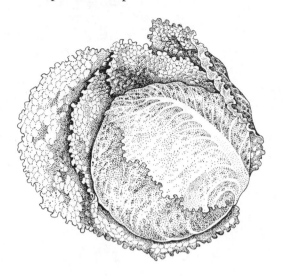

Other names: Curly cabbage, *chou de Milan, chou de Savoy.*

How grown: From seed.

Availability: Fall through spring.

Peak of freshness: Tender leaves with no yellowing.

To prepare: Wash. Remove any tough outer leaves. Some people remove the core as well.

Savoy cabbages are very popular in Italy, which probably accounts for their Mediterranean names, *chou de Milan* and *chou de Savoy* (the city of Milan was formerly a possession of the duchy of Savoy). Savoy cabbages have curly or ruffled leaves and the term *savoyed* is now used to refer to this characteristic in other vegetables. Europeans produce a variety of Savoy cabbages, some with tall loose heads and gray-green leaves that resemble those of romaine lettuce, others with tight heads surrounded by huge open leaves.

Savoy cabbages are more tender than regular cabbages and are milder in flavor. They are spectacular stuffed with rice and ground pork, beef, or veal and braised in stock or steamed. They may also be used interchangeably with regular cabbages.

Thai Sweet and Sour Salad

This Thai salad combines the rich flavor of sausage, the sharp taste of onions and scallions, and a sweet and sour dressing. It also uses a yellow cucumber, which is simply a fully matured cucumber. It adds a honeyed taste.

Serves 4 as a first course

½ pound ground pork
3 tablespoons dried shrimp
½ cup boiling water
Butter lettuce leaves
2 cups thinly sliced red cabbage
1 older yellow cucumber, peeled,
    seeded, and grated, or one
    green cucumber, thinly sliced
1 medium white onion, sliced
2 tablespoons chopped scallion
¼ cup chopped fresh mint, about
    1 bunch
¼ cup chopped fresh cilantro,
    about 1 bunch

DRESSING

2 small fresh hot peppers such as
    Thai or jalapeño, *seeded and
    chopped*
¾ cup rice wine vinegar or
    distilled vinegar
2 tablespoons sugar

In a sauté pan or skillet, cook the pork until it loses its pink color, crumbling it with a spatula. Drain off the fat and set the pork aside. Cover the shrimp with the boiling water and let them soak for 15 minutes. Drain.

Layer a serving plate with the lettuce leaves. Make mounds of the cabbage, cucumber, and white onion. Sprinkle the pork over the vegetables. Top with the scallion, dried shrimp, mint, and cilantro. Mix the dressing, pour over the salad, and serve.

CAULIFLOWER

Brassica oleracea Botrytis Group

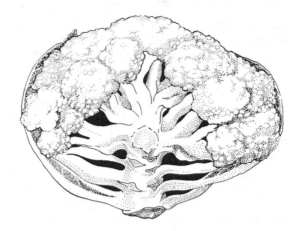

How grown: From seed.

Availability: All year, but especially late fall through spring.

Peak of freshness: Look for white- or cream-colored heads without brown tinges. The curd should be closely packed, not mealy or separated. The leaves surrounding the head should not show signs of drying. Cauliflower should be handled carefully, as it bruises easily.

To prepare: Wash. Trim the stem end and any leaves. Use whole, or separate into florets by breaking or cutting with a knife.

The cauliflower was also developed from the wild cabbage and is considered the aristocrat of the *Brassica* genus. Its reputation has been helped by its mild flavor and by its fine creamy white head, which is produced by blanching. The plants are large and spreading. Each stalk produces a single head surrounded by large green leaves, which are tied closed over the head to maintain its white color. To grow a perfect cauliflower requires a lot of work, and it usually commands a higher price than its other cabbage relatives. The florets of the cauliflower are composed of thickened flower stems. Its color, relatively rare among vegetables, can always be used to advantage at the table. Purple cauliflower, not readily available in the United States, is fairly common in Southern Italy.

Cauliflower is used raw or cooked in salads and with dips. It is frequently sautéed in combination with colorful vegetables such as red bell pepper and broccoli. Steamed or blanched cauliflower is fine with just a squeeze of lemon, or it can be marinated in a vinaigrette with parsley.

Cauliflower with Hot-Pepper Pork

Hot peppers and a marinade give a new dimension to otherwise bland cauliflower.

Serves 4 as a side dish, 2 as a main course

MARINADE

1 teaspoon cornstarch
½ teaspoon dry red wine
½ teaspoon sugar
1 teaspoon peanut oil

½ pound lean pork, cut into
  ½-inch cubes

SAUCE

2 teaspoons cornstarch
1 cup chicken stock
1 teaspoon dark soy sauce
½ head cauliflower
3 scallions
5 fresh hot red peppers such as
  Thai, jalapeño, or chimayo
3 tablespoons peanut oil
2 tablespoons dry red wine
1 teaspoon dark soy sauce

Mix all the ingredients for the marinade together and marinate the pork for 1 hour. Mix the sauce ingredients and set aside. Break the cauliflower into bite-sized pieces. Flatten the scallions with the side of a knife and cut into 2-inch lengths. Seed the peppers and cut them into thin slices lengthwise.

Heat the peanut oil in a wok or large skillet until it just begins to smoke. Add the cauliflower and stir-fry for 3 minutes. Add the peppers and cook another minute. Remove the cauliflower and peppers from the wok with a slotted spoon and reduce the heat to medium. Add the pork and stir-fry for 2 minutes. Add the wine, soy sauce, and scallions and cook for 2 minutes. Add the sauce mixture and return the cauliflower and peppers to the wok. Cook until the sauce thickens and serve over rice.

Chicken Breasts Stuffed with Curried Cauliflower and Mint

In this dish cauliflower takes on the yellow hue of the turmeric, contrasting with the carrot and green mint.

Serves 4 as a main course

4 chicken breasts, boned and
   skinned

MARINADE

½ cup peanut oil
4 small dried hot peppers
Leaves from 4 mint sprigs

STUFFING

2 tablespoons peanut oil
5 to 6 cauliflower florets, minced
1 small carrot, minced
5 green snap beans, thinly sliced
4 small fresh hot red peppers
   such as Thai or jalapeño,
   seeded and chopped
1-inch piece of fresh turmeric,
   minced, or 1 teaspoon dried
   turmeric
6 freshly ground coriander seeds
3 tablespoons water
6 to 8 fresh mint leaves from
   marinade, above

Mint Sauce, page 148

Pound the chicken breasts to a thickness of about ¾ inch with the side of a cleaver. Mix the ingredients for the marinade and marinate the chicken in the refrigerator for at least 4 hours.

Light a charcoal fire in an open grill. To make the stuffing, heat the oil in a wok or skillet and add the vegetables, turmeric, and coriander seeds. Sauté for 3 minutes, then add the water and cook until the vegetables are tender, about 4 or 5 minutes. Allow to cool. Drain the chicken, reserving the marinade. Lay each breast flat and make a lengthwise strip of 2 or 3 tablespoons of the stuffing. Cover each with several mint leaves from the marinade. Fold over the breast and seal with a needle and thread or by weaving in several wooden skewers. When the charcoal is covered with gray ash, grill the chicken breasts 6 to 8 minutes per side, basting frequently with the marinade. Serve with the mint sauce.

CIMA DI RAPA
Brassica Rapa Ruvo Group

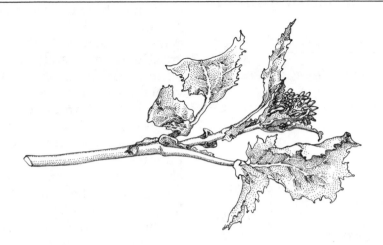

Other names: *Broccoli de rabe, cima di rabe, raab, rapini,* turnip tops.

How grown: From seed.

Availability: Fall through spring.

Peak of freshness: Look for a few fresh yellow flowers on the green florets, and for dark-green leaves and strong stalks. Usually sold as stalks 12 to 18 inches long. Avoid those that have wilted leaves or droopy florets.

To prepare: Wash. Trim stem ends. Remove large leaves and up to 6 inches of tough stalks.

Cima di rapa is loved by Italians and by those of Italian descent with good reason. Both sweet and bitter, green and yellow, soft and crunchy, it appeals to all the senses, especially when braised in olive oil and garlic. Not really a member of the broccoli subgroup at all, but belonging to the turnip subgroup (the name means "top of the turnip"), *cima di rapa* is nevertheless classified with the broccolis, most likely because with its leafy stalks and tiny scattered florets it resembles sprouting broccoli in shape. The plants grow up to 4 feet high and are somewhat weedy looking, with green florets and yellow flowers.

Today *cima di rapa* is becoming more widely available in Italian produce markets and specialty shops, and it will most likely be an important vegetable in the near future.

Cima di rapa must be cooked slowly, or it will acquire a bitter taste. When raw, however, it is not bitter and even the stalks are quite tender. Substitute it for greens in Posole, Mustard Greens, and Chimayo Peppers (page 73), and cook 20 minutes instead of 5.

Cima di Rapa Braised with Garlic

Cima de rapa *acquires a delicious, nutty taste with slow braising. This dish wonderfully complements a sweet-flavored meat such as pork or duck.*

Serves 4 as a side dish

*4 pounds cima di rapa
¼ cup olive oil
2 garlic cloves, smashed
Salt and pepper to taste
½ cup fresh-grated Parmesan
   cheese*

Wash the *cima di rapa,* but do not dry it. Remove the very tough stems and very large leaves. Some leaves and stalks should remain. Add the olive oil, garlic, and *cima di rapa* to a wok or large pot. Cover and cook slowly for about 40 minutes or until tender, stirring occasionally. Add water, if necessary, to keep the *cima di rapa* from sticking. Season to taste. Serve in a warmed earthenware bowl, topped with Parmesan cheese.

Cima di Rapa and Polenta Casserole

The polenta, layered on top of the vegetables, seals in their flavor.

Serves 4 to 6 as a side dish

*1 cup polenta (coarse cornmeal)
5 cups water
1 teaspoon salt
2 tablespoons olive oil
1 tablespoon chopped garlic
1 medium yellow onion, chopped
1½ pounds cima di rapa, chopped
2 green and 1 red or 3 red
   tomatoes, peeled, seeded, and
   chopped
Salt and pepper to taste*

Preheat the oven to 350°.

Dissolve the polenta in 1 cup of the water. Bring the remaining 4 cups of water to a simmer in a large saucepan. Add the polenta and salt and simmer, stirring frequently, until the polenta is very stiff, about 20 minutes (a wooden spoon should stand up in it).

Heat the oil in a sauté pan or skillet and sauté the garlic and onion until the onion is translucent. Add the *cima di rapa* and tomatoes and sauté until the greens have wilted. Pour the vegetables into a strainer and press out the excess liquid with the back of a wooden spoon. Don't press too hard or you'll smash everything. Pour the vegetables into a medium-sized casserole. Season with salt and pepper. Cover with the polenta. Bake uncovered for 30 minutes or until the polenta forms a crust and begins to brown. Serve hot or at room temperature.

CRESSES

There are several cresses, but only two are readily available in our markets: garden cress and watercress. The third, sometimes called upland cress, is usually found wild. Garden cress is most commonly sold as a sprout, often in combination with mustard. In British markets you can buy small containers of half cress and half mustard to harvest for salads and tea sandwiches. Watercress has a more pronounced taste than garden cress. It is cultivated in streams, and anyone lucky enough to have an unpolluted creek nearby can grow it. It should be harvested in the wild with caution, as some foragers have gotten tapeworm from picking it in polluted waterways.

COMMON CRESS

Barbarera verna

Other names: Land cress, upland cress, pepper grass, winter cress.	**Availability:** Year round.
	To prepare: Wash. Trim stem ends.
How grown: From seed.	

The strongest of the cresses and almost never found in the market, although it grows wild in Europe. Its leaves resemble those of a small radish. It has a peppery, somewhat hot taste, which increases as it matures. Use as you would garden cress.

GARDEN CRESS

Lepidium sativum

Availability: Fall through spring.

Peak of freshness: The smaller the better. Buy in combination with mustard when just a half-inch high.

To prepare: Trim stem ends.

Garden cress is easy to grow and has been cultivated in Europe since the time of the Greeks. Some kinds are curly, others have a flat leaf. Like parsley, it can be used cooked as an herb or raw as a vegetable. We prefer it mixed with other greens in a salad or on sandwiches.

WATERCRESS

Nasturtium officinale

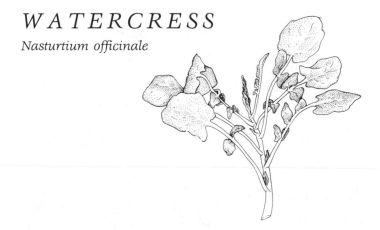

Availability: All year.

Peak of freshness: Avoid watercress with yellow or slimy leaves.

To prepare: Wash. Soak watercress for 10 minutes in a solution of 8 parts water to 1 part white vinegar. This removes clinging insects that even repeated washings in water will not get rid of. Trim stem ends or remove.

Watercress usually grows to 8 or 10 inches long, with round, dark-green leaves the size of a dime on succulent stems. The taste is peppery, but not hot.

Watercress is traditionally used in sandwiches and in salads. It can be substituted in Parsley Salad (page 94) and Sorrel Purée (page 251).

Watercress and Water Chestnut Salad

This is one of several recipes in this book courtesy of Bruce Cost, author of Ginger East to West *(Berkeley: Aris Books, 1984).*

Serves 4 as a first course

10 fresh water chestnuts
2 pounds (3 bunches) watercress,
  stemmed and minced
2 teaspoons light soy sauce
2 tablespoons Asian sesame oil
1 teaspoon salt
1½ teaspoons sugar

Peel and mince the water chestnuts. Add to the watercress. Mix the rest of the ingredients together and pour over the salad. Toss thoroughly and serve immediately.

Watercress and Horseradish Mousse

This mousse is elegant and easy to prepare. Try it with a sharply season-ed dish such as steak au poivre *or a plain poached fish fillet.*

Makes 2 cups

2 bunches watercress (about 1
  pound)
½ cup heavy cream
¼ cup freshly grated horseradish
Salt and white pepper to taste

Remove the stems from the watercress. Purée the watercress in a blender or food processor. Whip the cream. With a wooden spoon, blend the watercress purée and the horseradish into the cream. Season with salt and pepper. Serve slightly chilled.

Watercress and Herring Salad

This winter salad is especially delicious with fresh herring, which often shows up in fish markets in December and January.

Serves 4 as a first course

4 fresh herring, anchovies, or sar-
  dines, or 1 small jar herring
  pickled in vinegar, drained
1 quart water
2 tablespoons fresh lemon juice
2 bunches watercress (about 1
  pound), stemmed
½ purple onion, cut into thin
  slices

DRESSING

1 teaspoon stone-ground mustard
¼ cup heavy cream
1 tablespoon fresh lemon juice
½ teaspoon salt

To clean the fish, make a slit in each fish from the vent (the anus) to below the head. Cut through the backbone just behind the head and pull the head and entrails out. Remove the dark strip of blood along the backbone. Rinse the fish under cold water. Place the fish cavity-side down on a cutting board. Press firmly down on the fish. Turn over and pull out the backbone. Bring the water to a simmer in a large pot. Add the lemon juice. Poach the fish 2 or

3 minutes, or until the flesh is opaque in the center. Remove the fish, drain, and skin. Cut the fish in half lengthwise and then into ½-inch-wide pieces.

Make bed of watercress. Mound the poached fish or pickled herring in the center and surround with a circle of onion rings. Mix the dressing, pour over the salad, and serve.

HORSERADISH

Armoracia rusticana

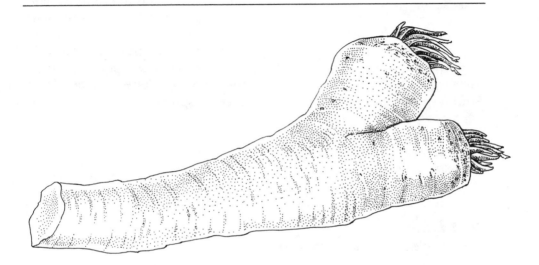

How grown: From root cuttings.

Availability: Fall through early spring.

Peak of freshness: Look for roots that are smooth, unblemished, and 6 to 12 inches long.

To prepare: Scrub the root and peel the skin. It is best to wear rubber gloves while preparing horseradish, and be careful not to rub your eyes.

Horseradish is a hardy, ragged-looking plant that grows in all the cool regions of the United States and in many parts of Europe. Its characteristic hot flavor is produced by mustard oil, which is common to the brassicas. Horseradish does not produce reliable seeds, and propagation comes from root cuttings that develop into brown-skinned roots in the fall.

Horseradish root may be grated and served alone or combined with mustard or cream or mayonnaise to produce the spicy sauce commonly served with boiled and pickled meats.

Frozen Horseradish Garnish

Most of us are familiar with horseradish and whipped cream. Serve this variation with a standing rib roast, a grilled steak, or even beef stew.

Makes 3 cups

1 cup ricotta cheese
1 cup heavy cream
Cayenne to taste
¼ teaspoon salt
3 tablespoons chopped fresh
    chives
4-inch piece horseradish
2 tablespoons tarragon vinegar
2 teaspoons sugar

Beat the ricotta cheese until very soft with a wooden spoon or in a blender or food processor. Whip the cream until stiff. Stir it into the ricotta cheese in a mixing bowl. Add the cayenne, salt, and chives.

Peel and coarsely grate the horseradish root. Combine it with the vinegar and sugar. Blend the horseradish mixture with the other ingredients. Spoon it into a container, cover, and freeze until hard, about 3 hours. Mix it again with beaters or a food processor and return it to the freezer until ready to serve. Scoop out portions with a melon baller. Serve on a bed of lettuce or spinach.

KALE

Brassica oleracea (many groups)

Collard Green

Kale

Other names: Collards, Scotch kale, greens.

How grown: From seed and from transplants.

Availibility: Fall through spring.

Peak of freshness: Gray-green curly leaves 6 to 14 inches long. Leaves should not be limp.

To prepare: Wash. Discard any discolored leaves. Trim away tough stem ends.

There are many kinds of kale, including collards, Scotch, blue, and ornamental kale. They differ in the shapes and colors of their leaves and their growth habits. Collards are the tallest of the lot; the others exhibit more spreading leaves. Ornamental kale has highly colored leaves: rosy red, pink, white, and yellow. It is now being marketed as "salad savoy," and while termed edible, its best use is decorative. In spite of the differences between collards and kales, they may be treated in the same manner culinarily. The leaves of these plants are best young.

The reputation of Southern cuisine is not only based on jambalaya, pecan pie, and black-eyed peas, but also on kale (commonly called collards there). Kale helps ring in the new year in many Southern homes. It is still the standby for boiled greens, but cooks are finding other uses for it. Young kale leaves can be stir-fried or used in soups, and large leaves can be stuffed.

Kale can be used in Posole, Mustard Greens, and Chimayo Peppers (page 73) and in Cima de Rapa and Polenta Casserole (page 63).

Kale Soup

This simple, hearty Portuguese soup uses fresh kale, the younger the better.

Serves 4 as a first course, 2 as a main course

½ pound kale, stemmed
½ pound chorizo or other spicy sausage
3 red potatoes, peeled and cut into ½-inch slices
5 cups chicken stock
Salt
4 slices toasted French bread
Black pepper to taste

Mince the greens by hand or with the metal blade of a food processor. Prick the sausages with a fork in several places and simmer them in a small pot of water for 15 minutes. Drain and cut the sausage into thin slices.

In a medium saucepan, boil the potatoes in salted water to cover for 10 or 15 minutes or until the slices are easily pierced with the tip of a knife. Purée the potatoes and a little water in a blender or food processor. You should end up with a very thick paste.

In a large saucepan, simmer the kale in the chicken stock for 5 minutes. Add salt to taste. Serve in warm bowls over toasted French bread, sprinkled with black pepper.

KOHLRABI

Brassica oleracea Gongylodes Group

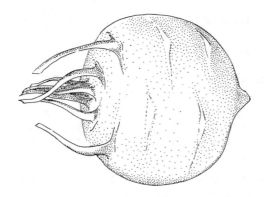

How grown: From seed.

Availability: Late spring, then again in fall and winter.

Peak of freshness: Small bulbs not over 2 to 3 inches in diameter, and not woody. Look for fresh leaves if they are intact.

To prepare: Trim ends and peel away the skin. To crisp uncooked kohlrabi, soak in ice water for 15 minutes before serving.

Kohlrabi has a peculiar shape: it is the stem that is swollen rather than the root. The leaves attach directly to the top of the bulbous stem, and, should you grow this unusual vegetable, you'll notice the root dangling below the bulb. In most markets both the leaves and the root are removed, which is a pity as the tender leaves make a tasty addition to stir-fries. In Europe, where this vegetable originated, the young leaves are a popular green. Today, kohlrabi is a minor vegetable crop in the United States. It has been introduced into China where it has become popular, its flavor being not unlike Chinese broccoli.

Although it is biennial by nature, it is best treated as an annual plant. Kohlrabi can be picked as soon as two months after seeding, with bulbs about 2 inches in diameter. At that stage the stem is tender and the skin not yet thickened. Depending on the variety, the skin may be purple, green with a hint of rosy red, or light green. The interior flesh is always white, and its flavor is dependent on the age of the plant rather than the color of the skin.

Kohlrabi has the succulent crunchy texture and sweet cabbage flavor common to the brassicas. It is commonly eaten raw in salads or with dips. Young kohlrabi may be quickly stir-fried, and the older vegetables can be steamed or blanched until tender. Kohlrabi is interchangeable with turnips in most recipes.

Lamb and Kohlrabi Tajine

This Moroccan stew of lamb perfumed with saffron and ginger is often made with cardoon. It can be prepared with a number of other vegetables including fennel, turnip, artichoke hearts, and celeriac. Saffron imparts a lovely golden color to all the ingredients.

Serves 6 as a main course

¼ teaspoon saffron threads
1 cup boiling water
2 tablespoons olive oil
2 tablespoons chopped garlic
1 teaspoon ground ginger
2 pounds lamb stew meat, cut into 2-inch cubes
Salt and pepper to taste
2 pounds kohlrabi, peeled and cut into thin slices
½ pound whole green olives (about 1 cup)
1 tablespoon fresh lemon juice

Cover the saffron threads with the boiling water and soak them for 30 minutes.

In a large Dutch oven heat the oil and sauté the garlic over medium heat for 3 minutes. Add the ginger and cook for 2 minutes. Add the meat, saffron and its liquid, and salt and pepper and cover with water. Simmer covered for 1½ to 2 hours. The meat should pull apart easily. Add the kohlrabi and green olives and simmer for 20 minutes or until the kohlrabi is tender. Add the lemon juice and serve over a bed of rice or *couscous*. This dish is excellent reheated the next day.

MUSTARD GREEN

Brassica juncea, B. Rapa, B. nigra, B. hirta

Other names: Greens.

How grown: From seed.

Availability: All year, but most common in winter and spring.

Peak of freshness: Green leaves without discoloration and never limp. Size depends upon type of mustard, but small leaves are generally less pungent.

To prepare: Wash. Discard discolored or wilted leaves. Cut away tough fibers and stems.

Mustard greens are a long-time favorite in the United States, and many a cook has gathered wild mustard greens in early spring. There are many kinds of mustards. Black mustard grows wild in many regions, having arrived in the United States with the first European immigrants over three hundred years ago. There are also several types of improved mustards that are commercially grown and which home gardeners plant in fall or early spring for their tender leaves. The bright-green leaves of those plants are slightly frilly or curled when young and make both tempting salads and cooked greens. Mustard greens may be treated like any other green, especially chard and Chinese mustards. The seeds of white and black mustard are harvested and ground into mustard powder. It is frequently flavored with horseradish, fine vinegars, and white wines and herbs.

Posole, Mustard Greens, and Chimayo Peppers

Posole *is the Spanish name for hominy, white corn kernels with softened outer skins. Posole is commonly found canned in the market, though it is sold in dried form in some markets in the Southwest. Posole and hominy are almost identical. The kinds of corn used in the preparation of each may be slightly different.*

Serves 4 as a side dish

1 cup dry posole, or 2 cups canned posole or hominy
3 cups water
1 pound mustard greens
Salt to taste
2 red chimayo peppers, chile de arbol, or other thin hot red peppers, seeded and cut into strips
2 garlic cloves, minced
3 tablespoons butter

If using dry *posole*, soak it overnight, then drain and rinse it in cold water in a colander. Place the *posole* and 3 cups water in a large pot and simmer for about 40 minutes or until tender. Drain, reserving ½ cup of the cooking liquid; set the *posole* aside.

Cut the mustard greens into shreds. Steam the greens for 3 minutes. Place the cooked vegetables in a colander and squeeze out the remaining water with the back of a wooden spoon. Combine the *posole*, greens, and ½ cup liquid in a saucepan and simmer for 5 minutes. If using canned *posole* or hominy, drain all but ½ cup of its liquid and add to the greens after 3 or 4 minutes. Add salt.

Sauté the peppers and garlic in butter in a sauté pan or skillet until lightly browned. Pour the *posole* into a warm serving bowl. Top with the pepper-garlic mixture and serve at once with warm tortillas.

Roast Duck and Mango Salad on a Bed of Greens

Duck is a perfect complement to bitter greens. Buy an already cooked duck in your local Chinatown, or roast your own. Bruce Cost, who created this recipe, believes the former is preferable because the cost of cooked meat is less than you would pay for an uncooked bird, and you don't have to deal with the fat.

Serves 8 as a first course, 4 as a main course

1 roast duck
2 ripe medium mangos
2 bunches bitter greens such as mustard greens or turnip greens, stemmed
3 scallions, white part only, minced
2 tablespoons minced fresh mint
2 tablespoons sherry vinegar
1½ tablespoons olive oil
½ teaspoon black pepper

Remove the skin from the duck, reserving the skin from the breast. Remove the meat from the breast and thighs of the duck. Cut the duck meat into thin strips 1½ inches long and ¼ inch wide, and place in a ceramic or glass bowl. Core the mangos, remove the flesh from the skin, and cut into similar-sized strips. Add the mangos to the bowl with the duck.

Cut the skin of the breast into thin strips and cook over medium heat in a dry skillet until it begins to crisp. (Like bacon, it will cook in its own fat.) Remove the skin cracklings and drain on paper towels. Reserve ½ tablespoon of the fat.

Arrange the greens on a serving dish. Add the scallions, mint, and cracklings to the mixing bowl with the duck and mango. Add the vinegar, oil, pepper, and reserved fat. Toss well, spoon onto the greens, and serve.

RADISH

Raphanus sativus

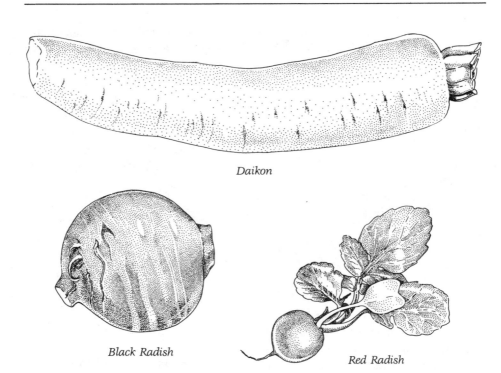

Daikon

Black Radish

Red Radish

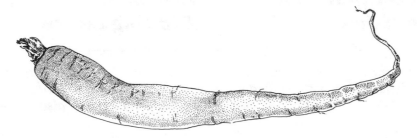

Long Red Radish

How grown: From seed.

Availability: All year.

Peak of freshness: Radishes should be crisp, not limp. Their interior should not be pithy, dry, or hollow, which indicates age and most likely a hotter-than-desired taste.

To prepare: Wash. Trim the root tips and leaves. Many people choose to leave the smaller leaves attached.

Radishes are appreciated for their peppery taste and crisp texture. Generally speaking, radishes grown in hot weather with little irrigation taste quite hot, while those grown in the cool, wet weather of early spring will have a milder taste. Radishes are available in a wide range of colors, from white to black with all shades of red in between. Asian radishes are called *daikons*, and these radishes produce roots from 2 to 4 inches in diameter and 6 to 20 inches long. Strictly speaking, they belong to a separate subspecies. One exotic Asian variety has either red skin with green flesh or green and white skin with a red flesh.

In the United States radishes are usually eaten raw, but in Scandinavia they are cooked in spring soups; in Mexico they are often cooked as we would carrots; and in parts of Africa radish tops are cooked and served as greens with a spicy sauce.

Sweet and Sour Radishes

Serve these as you would sweet pickles, to accompany a broad range of dishes.

Makes about 3 cups

30 radishes with greens attached
1 teaspoon salt

MARINADE

1 tablespoon medium soy sauce
2 tablespoons rice wine vinegar or distilled vinegar
1 teaspoon shao hsing or dry sherry
1 teaspoon sugar
2 tablespoons Asian sesame oil
1 tablespoon water

Thin the radish leaves by removing the larger ones. Smash each radish, using the side of a chef's knife (don't crush the radishes, just break them open in 2 or 3 places). Mix the salt with the radishes and set aside for 10 minutes. Transfer the radishes to a flat-bottomed bowl. Mix the marinade ingredients together and pour over the radishes. Let stand for 20 minutes or more.

Daikon Dipping Sauce

Serve this sauce with strong-flavored fish such as tuna, bluefish, or mackerel. It can also be served over rice.

Makes about 2 cups

About 1/2 pound daikon (1 cup grated)
½ cup water
2 tablespoons medium soy sauce
1 teaspoon grated fresh ginger
1 teaspoon fresh lemon juice, rice wine vinegar, or distilled vinegar
½ teaspoon wasabi (green horseradish powder found in Asian markets)

Grate the daikon and squeeze it in paper towels to remove any excess moisture. Combine all the remaining ingredients and serve at room temperature. You may add more wasabi if you prefer a spicy sauce.

ROCKET
Eruca sativa

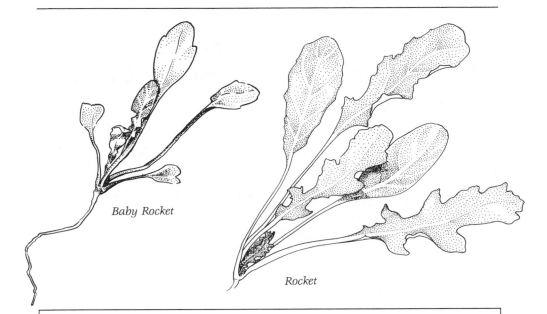

Baby Rocket

Rocket

Other names: *Roquette, arugula, rucolo.*

How grown: From seed.

Availability: All year.

Peak of freshness: The leaves should be dark green and somewhat smooth. A furry underside indicates toughness.

The leaves become bitter after the plant has flowered.

To prepare: Wash. Trim stems. Discard discolored or wilted leaves. Small leaves may be used whole; larger leaves are usually chopped before being added to salads.

For centuries no one bothered to cultivate this sturdy wild plant, which grew plentifully throughout most of the year along the rocky hillsides of the Mediterranean basin. Today rocket is one of the most popular salad greens in Europe and is becoming known in America. Large suppliers are beginning to grow it here in greenhouses to ensure a year-round supply. It may be harvested as an entire plant, or individual leaves may be cut from the plant. As it goes to flower, the flat, open plant becomes leggy and will grow to a foot or more in height.

Rocket leaves and flowers give a spicy, peppery taste to mixed salads, complementing both bland butterhead lettuce and bitter chicories. Although best used in salads when the serrated leaves are only 2 to 3 inches long, large rocket leaves are wonderful for wrapping around bits of fish or meat. In addition, the large leaves can also be used in sauces or stir-fries as you would use parsley or cilantro. Rocket can be cooked as a potherb. In India it is grown primarily for its oil, which is obtained from the seeds; the leaves are not used.

Rocket, Blood Orange, and Caper Salad

The sweetness of blood oranges (use only a fully ripened, slightly soft orange), the acidity of vinegar and capers, the spiciness of garlic, and the slight bitterness of rocket combine here to create an intriguing complexity.

Serves 4 as a first course

1 cup rocket sprigs
1 blood orange or 1 small sweet grapefruit, peeled and cut into thin slices

VINAIGRETTE DRESSING
4 tablespoons virgin olive oil
1 tablespoon sherry vinegar
½ teaspoon minced garlic
1 teaspoon capers with their juice

Arrange 10 of the rocket leaves on the plate. Remove the stems from the remaining rocket and tear the leaves into small pieces. Cover the whole leaves with the torn rocket. Fan out the orange slices in a half circle. Mix the dressing ingredients together, pour over the salad, and serve.

Mediterranean Plowman's Lunch

This is a Southern French version of the classic English Ploughman's Lunch of Stilton or Cheddar cheese, thick slices of fresh bread, and slices of tomato and lettuce.

Serves 1 as a main course

1 small goat cheese
1 egg, beaten
¼ cup fine dry bread crumbs
1 tablespoon olive oil
10 rocket leaves
3 thin slices purple onion
Ten niçoise olives

Flatten the goat cheese a bit. Dip it in the egg and then in the bread crumbs; repeat this procedure.

Heat the olive oil in a sauté pan or small skillet and sauté the goat cheese until nicely browned.

Arrange the rocket leaves on a plate. Place the goat cheese at one end. Fan the onion slices out in a half circle leading to a mound of olives at the other end of the plate. Serve while the goat cheese is still warm.

RUTABAGA

Brassica Napus Napobrassica Group

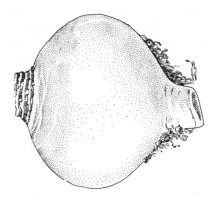

Other names: Swede turnip, Swede.

How grown: From seed.

Availablility: All year, but it is freshest in fall and winter.

Peak of freshness: The roots should be firm, not spongy.

To prepare: Scrub the skin and remove the leaves. Trim ends. Peel the skin after cooking.

The rutabaga developed as a cross between the turnip and the wild cabbage during the Middle Ages. It has a distinctive, starchy cabbage flavor, and it is popular with Europeans who serve it as a purée or sautéed in slices. Rutabaga can also be served in a cooked salad such as a Macedoine (page 161). Its leaves are waxy and stiff and are not usually eaten.

RUTABAGA AND TURNIP: NON-IDENTICAL TWINS

Take a close look at these two root vegetables and you'll find the following differences:
1. The neck of the rutabaga is fatter than that of the turnip.
2. Rutabagas have a yellow flesh that is firmer than the white meat of the turnip.
3. Rutabagas commonly have purple-yellow skin, while turnips have white skin blushed with rose, purple, or green at the neck.

Pan-Fry of Rutabaga with Parsley Sauce

This recipe can be made with other roots: turnips, carrots or parsnips, or all four together. Sweet potatoes also work well with the parsley sauce.

Serves 4 as a side dish

8 rutabagas
3 tablespoons butter

PARSLEY SAUCE

2 tablespoons butter
1 cup parsley sprigs, minced
  (about 1 bunch)
¼ cup dry white wine
⅓ cup heavy cream
Salt to taste
White pepper to taste

Steam the rutabagas for about 10 minutes or until tender. Peel them and cut into 3-inch-long pieces. Melt the butter in a sauté pan or skillet and sauté the rutabaga pieces in the butter, browning them on both sides.

While the rutabaga is steaming, make the sauce. Melt the butter in a heavy saucepan. Add the parsley and sauté for 2 minutes. Add the wine and simmer for 15 minutes. Add the cream, salt, and white pepper. Stir and keep warm. Pour the sauce into a small pitcher and serve alongside the rutabaga while hot.

TURNIP

Brassica Rapa Rapifera Group

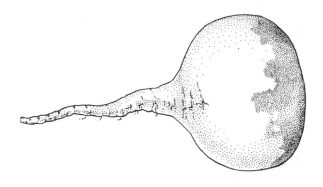

How grown: From seed.

Availability: All year, but cool months produce the sweetest, crispest roots.

Peak of freshness: Turnips should be smooth, firm, and not rubbery.

To prepare: Wash turnips gently: the skins may scar if they are young. The greens may be left attached on very young plants. Trim the root ends.

The turnip first grew wild somewhere in Asia, and wild turnips still grow on the steppes of Siberia. Today they are grown worldwide. In the United States turnips do best in the south during the fall and winter, though they are also grown in the north during the summer.

Spring and fall turnips are pleasantly radishlike, but summer turnips, like radishes, can be hot. Turnips are versatile: Asians treat them like *daikon* radishes and use the greens of the young turnips as well, stir-frying them or adding them to soup. The greens are also popular in the South cooked with pork. Baby turnips are sweet and can be steamed and eaten whole with the leaves attached, topped with a little olive oil. Turnips can be substituted in Lamb and Kohlrabi Tajine, page 71. Puréed turnips often accompany a pork or lamb roast and may be made into cream of turnip soup.

Turnips with Prosciutto and Gruyère

In this dish cooked turnips are sliced, then layered with prosciutto and Gruyère.

Serves 4 as a side dish, 2 as a main course

4 large turnips
¼ pound Gruyère or Emmenthaler cheese, cut into thin slices
2 ounces thin-sliced prosciutto, cut into 1-by-2-inch pieces
2 tablespoons grated Parmesan
2 tablespoons dry bread crumbs
4 parsley sprigs

Steam the turnips until tender, about 30 minutes. Allow to cool. Preheat the oven to 350°. Peel the turnips and cut each one into 3 or 4 horizontal slices. Place the bottom slice of each turnip in a deep baking dish. Add 1 piece of cheese and 1 of prosciutto on top of each turnip slice. Continue layering until you have used all the turnips, cheese, and prosciutto. Secure each completed turnip with a 4-inch piece of bamboo skewer. Sprinkle the tops with the Parmesan and bread crumbs. Cover the baking dish. Bake for 25 minutes, or until the cheese is melted and the turnips heated through. Serve each turnip topped with a sprig of parsley.

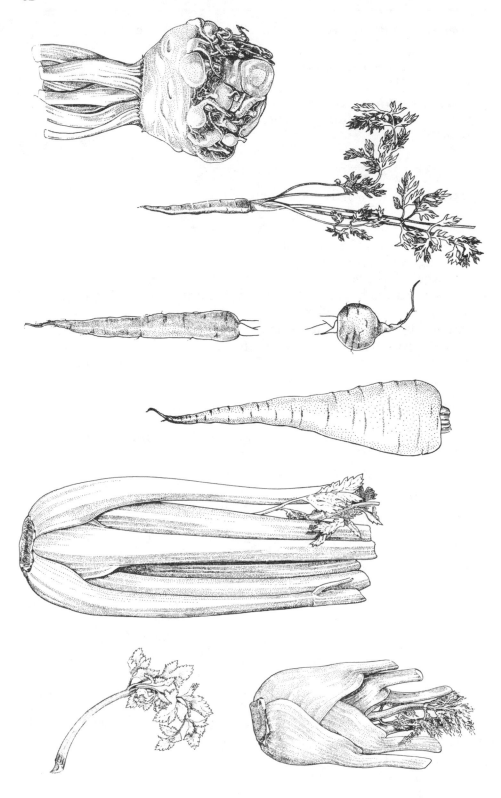

Carrot Family

Umbelliferae: Carrot, Celeriac, Celery, Fennel, Parsley, Parsnip

*T*he Umbelliferae family takes its name from its flowers, which are clustered together in umbels, formations shaped like upside-down umbrellas. Each umbel contains several hundred white, cream, yellow, or pink flowers. All the umbelliferae are strong smelling, especially in their wild state.

Many of the members of this family, such as dill and angelica, are used as herbs. Fennel and parsley are used both as herbs and as vegetables. In fact, even the common carrot was for many centuries employed only as a medicinal herb. Nicholas Culpepper, in his famous *Herbal*, informs us that the seed of the wild carrot in particular is useful for treating colic and kidney stones; that if the seeds are boiled in wine and then taken, they will aid conception; that carrot leaves applied with honey are useful in treating wounds.

CARROT

Daucus carota var. *sativus*

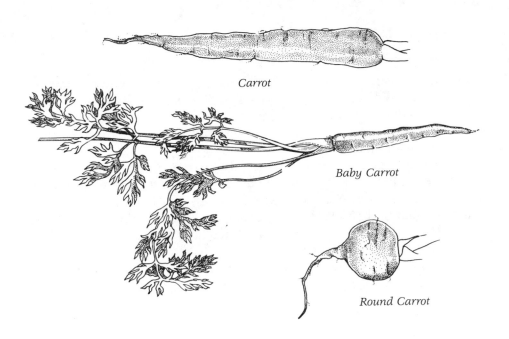

Carrot

Baby Carrot

Round Carrot

How grown: From seed.

Availability: All year.

Peak of freshness: Carrots should have a medium- to dark-orange clear skin, with no sign of whiteness or drying.

Freshness is sometimes indicated by attached leaves.

To prepare: Wash. Scrape or peel the skin lightly with a sharp knife or potato peeler. Trim the leaf end.

It's hard to imagine a carrot being any color besides orange, but until the beginning of this century other colors were readily available as well. Cooks and gardeners could choose from red, white, purple, and, of course, orange. Today, some British gardeners still grow a few white carrots, which have a stronger flavor, to add to a dish of orange ones.

Most of the carrots available in American markets are grown in one of two areas: California or southern Florida. Generally these carrots are the long, pointed Imperator types. The short stubby types and baby fingerlings commonly found in Europe are increasingly available in our markets, but the 18-inch-long Asian carrot is still rarely seen.

Although numerous kinds of carrots exist, each with different characteristics, the shopper can only distinguish taste by experimentation; shape or color is not a consistent guide in determining quality. If possible, find a market that carries several different kinds. Taste them all cooked and raw and make your own choice. Carrots are often selected for aesthetic as well as culinary reasons: baby or French Round carrots look attractive in delicate sauces or arranged on a plate, while large wide carrots are good for Chinese diagonal slicing.

Carrots are among the most versatile of vegetables. They can be used in salads with other vegetables or with nuts or fruit. They can be steamed, sautéed, puréed with cream and butter, baked as in Sweet Potatoes with Three Kinds of Ginger (page 289), used in Gratin of Winter Roots (page 96), or substituted for beets in Beet-Fennel Gratin (page 103). Carrots can be used in place of pumpkin in Leek and Pumpkin Soup (page 134) and instead of rutabaga in Pan-Fry of Rutabaga with Parsley Sauce (page 80).

Pickled Carrots

In Mexico, steamed tacos are often served with a side dish of pickled carrots, along with shredded lettuce and a salsa, page 221.

Makes 2 pints

*4 long carrots, or 2 dozen small
   round carrots
1 white onion
1¾ cups water
2 teaspoons salt
¾ cup distilled vinegar
2 fresh jalapeño peppers
6 peppercorns*

Slice the long carrots into ⅜-inch-thick pieces; leave round carrots whole. Slice the onion into ¼-inch rings. In a medium saucepan, bring the water and salt to a boil. Add the onion and carrots and cook for 4 minutes. Remove the pan from the heat and add the remaining ingredients. Allow to stand for several hours or overnight. Pour into two sterilized pint jars and cover. Pickled carrots may be refrigerated for up to 1 week.

Carrots with Cumin

Moroccan cooks are fond of combining carrots with cumin, as are Indian chefs. The sweet taste of the vegetable combines nicely with the deeply pungent flavor of cumin. This dish can be served with grilled meat or fish or with a curried lentil dish.

Serves 4 as a side dish

4 large or 16 baby carrots
1½ cups vegetable or chicken
  stock
2 tablespoons butter
1 large yellow onion, chopped
1 teaspoon chopped garlic
3 small fresh hot peppers such as
  jalepeño or serrano, seeded
  and chopped
1 teaspoon cumin seeds
Salt to taste

Cut the large carrots into sticks 2 inches long and ¼ inch wide; leave baby carrots whole. Bring the stock to a boil in a medium saucepan and simmer the carrots for 5 minutes or until almost tender. They should still be firm in the center when pierced with the tip of a knife. Reserve ½ cup of the cooking liquid.

Melt the butter in a heavy skillet and add the onion, garlic, and peppers. Sauté until the onion is translucent. Add the cumin and cook for 1 minute. Add the reserved cooking liquid, carrots, and salt. Cook over medium heat for about 3 minutes or until the carrots are tender.

Boeuf aux Carottes

This hearty country French stew is often served at small, out-of-the-way cafes whose cook-owner will prepare a midday meal on request. This dish can be served immediately, but the flavor improves so much after a day or two that we recommend making it two days before serving, then reheating it slowly in the oven, tightly covered.

Serves 6 as a main course

2 tablespoons olive oil
1 large yellow onion, chopped
1 tablespoon chopped garlic
1½ pounds stewing beef, with
  some fat left on, cut into
  2-inch cubes
2 cups dry red wine
2 pounds carrots, cut into 1-inch
  lengths
1 tablespoon minced fresh
  thyme, or 1 teaspoon dried
  thyme
Salt and pepper to taste

Heat the olive oil in a large Dutch oven or other heavy heatproof casserole. Cook and stir the onion and garlic over medium heat until translucent. Remove the onion and garlic from the pot with a slotted spoon. Add the meat and cook over high heat, stirring frequently, until the meat is browned. Remove the meat from the pan. With the heat on high, add a little of the red wine and stir and scrape the stuck bits from the bottom of the pan. This helps make a nice, dark sauce. Add the carrots, thyme, salt, pepper, and remaining red wine. Reduce the heat and cover. Cook for 1 hour, stirring every 15 minutes. Taste for seasoning and add more salt and pepper if neces- sary. Cook for another hour. The meat should be tender enough to cut with a fork.

CELERIAC

Apium graveolens var. *rapaceum*

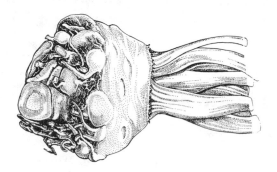

Other names: Celery root, turnip-rooted celery, knob celery.

How grown: From seed.

Availability: Fall and winter.

Peak of freshness: Firm, not spongy. Do not be alarmed by the irregular side roots, misshapen and dirty appearance, and pungent smell. These are characteristics of a fresh celery root.

To prepare: Wash. If using raw, peel off the skin and any side roots with a sharp stainless steel knife (iron discolors celeriac). Remove any stalks remaining at the root top. Store the root in acidulated water until ready to use. Celeriac may also be cooked first, then peeled.

What would a tray of *crudités* in a French provincial restaurant be without a *remoulade* of *céleri-rave*? Perfectly julienned, pale and creamy white, the crunchy celeriac, tossed with a vinaigrette and served next to grated carrots, beets, and sliced tomatoes, is the first course of many a simple meal.

Celeriac is best known in Northern Europe, where it has long provid- ed fresh winter fare. It is commonly used in soups, stews, and salads. It has a delightful crunchiness and celerylike flavor, and is an excellent com- panion to wild game.

Celerylike stalks top the crown of the celeriac root, which grows to the size of a large coconut. Celeriac is grown for its root, not its stalk.

It is regaining its popularity in the United States; during the thirties and forties celeriac was a frequent Sunday supper dish, served in a salad with chopped green onion and canned red pimiento (see below). Celeriac can be puréed with cream and butter. It can be substituted for fennel in Beet-Fennel Gratin (page 103), and substituted for or added to celery in poultry stuffings and in Chicken and Celery Braised in Cream (page 90).

Old-Fashioned Celeriac Salad

Serves 4 as a side dish

2 medium or 3 small celeriac
    roots
½ cup chopped scallions
¼ cup chopped roasted and
    peeled pimiento (see page 203)
Salt and pepper to taste
¼ cup vinaigrette dressing (page
    94) or mayonnaise (page 161)

Boil the celeriac in salted water to cover for 45 minutes or until tender. Drain and cool. Peel and cut into ½-inch cubes. Combine with the scallions, pimiento, and salt and pepper and toss with dressing. Refrigerate for 2 hours or more to develop the flavor.

Celeriac, Cranberry, and Apple Salad with Honey

Serves 4 as a side dish

1 celeriac root (about 1 pound)
½ pound fresh cranberries
½ cup water
¼ cup honey
2 red apples such as Winesap or
    Jonathan, unpeeled and cut in-
    to ¼-inch cubes
Juice of ½ lemon
Radicchio or lettuce leaves

Peel the celeriac and cut into ¼-inch cubes. Steam 5 minutes or until just tender. Boil the cranberries in ½ cup of water for 5 minutes. Drain and chop coarsely, using a knife or a food processor with a metal blade. Add the honey to the cranberries and let them stand for 1 hour. Combine the celeriac, cranberries, apples, and lemon juice. Spoon onto radicchio or lettuce leaves. This salad may be served chilled or at room temperature.

CELERY

Apium graveolens var. *dulce*

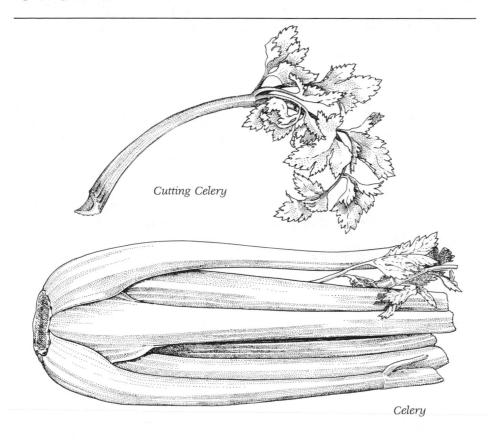

Cutting Celery

Celery

How grown: From seed.

Availability: Year round.

Peak of freshness: Celery stalks should be crisp. Avoid those with any signs of drying, as they will be tough.

To prepare: Wash. Trim the ends off the stalks, pulling off any strings from the outer stalks. Trim the bulb end.

A native of the boglands of Eurasia, celery was well known in the Middle Ages as a medicinal plant, but it wasn't used as food until much later.

European cutting celery and Asian *kintsai* celery are closely related to wild celery and consequently have very thin, reedy stalks. They are used primarily for their pungent leaves, which give a distinct flavor to stews and soups.

The stalk celery with which we are so familiar is a relatively recent newcomer to kitchens, appearing around the turn of the century. A hundred years ago the only way to produce the thick mild-flavored pale-green stalks was to blanch them in trenches or by wrapping. Today selected strains are self-blanching. Celery comes in different colors, ranging from yellow to dark green to green tinged with red or pink. The red and pink celeries are most frequently grown in Britain and Northern Europe. Americans prefer the light green or yellow types.

Celery and Scallop Salad

Serves 6 as a first course

1 large or 2 small bunches celery
  (2 pounds)
½ pound sea scallops, cut in half
  crosswise
1 red bell pepper, seeded and cut
  into strips
1 tablespoon sesame seeds

DRESSING

1 tablespoon Asian sesame oil
1½ tablespoons medium soy
  sauce
2 tablespoons aji pon vinegar
1 teaspoon sugar
½ teaspoon salt

Lettuce leaves

Remove the leaves from the celery. Cut the celery diagonally across into thin slices. Steam for 1 minute. Remove from the heat and rinse under cold water. Drain; set aside.

Poach the scallops in simmering water until just cooked, about 2 minutes (if you are working with very large scallops you may need to cook them another minute). Allow them to cool. In a stainless steel or glazed ceramic bowl combine the celery, scallops, and peppers.

Toast the sesame seeds in a small skillet over low heat, stirring frequently so they brown evenly. Mix the dressing, pour it over the scallops and vegetables, and toss thoroughly. Let the salad stand for 30 minutes. Serve on a bed of lettuce garnished with the sesame seeds.

Chicken and Celery Braised in Cream

Celery has a wonderfully delicate flavor that is brought out by slow cooking.

Serves 4 as a first course, 2 as a main course

1 whole chicken breast, skinned,
  boned, and cut into 1-inch
  cubes
½ cup unbleached all-purpose
  flour
6 celery stalks, cut into strips 1/2
  inch wide and 3 inches long
½ cup heavy cream
1 teaspoon paprika
Salt and pepper to taste

Preheat the oven to 350°.

Dredge the chicken cubes in the flour. Steam the celery stalks for 3 minutes. Add the chicken, celery, cream, paprika, salt, and pepper to a Dutch oven. Cover and bake for 20 minutes. Serve over rice.

FENNEL
Foeniculum vulgare

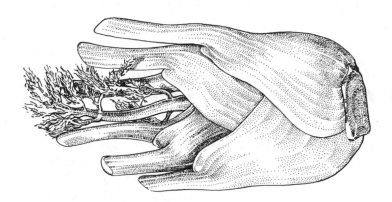

Other names: Sweet anise, *finnochio*, Florentine fennel.

How grown: From seed.

Availability: Late summer, fall, winter, early spring.

Peak of freshness: The cut edges should appear fresh, with no sign of drying or brownness. The bulb should be compact, not spread at the top. Spreading indicates an overly mature bulb, which will be woody inside.

To prepare: Wash. Trim the bottom and top. Remove the outer pieces if they are bruised.

Bite into a *boudin* sausage made Cajun, Spanish, or French style, and one of the first flavors to tickle your senses will be that of fennel, a slightly sweet, slightly licorice taste that is distinctive and pleasurable to most people.

Fennel is a Mediterranean favorite that was first planted in the United States in the 1800s. The bulb develops above the ground, with stalks topped by feathery leaves. It has naturalized to a great extent and now grows wild across the California countryside. Although it is a popular European vegetable, fennel has only recently become readily available in the United States. For many years it could be purchased only in Italian or specialty produce markets.

There are two basic types of fennel: the heading type (the herb), which is used primarily to produce seeds, and the bulbous type (the vegetable), which produces a bulb used raw or cooked in a variety of preparations. The bulbs of both cultivated fennels have tightly wrapped celerylike stalks, and the leaves, seeds, and stalks of both types may be used in cooking.

Fennel is delicious raw. In Italy the unadorned bulbs are served as part of an antipasto. It can be chopped and added to salads. In the Mediterranean region, the branches are often used to stuff fish, to flavor fish soup, as a bed of grilled fish or sausages. Fennel can be substituted in Cream of Lettuce Soup (page 285). It can be baked simply with butter and Parmesan cheese. Fennel can also be puréed, grated, and grilled.

Fig Salad with Fennel Leaves

This rich, tart dressing could also be served with slices of cucumber or jicama.

Serves 4 as a first course

DRESSING

2 tablespoons crème fraiche
Juice of 1 lemon
1 teaspoon grated lemon zest
2 tablespoons olive oil
Pepper to taste

3 tablespoons chopped fennel
   leaves
8 figs, washed and cut in
   quarters

Combine the dressing ingredients and add 2 tablespoons of the fennel leaves. Place 2 figs on each plate and pour the dressing over. Garnish with the remaining fennel leaves.

Fennel and Tuna Salad

This salad is a variation of the classic fennel-seafood combination.

Serves 4 as a first course

½ pound tuna fillet
1 cup thinly sliced fennel
2 lemons, very thinly sliced
¼ cup virgin olive oil
1 teaspoon fresh minced thyme,
   or ½ teaspoon dried thyme
Salt and pepper to taste

Light a charcoal fire in an open grill. When the charcoal is covered with gray ash, grill the tuna fillet 3 to 4 minutes per side. The meat should still be pink inside. Cut the fish across the grain into ½-inch slices.

Arrange the fennel slices on individual plates. Cover with a layer of lemon slices. Place slices of tuna on top of the lemon. Drizzle each plate with 1 tablespoon of the olive oil, a bit of fresh thyme, and salt and pepper. As you eat the salad try to take a slice of lemon, a bit of fennel, and a piece of tuna with each bite.

Fennel with Tomato

Serves 4 as a side dish

4 small or 2 large fennel bulbs
3 tablespoons olive oil
1 tablespoon chopped garlic
4 fresh tomatoes, peeled and
  chopped
Salt and pepper to taste
¼ cup dry bread crumbs
2 tablespoons butter, cut into
  small pieces

Preheat the oven to 350°.

Cut the stalks from the fennel and reserve for another use. Slice the bulbs lengthwise into ½-inch-wide strips. Heat the olive oil in a sauté pan or skillet, add the fennel and garlic, and sauté over medium heat for 3 minutes. Add the tomatoes, cover, and cook slowly for 10 minutes. Season to taste. Transfer the fennel-tomato mixture to an ovenproof casserole. Top with bread crumbs and butter. Bake for 20 minutes and serve.

PARSLEY

Petroselinum crispum

How grown: From seed.

Availability: All year.

Peak of freshness: The leaves should be green, never yellow.

To prepare: Wash thoroughly. Discard any discolored leaves and cut off stems.

The Greeks thought that parsley was evil because the mythical infant Archemorus was eaten by serpents as he lay enveloped in a field of parsley. Obviously, this wonderfully aromatic, bright-green plant doesn't deserve its bad reputation.

Parsley is a native of the Mediterranean region and has been carried to most parts of the world. In Northern Europe it is grown in pots that are carried inside in cold weather, though it survives fairly cool temperatures well. Parsley is a biennial that tends to grow permanently wherever it is planted because it often reseeds itself.

Several kinds of parsley have been developed over the years. The most common are flat-leafed Genovese (also called Italian), giant, and common parsley. The curly leaved parsleys are milder in flavor than those with flat leaves.

Until recently, parsley was considered an herb only, but its use as a vegetable is on the rise. It is the basis for a number of sauces, including *salsa verde* and shallot-parsley butter. It may be deep-fried with a tempura batter or made into a tangy cream soup.

Parsley Salad

America's most popular herb is also a vegetable. Coupled with a vinaigrette made with subtle champagne vinegar and shallots, it makes an unusual first course by itself or to accompany pâté, and it can also serve as a sauce for oysters or clams on the half shell.

Serves 4 as a first course

VINAIGRETTE
¼ cup virgin olive oil
1 tablespoon champagne vinegar
1 teaspoon chopped shallot
Salt and pepper to taste

2 cups loosely packed Italian
    parsley sprigs (about 2 bun-
    ches), minced
1 hard-cooked egg, chopped

Mix the olive oil, vinegar, shallots, and salt and pepper together. Pour this vinaigrette over the parsley. Place the parsley on a serving dish and refrigerate for 30 minutes. Mound the egg in the center and serve.

PARSNIP
Pastinaca sativa

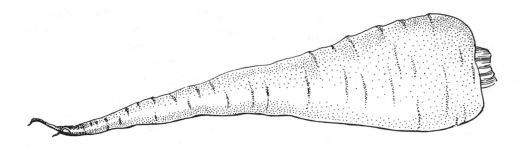

How grown: From seed.

Availability: Fall through spring.

Peak of freshness: Look for straight, 5- to 10-inch smooth-skinned roots that do not bulge excessively at the crowns. Avoid limp and wilted roots.

To prepare: Scrub; trim both ends.

In Europe the parsnip was one of the main sources of carbohydrates until it was replaced by the more versatile potato in the 1600s. Parsnips have not been altered much since then by the efforts of agricultural researchers, perhaps because they are currently somewhat out of favor.

Many farmers of the older generation believe that frost improves the flavor of parsnips, and therefore they leave their crop in the ground until after the first cold spell. Home gardeners might want to try this technique.

The parsnip closely resembles the carrot in taste and the sweet potato in texture. It can be substituted in many root recipes, including Boeuf aux Carottes (page 96), Sweet Potato with Three Kinds of Ginger (page 289), Taro Root Stewed with Duck (page 292), and Pan-Fry of Rutabaga with Parsley Sauce (80).

Gratin of Winter Roots with Wild Mushrooms

This is a colorful dish with a top layer of sorrel or spinach.

Serves 6 as a side dish

2 each *parsnips, turnips,*
    rutabagas, and sweet potatoes
2 *bunches sorrel, or 1 bunch*
    spinach
½ *pound wild mushrooms,*
    thinly sliced
1½ *cups heavy cream*
Salt and pepper to taste

Preheat the oven to 375 °.

Peel the root vegetables and cut them into ½-inch-thick slices. Destem the sorrel or spinach. Cover the bottom of the baking dish with a layer of mixed roots and a handful of mushroom slices. Alternate layers until you have used up all the roots and mushrooms. Pour in the cream. Sprinkle with salt and pepper. Cover the top with the sorrel or spinach leaves. Cover the casserole and bake until the roots are tender, about 45 minutes. Take the casserole to the table and serve each person a multilayered piece.

Corn

Zea mays

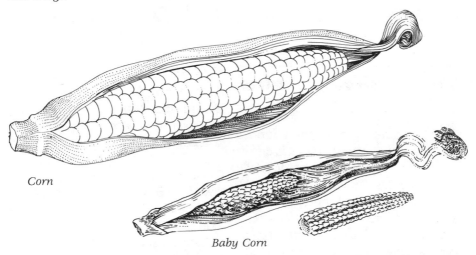

Corn

Baby Corn

C orn is not strictly a vegetable, but a member of the grass family that originated in South America. Almost anyone who has tasted different kinds of sweet corn will have his or her favorite. Some insist that white corn, particularly Country Gentleman, is the acme of flavor; others prefer Silver Queen or Platinum Lady. Still others adore yellow corn. And the debate goes on every summer. Everyone does agree that sweet corn is best eaten at its peak before the sugar turns to starch, a process that starts as soon as the corn is picked. A recent development may give those who live some distance from a cornfield a chance to taste sweet corn at its peak. Scientists have developed a double sugar gene so that the corn has an extended period of prime quality.

Although canned baby corn has been available for some time, baby corn has only become available fresh within the last year or so and on a limited basis. Treat it as you would any fresh corn, but eat the cob along with the kernels.

Young corn is delicious grilled. Try accompanying it with a spicy butter such as one made with *jalapeño* and lime juice. Corn with larger kernels is best boiled or steamed, or cut off the cob and sautéed or added to salads.

How grown: From seed.

Availability: At peak in summer.

Peak of freshness: Fresh-picked is best. Otherwise look for firm, smallish kernels, with no mold or decay at the tip of the cob,

and avoid brownish silk or tassels.

To prepare: Roast in the husk or peel it away (shuck) and remove the corn silk. Trim both ends to use whole, or cut the kernels off.

Thai Cabbage Salad

Thai cuisine is renowned for its salads, which usually include either meat or fish as well as a wide range of vegetables. The dressing is nearly always a combination of fish sauce and lime juice as well as fresh herbs. Thai salads are composed of contrasting tastes, textures, and colors. Seasonal substitutions are the rule rather than the exception, and nearly any raw or cooked vegetable may be served in this manner.

Serves 4 as a first course

2 medium ears of corn
Lettuce leaves
1 cup each chopped purple and
  green cabbage
¼ cup chopped roasted skinned
  peanuts
1 tablespoon chopped fresh mint
1 tablespoon chopped fresh
  cilantro

DRESSING

¼ cup fish sauce
2 tablespoons fresh lime juice
1 teaspoon sugar
1 teaspoon chopped purple onion

Cook the corn in boiling water to cover for 3 to 5 minutes; drain and cool. Cut off the kernels and set aside.

Cover a serving tray with lettuce leaves. Place the cabbage and corn in separate mounds on top of the lettuce. Scatter the peanuts, mint, and cilantro over. Mix the dressing and pour it over the salad. Serve immediately.

Grilled Corn and Okra Served on a Bed of Onion Salad

This dish is best with baby corn, though very young corn is also delicious. Baby corn is about 2 inches long and ½ inch in diameter, yet the kernels are perfectly formed and the cob is entirely edible. Not all corn when it is immature will exhibit these characteristics. You can also grill regular-sized ears of corn separately—do not try to skewer them or they will break apart.

Serves 4 as a side dish

16 ears of baby corn, shucked, or
    8 young ears of corn, shucked
    and cut in half crosswise
1 pound young okra
¼ cup olive oil
2 teaspoons minced fresh
    oregano
Salt and pepper to taste

ONION SALAD

4 medium purple onions,
    chopped
2 tomatoes, peeled, seeded, and
    chopped
1 cup minced fresh Italian
    parsley
1 tablespoon olive oil
1 tablespoon red wine vinegar
Salt and pepper to taste

1 tablespoon minced fresh
    Italian parsley for garnish

Marinate the corn and okra in the olive oil, oregano, salt, and pepper for 2 to 4 hours. Combine all the ingredients for the salad and refrigerate for 1 hour.

Light a charcoal fire in a open grill. Drain the corn and okra and alternately skewer them on small wooden skewers, passing the skewers crosswise through the centers of the vegetables.

When the charcoal is covered with gray ash, grill the vegetables, turning them frequently and basting with the marinade.

Ring the outside of the serving plate with the onion salad. Remove the corn and okra from the skewers and mound them in the center of the plate. Garnish with the parsley and serve.

Goosefoot Family

Chenopodiaceae: Beet, Chard, Spinach

*T*he goosefoot family undoubtedly got its name because of the leaves of its members, which resemble the thick, webbed skin of the goose's foot. Although this family also includes a few weeds, it is better known for its vegetable members. Spinach, chard, and beets are the most common, but lesser-known potherbs such as orach, lambsquarter, and Good King Henry also belong to the goosefoot family. All the family members have small flowers that are often strong-smelling. If you travel by a field of sugar beets that has gone to seed, you will notice the almost sickeningly sweet odor given off by the small flowers borne on tall stalks.

Chenopods are distributed worldwide. Chard, beets, and spinach have been eaten for centuries in Eurasia, and the commentaries of Aristotle have a reference to red chard. In India today goosefoot members are used for medicines and in salads and stews.

BEET

Beta vulgaris Crassa Group

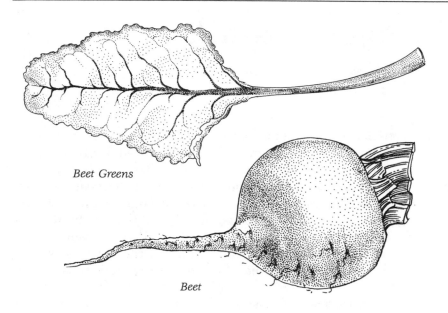

Beet Greens

Beet

How grown: From seed.

Availability: Fall through spring.

Peak of freshness: Beets should be firm, with a root tip that is short and not too hairy. If it has a hairy tip, the beet had to struggle to grow and might be tough.

The beet top should not be a dryish brown, as this indicates the crown was not underground and will probably be tough as well.

To prepare: Scrub well and trim both ends. Beets may be peeled before or after cooking.

The Greeks were fans of the beet as early as the fourth century B.C. Invading Southern European armies took the beet north with them, and it became such a staple food that today we tend to associate beets with cold climates, where they can grow almost year round.

The red color of beets is produced by betanin. Today yellow, or golden, beets are becoming popular. They resemble red beets in every way except for the lack of betanin. Beet leaves are often ignored by cooks, even though they are delicious. When tender the leaves have a lovely tart taste that combines well in a salad with less flavorful greens.

Beets are commonly boiled and used in salads, baked in gratins and used in soups.

Beet-Tomato Chutney

Serve this chutney hot or at room temperature as an accompaniment to a fish or meat curry.

Makes about 6 cups

1 tablespoon chopped garlic
3 tablespoons chopped fresh
   ginger
3 tablespoons oil
1 tablespoon fresh chopped
   turmeric, or 1 teaspoon ground
   dried turmeric
1 teaspoon ground cumin
2 pounds beets, peeled and cut
   into ½-inch cubes
1½ pounds tomatoes, peeled,
   seeded and chopped
Salt and pepper to taste

In a sauté pan or skillet, sauté the garlic and ginger in the oil over medium heat until nearly tender. Add the turmeric and cumin and cook 2 minutes longer. Add the beets, tomatoes, salt and pepper, and water to cover. Simmer 30 minutes or until the beets are tender.

Beet-Fennel Gratin

This cold-weather gratin should be baked in a dish that can be brought to the table. Cubes of potato or celeriac can be substituted for the fennel. The resulting dish is a hearty deep red and very warming.

Serves 6 to 8 as a side dish

3 pounds beets, peeled
½ cup freshly grated Parmesan
   cheese
1 pound fennel stalks, thinly
   sliced crosswise
2 cups half and half
Salt and pepper to taste
¼ cup dry bread crumbs
Fennel leaves or parsley sprigs for
   garnish

Boil the beets in salted water to cover for 20 minutes or until tender, then drain and cut into ½-inch cubes. Preheat the oven to 350°.

Cover the bottom of the buttered baking dish with half of the beets. Sprinkle with 2 tablespoons of the Parmesan cheese. Cover with the fennel. Sprinkle again with 2 tablespoons of Parmesan. Add the remaining beets and Parmesan. Add the half and half. Season with salt and pepper. Cover with bread crumbs. Bake for 30 to 40 minutes. Serve garnished with fennel leaves or parsley.

Beet Pasta with Grilled Salmon and Basil-Cream Sauce

Cooked beets turn pasta a luscious rose color. Salmon and basil add more bright hues to this special summer dish.

Serves 6 or more as a first course, 4 as a main course

PASTA

½ pound beets
2 cups semolina flour
2 cups unbleached all-purpose flour
3 to 4 large eggs

FISH STOCK

2 to 3 pounds salmon bones and/or heads
2 medium yellow or white onions, cut in half
2 carrots, scraped and chopped
1 bay leaf
½ cup parsley sprigs
2 cups dry white wine
Water to cover

BASIL-CREAM SAUCE

1 cup heavy cream
1 cup fish stock
¼ cup basil leaves
Salt and pepper to taste

1 pound salmon fillet
¼ cup olive oil
¼ cup basil leaves
1 gallon water
Salt to taste
2 tablespoons basil leaves for garnish

Cook the beets in boiling salted water to cover for 20 minutes or until tender; cool, peel, and grate. Mix the beets and flours by hand with a wooden spoon in a large bowl or in a food processor with a pastry blade. When the beets are thoroughly combined, add the eggs one at a time. The dough should be moist without being wet. Remove the dough from the bowl or food processor, form it into a ball and knead vigorously on a lightly floured surface until the dough becomes elastic (1 to 2 minutes for the processed variety, about 5 minutes for the hand-mixed dough). Refrigerate for 1 hour or more wrapped in plastic. Flatten and cut into linguine or spaghetti.

Any part of the fish except the entrails and the gills is suitable for stock, or *fumet*, as it is also called. Fish stock does not require long, slow cooking. One half-hour over a moderate flame develops the flavors fully. Fish stock keeps frozen up to 2 months. To make the stock, simmer all the ingredients for 30 minutes in a stockpot. Skim the foam off as it forms. Strain the stock through a fine sieve.

To make the sauce, in a heavy saucepan combine all the sauce ingredients and cook to slowly reduce the liquid by one-half. Strain through a sieve. The sauce can be made ahead of time. Dot the top with small pieces of butter to prevent a skin from forming. Reheat in the top of a double boiler.

Marinate the salmon with the olive oil and basil for at least 1 and preferably 4 hours, turning several times.

Make a fire in an open grill with mesquite charcoal or a mildly flavored hardwood charcoal such as oak. Place the grate about 12 inches from the coals. When the coals are covered with gray ash with no open flame you are ready to cook the fish. Grill the salmon for about 6 minutes total, turning once and basting with the marinade frequently. Cook the fish until a thin wooden skewer easily pierces the thickest part of the fillet. Remove to a warm platter.

Cook the pasta in vigorously boiling salted water until just *al dente*, 1 to 2 minutes. It will continue to cook on the serving platter. Cut the salmon into 1-inch-thick slices crosswise. Arrange it across the top of the pasta. Cover with the cream sauce. Garnish with basil leaves and serve immediately on warm plates.

CHARD

Beta vulgaris Cicla group

> ***Other names:*** Swiss chard, spinach beet, leaf beet.
>
> ***How grown:*** From seed.
>
> ***Availability:*** Fall through spring.
>
> ***Peak of freshness:*** Clear white or red ribs, showing no brownish discoloration. The leaves should be crisp and semi-savoyed.
>
> ***To prepare:*** If the leaves are large, remove and chop the midribs. They will take longer to cook than the leaf sections. Cut from the base of the leaf upward along the edge of the rib on both sides.

Chard is a type of beet that has been selected for its leaf development rather than for its root. There are many varieties of chard, though only two general categories are available in the United States: red and green. The green types have white mid-ribs, and leaves that vary in color from dark to light green. Red chard has cherry-red mid-ribs. Chard, regardless of color, is just the right tartness to combine with sweet ingredients such as raisins. Mediterranean cooks frequently use chard with fruits or sugar as well as with raisins. Chard is usually steamed, used in soups, or stir-fried. Chard leaves with their ribs removed may be substituted for spinach and other leafy greens in most recipes. Very young chard may be served raw in a salad.

Provençal Chard Soup

Serves 4 as a first course

3 tablespoons olive oil
1 small yellow onion, minced
1 teaspoon chopped garlic
2 medium carrots, cut into
    ¼-inch slices
10 medium or 5 large chard
    leaves, minced
2 large red potatoes, peeled and
    cut into ½-inch cubes
3 cups chicken stock
3 cups water
Salt and pepper to taste

Heat the olive oil in a heavy stockpot. Add the onion, garlic, and carrots and sauté for 3 minutes. Add the chard, potatoes, and stock and water. Simmer for 45 minutes. Season with salt and pepper and serve.

Curried Chard and Shark Pie

In this dish, chunks of firm-fleshed fish, tomatoes, and curry spices are wrapped in a envelope of chard and baked in a flaky pie crust.

Serves 8 to 10 as a first course, 6 as a main course

½ pound chard
A double recipe, minus the
    sugar, of the pie dough for
    Tomato Tart, page 227
3 tablespoons oil
1 yellow onion, chopped
1 tablespoon chopped garlic
1 tablespoon chopped fresh
    ginger
1 teaspoon freshly ground cumin
1 teaspoon grated fresh turmeric,
    or ½ teaspoon ground
    turmeric
1 teaspoon freshly ground
    coriander
Salt to taste
½ pound shark, swordfish, or
    halibut, cut into 1-inch cubes
1 medium tomato, peeled,
    seeded, and chopped

Preheat the oven to 350°.
Cut the chard leaves from the stems and tear each leaf into 4 or 5 pieces. Save the stems for another use.
Prepare the dough and cut it in half. Roll the half into a 12-inch circle on a floured board. Place the dough in a 9-inch pie pan, folding the edges under, and pierce with a fork in several places. Bake for 10 minutes or until it just begins to brown. Remove from the oven and set aside.
Heat the oil in a sauté pan or skillet. Add the onion, garlic, and

ginger and cook over medium heat until the onions are translucent. Add the spices and salt and cook another 2 minutes. Remove the pan from the heat.

Roll the other half of the dough into a 12-inch circle. Line the bottom of the pie with half the chard leaves. Place the shark and tomato on top of the chard and cover with the onion-curry mixture. Place the remaining chard leaves on top and tuck them in around the filling. Cover the pie with the top crust. Pinch the two crusts together around the edge. Cut off any overhanging top crust. Pierce the top crust with a fork in 5 or 6 places. Bake for 30 minutes or until browned. Serve hot or at room temperature.

Peppered Goat with Sultanas and Pine Nuts Served on a Bed of Chard

---

This dish was inspired by the sweet and sharp tastes of the Provençal tourte aux blettes: chard pie in a sugar crust, liberally laced with pine nuts and golden raisins.

Serves 4 as a main course

4 tablespoons butter
1 tablespoon olive oil
1 tablespoon minced garlic
1 medium yellow onion, chopped
1 pound goat or beef, trimmed of
    fat and cut into 1-inch cubes
2 teaspoons ground cumin
6 small fresh hot red peppers
    such as Thai, seeded and
    chopped
4 branches fresh thyme, or 1
    teaspoon dried thyme
1 cup chicken stock
1 tomato, chopped
½ cup sultana raisins
Salt and pepper to taste
½ cup pine nuts
1 pound chard

Melt the butter and olive oil in a pan large enough to hold all the ingredients. Sauté the garlic and onion over medium heat until the onion is translucent. Remove the garlic and onion from the pan with a slotted spoon. Brown the meat and remove it from the pan with a slotted spoon. Return the garlic and onion along with the cumin, peppers, and thyme. Sauté for 3 to 4 minutes over high heat. Add the chicken stock and tomato. Return the meat to the pan along with half the raisins and the salt and pepper. Simmer until the meat is tender, about 1 hour, adding a little more chicken stock, if necessary, to keep the meat covered. Just before serving, stir in all but a few of the remaining raisins and the pine nuts.

Cut the white stalks from the chard and cut them into ½-inch-wide strips. Steam the stalks and leaves until limp. Cover a serving platter with the chard, top with the hot goat mixture, and sprinkle with a few sultanas and pine nuts. Serve with a crusty bread and a robust red wine.

SPINACH
Spinacea oleracea

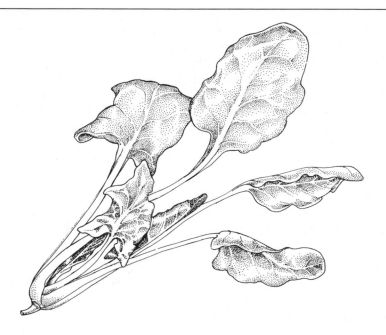

How grown: From seed.

Availability: All year.

Peak of freshness: Bright-green leaves, with no signs of sliminess either on leaves or stems.

To prepare: Few things are more disconcerting at the table than sandy spinach greens. Spinach is grown in sandy soil and must be rinsed repeatedly or plunged into several changes of water. Discard any wilted leaves. Trim stem ends and remove any tough stems.

It is generally believed that spinach originated in southwestern Asia, but it was unknown in Europe until the seventeenth century. Spinach quickly caught on as a cold-weather crop, because it grows rapidly in sandy soil as long as there is enough water and a few warm days.

There are several kinds of spinach; some have curly leaves, others smooth. Both kinds are treated the same in cooking.

Spinach is a versatile green, excellent cooked in gratins, stir-fries (with oyster sauce and garlic), stuffings, and pies, and raw in salads. Cream of spinach soup is a traditional winter dish. Spinach may be used interchangeably with sorrel and chard, and it can be substituted in Rocket, Blood Orange, and Caper Salad (page 78).

Pâté of Leafy Greens

You can make this pâté the day before you plan to serve it. Accompanied with a little crème fraîche *or freshly made ricotta, it makes a wonderful summer lunch.*

Serves 6 as a main course, 8 as a first course

4 cups spinach leaves (1 bunch)
2 cups watercress leaves
(2 bunches)
1 cup dandelion or chicory
greens
3 medium yellow onions, minced
1 tablespoon minced garlic
¼ cup butter
1 teaspoon chopped fresh thyme
leaves, or ½ teaspoon dried
thyme
1 tablespoon chopped fresh basil
½ teaspoon salt
4 slices dry white bread or
baguette, crusts removed
1 cup half and half
6 ounces ground sausage meat
4 large eggs, beaten
Lettuce leaves

Steam the greens in a basket until limp, about 2 minutes. Press out the water with a wooden spoon while the greens are still in the basket. Remove and chop the greens.

In a sauté pan or skillet, sauté the onions and garlic in butter over medium heat until the onions are translucent. Stir in the greens. Add the herbs and salt.

Soak the bread in the half and half for 15 minutes. Squeeze the liquid out of the bread with your hands. Cut the bread into small pieces. Mix with the greens.

Crumble the sausage and cook until it loses its pink color. Drain off any oil. Add the sausage to the greens. Pour the eggs into the greens-sausage mixture. Mix until well blended. Preheat the oven to 350°.

Butter the sides of a heavy mold 3 inches deep and 8 inches in diameter. Pour in the mixture and bake for 1¼ hours. Cool on a wire rack for 30 minutes. Refrigerate for 2 hours. Run a knife around the circumference of the mold. Place in a bowl of just-boiled water for 30 seconds. Turn upside down over a serving plate lined with lettuce leaves and tap gently.

Spinach Loaf

This dish comes from Italy and is often prepared in the fall.

Serves 6 or more as an appetizer, 4 as a first course

2 tablespoons butter
1 large yellow onion, chopped
1 tablespoon chopped garlic
6 cups chopped spinach leaves (2
to 3 bunches)
¼ cup pine nuts
2 slices toasted white bread, cut
into ½-inch cubes
⅓ cup plus 1 tablespoon milk
1 bunch parsley, stemmed and
minced
3 eggs, beaten
⅓ cup grated Romano or
Parmesan cheese
1 teaspoon salt
1 teaspoon ground nutmeg

Melt the butter in a sauté pan or skillet and sauté the onion and garlic over medium heat until the onion is translucent. Steam the spinach until wilted. Drain in a colander and press out the excess moisture with the back of a large spoon. Toast the pine nuts in a skillet until barely brown.

Soak the bread cubes in the milk until soft. Squeeze as much liquid as you can out of the bread. In a large mixing bowl, mix all of the ingredients together.

Lay an 18-inch square of cheesecloth on a cookie sheet. Pour the spinach mixture into the center of the cloth, letting the excess liquid run out. Roll the cloth into a sausage shape and tie the ends with cotton string. Let any remaining liquid drain out into the sink.

Heat 3 inches of water in the bottom of a steamer. When it comes to a full boil, place the cheesecloth-bound spinach into the steamer rack and let it steam for 40 minutes, or until the tip of a knife comes out clean from the center. Cool for a minute or two. Unwrap the spinach and serve hot or warm on a bed of polenta or mashed potatoes.

Spinach and Grilled Shrimp with Spicy Peanut Sauce

In Africa, peanuts and greens are often combined, and the result is unusual and delicious. Not everyone is fond of sauces made from peanut butter, but for those who are this dish is a treat.

Serves 4 as a first course

PEANUT SAUCE
¼ cup chopped yellow onion
1 tablespoon chopped garlic
3 small dried hot peppers, seeded and chopped
2 tablespoons oil
1 cup chicken stock
½ cup fresh salted peanut butter
Salt and pepper to taste

4 fresh serrano or jalapeño peppers
4 large shrimp
1 pound spinach, chopped

Light a charcoal fire in an open grill.

To make the sauce, sauté the onion, garlic, and dried peppers in the oil in a saucepan. When the onion is translucent, add the stock and peanut butter. Simmer 3 to 4 minutes, stirring frequently with a whisk, until the sauce begins to thicken. Season to taste and set aside.

While the coals are red, grill the fresh peppers until thoroughly blackened. Halve, seed, and chop the peppers. When the coals are covered with gray ash, grill the shrimp until just opaque.

Immediately steam the spinach in a basket for 3 minutes. Press out the excess moisture with the back of a large spoon. Make a bed of spinach on each plate. Arrange the chopped peppers and shrimp on top of the spinach. Top with the peanut sauce. Serve with rice.

Spinach Tamales

The dough for traditional tamales is made from masa de maiz, *a finely ground cornmeal that has been treated with lime water. In these tamales, polenta, popular in Italy, not Mexico, is used. The filling is European as well—feta cheese and spinach along with roasted hot peppers.*

Serves 8 as a main course

24 corn husk tamale wrappers
    (available in Mexican groceries
    and many supermarkets)
3¾ cups water
¾ cup polenta
1 teaspoon salt
½ pound spinach or chicory
    greens, stemmed
3 fresh pasilla peppers, roasted,
    peeled and seeded (page 203)
¼ pound feta cheese, cut into
    1-inch squares, ½ inch thick
Tomatillo Salsa, page 221

Separate the tamale wrappers and place them in a steamer basket over boiling water for 5 minutes. Steaming makes the wrappers pliable for folding.

Dissolve the polenta in ¾ cup of the water. Bring the remaining 3 cups water to a simmer in a medium saucepan. Add the salt and polenta and simmer for at least 30 minutes, stirring frequently. If the polenta becomes too thick, pour it into the top of a double boiler and keep cooking. The polenta is done when the grains are soft and of a thick consistency.

Steam the greens in a basket for 2 minutes. While the greens are still in the basket, squeeze out the water by pressing down on them with a large spoon. Chop the greens.

Cut the peppers into thin strips and mix with the greens. Spread the polenta into a 3-inch circle in the center of each corn husk. Place a slice of feta in the center of the polenta. Spoon 1 teaspoon of the greens-pepper mixture on top of the cheese. Fold the sides to the center, one side over the other. Then fold the top and bottom ends to the middle. Stack each folded tamale in the steamer, folded side down. Steam over the boiling water for 20 minutes. Serve with Tomatillo Salsa.

SPINACH ALTERNATES

For most of us spinach is spinach, what botanists refer to as the green leafy member of the goosefoot family. But there are other spinaches, by name at least, if not by family association, and at least four potherbs are commonly given that name, including Chinese spinach, Ceylon spinach, water spinach, and New Zealand spinach. All of these are tropical in origin, and they are more easily grown in warm weather than common spinach, which tends to bolt.

CEYLON SPINACH

Basella rubra

Other names: Malabar nightshade, *gendola, put, saan choy,* slippery vegetable.

How grown: From seed or cuttings.

Availability: Almost all year in tropical climates.

Peak of freshness: Look for large, fleshy leaves up to 7 inches long and 4 inches wide.

To prepare: Wash. Trim stem ends.

Although grown as a potherb, the primary use of Ceylon spinach is as the source of a dye that is extracted from its red berries and used in medicines and jellies. Ceylon spinach grows as a twisting vine, taking well to trellises. It grows vigorously in warm, wet weather, and among the few places it flourishes in America are southern Florida and Hawaii.

Ceylon spinach bears a strong resemblance to flowering white cabbage, though its taste is milder. It is mucilaginous, similar in texture to okra. It can be fried, stewed, or cooked in soups.

CHINESE SPINACH

Amaranthus tricolor

Other names: Amaranth, Jacob's coat, *een choy, tampala.*

How grown: From seed.

Availability: Early spring through late fall.

Peak of freshness: Each leaf should be tender and smooth. The stems should be firm.

To prepare: Wash. Trim stem ends. Peel stems, if large, and use along with leaves.

This plant has been grown for centuries in India, where its seeds are as important to the local diet as are its leaves. It is commonly called amaranth and is currently under intensive development because it is nutritious and easy to grow. The plants are upright, with branching stems and leaves no longer than 6 inches. The stems and leaves may be tinged with red. There are at least fifty kinds of amaranth that grow not only in the warm parts of Asia but also in tropical America and in Africa.

Chinese spinach is mild and slightly sweet. It is usually prepared simply. It can be quickly sautéed with mint and cashews or added to soups. It can be substituted in all spinach recipes.

NEW ZEALAND SPINACH

Tetragonia tetragonioides

Other names: Summer spinach.

How grown: From seed.

Availability: May through October.

Peak of freshness: Use the young leaves and shoots. Avoid large, mealy-looking leaves.

To prepare: Wash. Trim stem ends and remove large stems.

New Zealand spinach was brought back to England in 1770 by Captain Cook, who collected a number of plants for botanists back home. At the time it grew abundantly in New Zealand, Tasmania, and parts of Australia. It was first grown in England as a potherb in 1819. In recent years it has been receiving a lot of attention as a warm-weather spinach, as it flourishes in hot weather. New Zealand spinach is a large, sprawling plant that can be picked throughout the warm summer months. Its leaves are smaller and more glandular than regular spinach. Use it raw in salads, or substitute it in any spinach recipe.

WATER SPINACH

Ipomoea aquatica

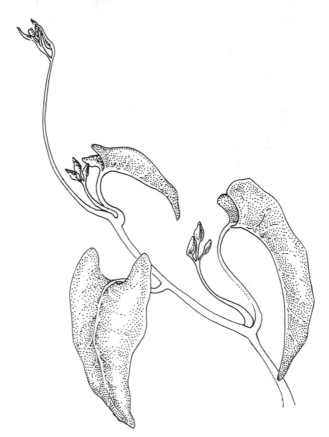

Other names: Swamp cabbage, *ong choy.*

How grown: From seed.

Availability: Early spring to late fall.

Peak of freshness: Look for small tender shoots and young leaves. The larger stems are too tough to bother with.

To prepare: Wash. Cut off tough stems and discard any discolored leaves.

The origin of water spinach is unknown, though it may first have grown in India. It is cultivated throughout tropical Asia, where it is grown by two methods: in rows or beds, with ample watering, or transplanted into swamps where it quickly establishes itself and grows to be quite large. The leaves are not as succulent or as full when grown in dry beds, but the young shoots are still tender and full of flavor. When cooked, the leaves of water spinach are tender, while the stems are firm. It is usually cooked with garlic and shrimp paste, and it may also be flavored with oyster sauce. It can be interchanged with spinach when very young.

Gourd Family

Cucurbitaceae: Bitter Melon, Chayote, Cucumber, Squash, Winter Melon (Wax Gourd, Fuzzy Melon)

The gourd, or cucurbit, family is large, with over 750 species scattered throughout the warm regions of the world. Most cucurbits, such as cucumbers, melons, and Asian gourds, originated in Africa and Eurasia, and it is only the pumpkins, squashes, and chayote that evolved in the Americas. Several wild cucumbers, however, quite different from the domesticated varieties of today, grew wild in North America and were a favorite food of the Indians.

The fruits of the cucurbits are the largest in the world. Most are succulent, and in the arid regions of Africa they are used as sources of liquid. There large watermelons sprout when the desert rains begin and mature as the dry season continues. During the ensuing dry season, the melons are opened up to quench the thirst of humans and animals alike. The cucurbits are able to withstand dry conditions because of a complex root structure. They require moisture when they first sprout up, but as the months go by, they require less and less. Melon growers actually withhold water from their plants to ensure that the melons do not become waterlogged and insipid-tasting.

The root system of cucurbits are matched above ground with trailing vines and large, lobed leaves. Gardeners can successfully trellis cucumbers, squashes, and melons because the vines grow so quickly and long. The flowers of most cucurbits are showy; many are yellow, a few are white. Cucumber blossoms tossed into a green salad make an attractive addition, while squash blossoms may be stuffed, served whole, or chopped.

BITTER MELON
Momordica Charantia

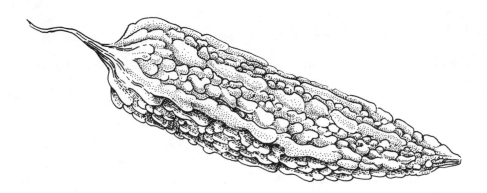

Other names: Balsam pear, bitter cucumber.

How grown: From seed.

Availability: Summer through winter.

Peak of freshness: Look for fruit with light-green, shiny skin, without brown spots.

To prepare: Wash. Cut in half and remove the seeds. Soak in salt water for 30 minutes or more for most recipes.

Bitter melon is native to tropical India and is now grown in warm regions of the United States. In Asia the tender shoots and immature leaves are considered superior to the fruit, but they are not sold in this country.

Bright yellow flowers decorate the vines of bitter melon. The female flowers soon develop into warty, ridged, light-green fruits 6 to 10 inches long and shaped like cucumbers. The flesh is silvery green and contains pale-brown seeds.

The fruit is bitter, as the name implies, and most recipes call for it to be soaked in salt water for 30 minutes or more. Immature fruits are less bitter than older ones. In India, bitter melon is sautéed with garlic and hot pepper and used in pickles. Bitter melon halves can be stuffed with any stuffing appropriate for squash and baked (be sure to soak them in salt water first; see above).

Bitter Melon with Beef and Black Beans

Bruce Cost adapted this recipe from a dish created by Virginia Lee, co-author of The Chinese Cookbook *(New York: Lippincott, 1972).*

Serves 3 to 4 as a main course

1 pound bitter melon
¼ cup salted black beans
¼ cup shao hsing *or dry sherry*
2 tablespoons minced garlic
4 or more small fresh hot peppers such as jalapeño or serrano, seeded and chopped
¾ pound flank steak, thinly sliced against the grain
2 teaspoons cornstarch
1 tablespoon Asian sesame oil
1 tablespoon dark soy sauce
2½ teaspoons sugar
1½ teaspoons salt or to taste
2 tablespoons chicken stock
1 cup oil

Cut the melon in half lengthwise. Scrape the white center of the melon thoroughly and discard the pulp and seeds. Cut the shell into slices ¼ inch thick and 1½ inches long. Blanch for 3 minutes, run under cold water, and drain. Set the melon aside.

With a cleaver or heavy French knife, lightly chop and then slightly crush the black beans. Combine with *shao hsing* or sherry and garlic and set aside. Seed the peppers, shred them the same size as the melon strips, and set aside.

Toss the flank steak with the cornstarch, sesame oil, and soy sauce and set aside. Blend the sugar, salt, and chicken stock.

Heat the oil in a wok until almost smoking and stir-fry the meat for about 15 seconds. It should still be pink. Remove the meat from the wok with a slotted spoon. Drain off the excess oil by placing the meat in a colander.

Remove all but 3 tablespoons of the oil from the wok. Heat until very hot. Add the black bean–garlic mixture and then the peppers. Stir-fry for 20 seconds. Add the seasoned chicken stock, then the beef and melon. Stir and cook until heated through. Serve over rice.

CHAYOTE

Sechium edule

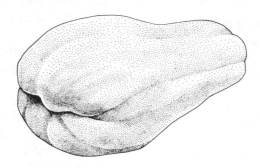

Other names: Vegetable pear, *christophine, brionne.*

How grown: The entire fruit is planted; within it is a single seed that sprouts during the warm season.

Availability: Late summer and fall.

Peak of freshness: Unblemished skins, with no browning.

To prepare: Wash. Split in half and remove the seed. Peel or serve stuffed.

In its tropical home of Central America, the *chayote* is a major source of food. All of its plant parts may be eaten. The starchy, tuberous roots, which develop after a plant is more that two years old, are thought by many to be the tastiest part, but these tubers are seldom seen in the market. Neither are the young leaves and shoots, which are snipped from the vines and added to soups.

The third part of the plant is the fruit. The trailing vine may bear either male or female fruit, or both. The smooth-skinned, slightly ridged and lumpy female fruit is preferable, as the male is less fleshy and covered with warty spines. The shell of both is inedible. It is impossible to predict whether a plant will yield fruit of both sexes or only one, so most gardeners start with at least three plants and cull any with male fruit only.

Chayote is exceedingly bland and should be combined with flavorful ingredients that both flavor the dish and bring out its mild taste. Cajun cooks prepare it with shrimp, tomato, and garlic.

Chayote Soup with Peppers

The bland chayote takes on the warm and spicy flavor of peppers in this Southwestern-influenced soup.

Serves 4 as a first course

1 yellow onion, chopped
3 fresh ancho peppers and 3 fresh jalapeño peppers, roasted, peeled, seeded, and chopped (page 203)
½ teaspoon dried oregano
2 tablespoons olive oil
2 chayotes (about 1 pound total), peeled and cut into ½-inch dice
1 quart chicken stock
1 avocado, cut into thin slices, for garnish
1 tablespoon cilantro leaves for garnish

In a large saucepan, sauté the onion, peppers, and oregano in olive oil until the onion is translucent. Add the chayotes and chicken stock and simmer covered until tender, about 15 minutes. Serve in warm bowls, garnished with a few slices of avocado and cilantro leaves.

CUCUMBER

Cucumis sativus

The cucumber has always had a big following, probably because of its cool, refreshing taste. It is often served to complement hot spicy foods. Because of its astringency, the cucumber is also used as a component in some cosmetics.

Cucumbers grow on vines with yellow flowers. They were among the plants growing in the hanging gardens of ancient Babylon, and today New Yorkers, continuing the tradition of urban farming, grow them in rooftop gardens. The British were among the first to improve bitter types into thin-skinned mild types. They are relatively easy to cultivate and are versatile in the kitchen.

Cucumbers are divided into two neat categories—pickling and slicing—and the two are not usually interchangeable.

PICKLING CUCUMBERS

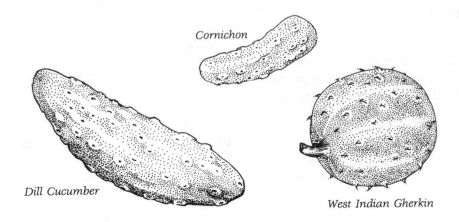

Cornichon

Dill Cucumber

West Indian Gherkin

How grown: From seed.

Availability: July and August.

Peak of freshness: Spiny, hard, light green and slightly warted.

To prepare: Wash, scrubbing slightly to remove any loose spines. Trim stem ends.

Pickling cucumbers include the French *cornichon,* the American dill, and the West Indian gherkin. They are usually identifiable by their sharp black or white prickles, called spines. The true gherkin species originated in the West Indies. The British love the gherkin pickled in sweet brine, and it is served in Indian and Pakistani curry houses in England and throughout the former British empire. The gherkin is only 2 inches long when mature. The *cornichon* pickle is made from very young fruits of black-spined pickling cucumbers that are packed in a brine heavily spiked with tarragon. *Cornichons* are a traditional accompaniment to pâté and many other dishes, including *pot au feu.* Their sharp flavor and crunchiness complement soft textures and rich flavors. They are so commonly used in France as to be comparable to our dill pickle.

SLICING CUCUMBERS

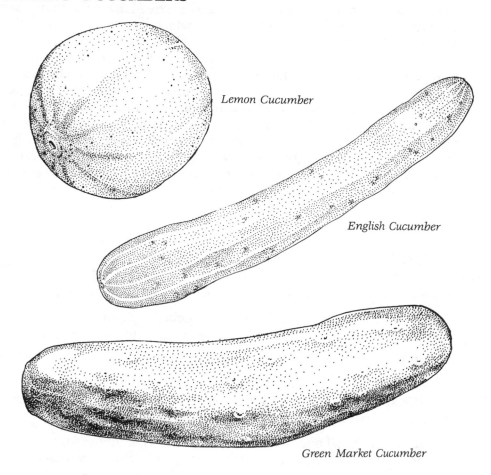

Lemon Cucumber

English Cucumber

Green Market Cucumber

How grown: From seed.

Availability: Summer. Hothouse cucumbers such as Green Market and Burpless are available all year.

Peak of freshness: Firm, but not hard. Cucumbers should not be pliable or have soft spots.

To prepare: Wash. Peel if desired. Many prefer leaving the skin, as today they are not usually bitter. Waxed skins should be peeled. (Skins that have been waxed are shiny and feel waxy; non-waxed cucumbers are duller and tend to be less plump.)

The skins of slicing cucumbers vary a great deal. Some are thin, others thick. The color may vary from light to dark green. Many of the cucumbers available in supermarkets have waxed skin, which lengthens shelf life. This skin should be peeled.

No matter what the shape, size, or color, slicing cucumbers share a crisp, crunchy texture and cooling taste appreciated by almost all the world's cultures. In the Middle East and India cucumbers are mixed with yogurt, mint, and coriander and served as a side dish to offset spicy foods. High tea would not be the same without cucumber sandwiches served on buttered crustless white bread. Cucumbers are an indispensable ingredient in Greek salads, along with tomatoes, feta cheese, red onion, and olives. Cucumbers can be sautéed or stir-fried as you would zucchini or other summer squash.

Slicing Varieties

APPLE OR WHITE: White skin, round, the size of a tennis ball.

ARMENIAN: 10 to 18 inches long, 1 to 2 inches in diameter, with a pale-green convoluted shape that results in scalloped edges when sliced.

BURPLESS: 8 to 16 inches long, 1½ to 2 inches in diameter, with a ridged green skin.

EDIBLE SKIN, ENGLISH: 8 to 16 inches long, 1 to 1½ inches in diameter. Dark green with a smooth skin and few seeds.

GREEN MARKET: The most common cucumber, 8 inches long and 1 to 1½ inches in diameter, with a dark-green, rather thick smooth skin.

LEMON OR YELLOW: Round, about the size of a tennis ball, with pale-yellow skin and some spines, which rub off easily.

Cornichons

Cornichons *are typically made from the Cornichon Vert de Petit Paris or Improved Bourbonne, among others. If you don't have access to these varieties, try using any tiny dill pickling varieties such as Spartan or Tiny Dill.*

Makes 2 pints

40 to 50 tiny pickling cucumbers
   (about 1 cup)
3 tablespoons salt
1 yellow onion, thinly sliced
4 tarragon sprigs
1 garlic clove, sliced
1 bay leaf, halved
4 black peppercorns
¾ cup boiling water
¾ cup distilled vinegar

Wash and dry the cucumbers. Put them into a glass or ceramic bowl, sprinkle with the salt, and let stand for 12 hours, adding the sliced onions for the last 6 hours.

Wash and dry the cucumbers. Divide the cucumbers and the onion slices equally into sterilized pint canning jars (the jars should be about one-quarter full). Add the tarragon, garlic, bay leaf, and peppercorns, placing them on top of the cucumbers. Pour half of the water and vinegar into each jar. Tightly close the jars so no moisture can get in.

In a large pot, boil the jars, covered with water, for 7 minutes. Remove from the water and allow to cool. Store in a cool place. The *cornichons* will be ready to sample in 3 weeks. They will keep in the refrigerator for months after opening.

Cucumber–Yogurt Salad

This cooling salad, known in India as raita, *is delicious with roasted or grilled meats and as an accompaniment to curries.*

Serves 6 to 8 as a side dish

1 medium cucumber, peeled, cut
   in half, and seeded
½ teaspoon salt
½ teaspoon cumin seeds
1 tablespoon minced fresh mint
Cayenne to taste
½ teaspoon salt
1 cup plain yogurt

Cover each cucumber half with ¼ teaspoon of salt. Place face down on a paper towel for 30 minutes. Wipe the salt off the cucumber with fresh paper towels. Finely grate the cucumber.

Roast the cumin seeds in a small skillet over medium heat until the seeds begin to brown. Cool to room temperature.

Combine all the ingredients and chill for 1 hour.

Cucumbers Stuffed with Tapenade and Goat Cheese

You can use a milder, easy-to-spread cheese such as cream cheese instead of goat cheese to make this lively summer appetizer. This recipe for tapenade was created by Maggie Klein and appears in her book The Feast of the Olive *(Berkeley: Aris Books, 1983).*

Serves 10 to 12 as an appetizer

Tapenade

One 2-ounce can anchovy fillets
½ cup California pitted black
    olives
¼ cup capers, drained
¼ cup olive oil
1 tablespoon Dijon mustard

One 4-ounce goat cheese
3 medium cucumbers
1 small purple onion, chopped

Drain and rinse the anchovies. In a blender or food processor, blend all the *tapenade* ingredients. If the *tapenade* is too thick, drizzle more olive oil into the mixture as you continue to blend for a few seconds more—it should be spreadable. Mix the *tapenade* and goat cheese together.

To stuff the cucumbers, cut off one end of each and scoop out the seeds with the handle of a fork or spoon. Spoon a bit of the filling into the opening with a spoon. Pack it down with the handle. Repeat until the cucumber is fully stuffed. Refrigerate for 1 hour.

Cut the cucumbers into thin slices and arrange in a circular pattern, garnished in the center with chopped purple onion. This dish can be dressed with a vinaigrette, if you like.

SQUASH

Curcubita pepo, C. maxima, C. moschata

Squash is indigenous to the Americas. The word squash comes from the Naragansett Indian word *askutasquash*. Indians used squash throughout the year, drying winter squash on sticks in the sun. Today we have fresh squash year round. The numerous kinds of squash are best described by the season in which they are harvested.

SUMMER SQUASH

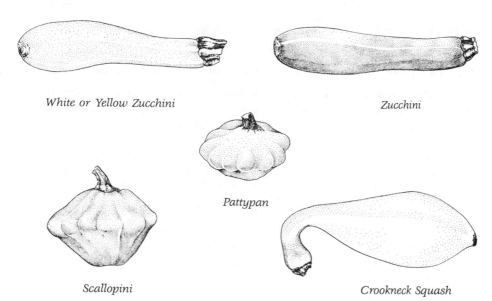

White or Yellow Zucchini

Zucchini

Pattypan

Scallopini

Crookneck Squash

Other name: Vegetable marrow.

How grown: From seed.

Availability: Most abundantly available in summer, though zucchini from Mexico are now available all year.

Peak of freshness: Firm and not over-large. Summer squash should not bend, especially crooknecks. No brown spots.

To prepare: Wash. Trim stem end. Do not peel.

Summer squash are eaten when they are immature; the skin is fine and thin and the seeds are barely developed. Most summer squashes grow on bushes rather than on trailing vines like the winter squashes, which makes them nice for home gardens. Native to the western hemisphere, summer squash so readily adapted to Mediterranean conditions that we think of zucchini, for example, as an Italian squash. Generally speaking, the flavor of summer squash diminishes as the size increases and the flesh loses its fine texture.

When large, summer squash are good for stuffing, as the firm skin holds its shape well when baked. Small squashes should be cooked quickly. Grated squash sautéed with garlic, peppers, and olive oil may be eaten alone or tossed with pasta. Whole squash steamed and served with butter is one of the highlights of summer. Mixing squashes in a sauté or stir-fry can produce a spectacular medley of colors. Tomato and garlic are traditional accompaniments to sautéed squash, along with basil. Zucchini may be added to summer salads along with or instead of cucumber.

Summer Squash Varieties

PATTYPAN: Also called bush scallop or custard marrow. Two to 4 inches in diameter with round, scalloped edges. Pale green or yellow.

SCALLOPINI: Shaped like a pattypan, but speckled green like a zucchini.

YELLOW CROOKNECK: Six to 8 inches long, with a bright-yellow, slightly bumpy skin, a bulbous base, and a narrow curving neck. Some strains have straight necks.

ZUCCHINI: Also called *courgette* or Italian squash. Four to 6 inches long in a large range of colors including white, pale gray, green, and yellow. Some zucchinis are round. Gray varieties are often more flavorful.

ZUCCHINI BLOSSOMS: Large gold trumpet-shaped blossoms. Female blossoms produce fruit and are most often sold attached to tiny zucchinis the size of a little finger. In Europe the male blossoms, which do not bear fruit, are sold as "bouquets" and used for stuffing.

Squash Blossoms

Few entrées are more stunning than a fan arrangement of tiny steamed summer squash, each crowned with its own golden yellow blossom. Unstuffed squash blossoms lend a striking color note to scrambled eggs, and they can be added to *quesadillas* along with onions. In Provençe and in Italy squash blossoms are made into a sweet by dipping the flowers in batter and deep-frying them, then covering them with powdered sugar.

STEAMING SQUASH WITH BLOSSOMS

Slice each blossom twice lengthwise, stopping short of the point where the fruit and blossom are attached. Once prepared to this point, the squash may wait up to 8 hours refrigerated before steaming. The squash should be steamed 2 to 3 minutes in a steamer. To serve, press the top of the blossom slightly to fan out the cut pieces.

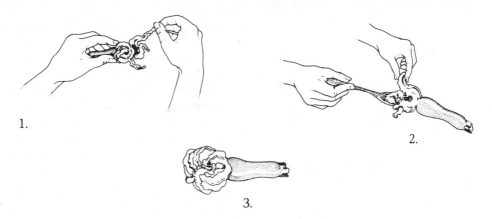

1.

2.

3.

STUFFING BLOSSOMS

A hearty stuffing for squash blossoms is the one used in Stuffed Pain de Sucre on page 275. Thus filled, the blossoms can be baked with an herbed tomato sauce after being dusted with Parmesan cheese.

No matter what stuffing you use, here is an easy way to fill them: Hold the base of the blossom with one hand and with the other open the blossom. Fill the flower up to the point where the petals begin to divide. Carefully twist the ends of the petals to seal the filling.

Baby Squash in Marinade

Choose from among your favorites; the following are suggestions. Squashes lend themselves especially well to this recipe, but you can add any other baby vegetables that appeal to you (see page 303 for a discussion of different kinds of baby vegetables).

Serves 4 to 6 as a side dish

4 each 2-inch-long zucchini and yellow straightnecks
4 each golden acorn squash, pattypans, scallopini, and round zucchini, all about 1 inch in diameter

MARINADE
½ cup olive oil
2 tablespoons wine vinegar
2 teaspoons minced fresh thyme, or 1 teaspoon dried thyme
4 bay leaves
1 branch rosemary, or ½ teaspoon dried rosemary
Salt and pepper to taste

Steam the squash for 2 to 3 minutes. Mix the marinade ingredients together in a ceramic or glass bowl large enough to hold all the squash. Add the squash to the marinade and turn them to coat. Cover the bowl and leave it at room temperature for 6 to 8 hours. Serve at room temperature.

Zucchini and Potatoes

This dish is simple to prepare, yet the flavor is interesting enough to serve with rich meat dishes.

Serves 4 as a side dish

2 large or 4 small red potatoes
2 large or 4 small zucchini
2 tablespoons butter
2 tablespoons olive oil
1 tablespoon chopped garlic
3 bay leaves
2 fresh thyme sprigs, or
  1 teaspoon dried thyme
Salt and pepper to taste

Peel the potatoes. Cut the potatoes and zucchini into ½-inch cubes. In a large, heavy saucepan melt the butter and add the olive oil. When the oil is hot, add the vegetables, garlic, bay leaves, and thyme. Cook over medium heat for 5 minutes, stirring the vegetables frequently. Season with salt and pepper. Cover, reduce the heat, and cook 25 to 30 minutes, checking occasionally to prevent sticking. When done, the zucchini will have disappeared, having provided the liquid for the potatoes to cook in, and the potatoes will be tender. Remove the bay leaves and thyme sprigs before serving.

WINTER SQUASH

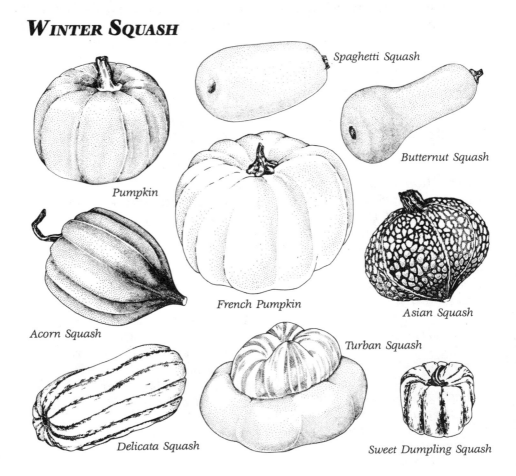

Spaghetti Squash

Butternut Squash

Pumpkin

French Pumpkin

Asian Squash

Acorn Squash

Turban Squash

Delicata Squash

Sweet Dumpling Squash

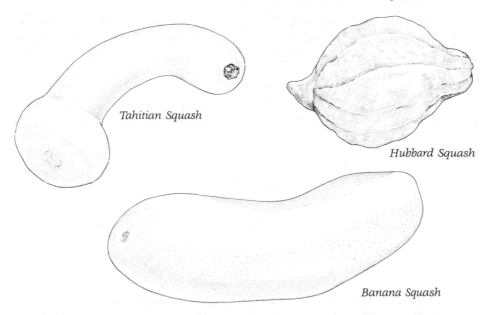

Tahitian Squash

Hubbard Squash

Banana Squash

Other names: Vegetable marrow.

How grown: From seed.

Availability: Fall and winter.

Peak of freshness: Skin should be hard with no sign of softness or mushiness.

To prepare: Cut in half or in slices with a sharp knife. Scrape out the seeds and trim away the rind.

The first waves of European settlers were overjoyed to find the winter squashes of America. These vegetables would keep for months protected by their thick, hard skins. They were often the only fresh vegetables available during the harsh New England winters. The large, mature seeds could be toasted and eaten, so nearly the entire vegetable was usable. Modern agriculture has passed over many of the winter squashes, so that only a dozen or so are now widely available. The Pilgrim favorites, with their blue, red, gray, and green skins, are fast disappearing. In other parts of the world, however, thick-skinned squashes are still widely available. The markets of Japan, Guatemala, and the Philippines are full of a bewildering array of exotic-looking hard-skinned squashes.

In Japan at Christmas and New Year's, many families serve *kabocha* squashes, which symbolize health and happiness for the coming year. *Kabocha* means "small winter squash." There are many different types but all may be marketed as *kabocha* squashes.

In the Philippines, thick slices of orange-fleshed squash are fried with garlic, onions, and pork chops. Southeast Asians frequently use winter squash in soups with coconut milk and tofu, and Central Americans often crystallize sweetened squash. Winter squash is most commonly baked stuffed or unstuffed, steamed, or puréed with cream and butter. The Italians stuff ravioli with puréed pumpkin and serve it with a cream sauce and Parmesan cheese.

Winter squash may be substituted in Sweet Potatoes with Three Kinds of Ginger, page 289, and in Pan-Fry of Rutabaga with Parsley Sauce, page 80, and added to Gratin of Winter Roots with Wild Mushrooms, page 96.

Winter Squash Varieties

ACORN: Yellow or dark green and gold. Six to 8 inches long, 4 inches in diameter. Deeply ridged. May be eaten as a summer squash when 2 to 3 inches long. It is pale yellow at this stage. Widely available in its mature stage.

ASIAN WINTER SQUASH: Not really a specific variety but a generic term for squash popular in Asia. Often convoluted, football shaped or flattened, weighing 5 to 15 pounds. Orange to yellow flesh, bland flavor.

BANANA: Up to 2 feet long. Yellowish-pink skin and orange meat.

BUTTERNUT: Light brown, shaped like a club with a spherical end, 8 to 12 inches long. Finely grained orange flesh with a seed cavity at the longer end.

DELICATA: Much the same color as Sweet Dumpling, but the shape is different, somewhat like a large cucumber. It is at its best when the skin is yellow with almost orange stripes. The flavor is less striking than Sweet Dumpling, and the meat is less dense.

HUBBARD: Large, often weighing 12 pounds or more. Gray-green, blue, or dark-green warted skin. Nutty flavor; good for pies.

PUMPKIN: May grow as large as over 100 pounds. Skin may be deep orange or buff, even white.

SPAGHETTI: Up to 1 foot long and 8 inches in diameter. Bright yellow, slightly ridged skin. The cavity is filled with long translucent threads, hence the name "spaghetti." Very bland.

SWEET DUMPLING: Actually classified as an Asian gourd, this extremely tasty squash is rarely more than 4 inches in diameter, an ideal size to serve two people. Its skin is creamy white with green stripes, and on full maturity becomes yellow with deep-orange stripes. It can be eaten at both stages, but the flavor is most intense at the yellow stage.

TAHITIAN: Up to 2 feet long with a bulbous bottom and a slightly curving neck. Seeds located only in the bottom cavity. Pale orange skin and meat. May be eaten as a summer squash when immature. At that stage the skin is green with yellow stripes and the meat is white. Flavorful; purées well.

TURBAN: Various shapes and colors, but always topped with a hat 6 to 10 inches in diameter. Very bland.

Roasted Pumpkin Seeds

This simple hors d'oeuvre is called pepitas *in Mexico.*

Makes 1 cup

1 cup seeds from a freshly cut
pumpkin or winter squash
2 tablespoons oil
Salt to taste

Preheat the oven to 325°.

Wash and dry the seeds. Heat the oil in a sauté pan or skillet and brown the seeds. Remove them with a slotted spoon and put on a cookie sheet in a single layer. Salt to taste and bake for 15 minutes or until crisp. Cool on paper towels.

Leek and Pumpkin Soup

Serves 4 as a first course

1 small 2-pound pumpkin, cut in
    quarters, seeded, and peeled
1 quart chicken stock made from
    chicken parts, leek tops, and 2
    inches sliced fresh ginger (see
    page 26)
2 large or 6 small leeks, cut into
    ½-inch slices
2 tablespoons butter
Salt and pepper to taste

Steam the pumpkin until just tender. A small pumpkin will yield at least 4 cups of meat. Reserve 2 cups for this recipe. Form the pumpkin into balls with a melon baller. In a large saucepan, bring the stock to a simmer. Cook the pumpkin in the stock until very tender, about 10 minutes.

Meanwhile, sauté the leeks in butter for about 10 minutes or until translucent. Add the leeks to the soup and season.

Pumpkin au Gratin

Any winter squash can be cooked in this manner.

Serves 4 to 6 as a side dish

One 2- to 2½-pound pumpkin
Flour
¼ cup olive oil
2 to 4 tablespoons minced garlic
2 tablespoons minced fresh
    parsley
Salt and pepper to taste

Preheat the oven to 325°.

Cut the pumpkin in half. Peel, seed, and cut the pumpkin into ½-inch cubes.

Toss the cubes in flour until evenly coated. Oil the bottom and sides of an ovenproof casserole with half of the olive oil. Fill the casserole with the pumpkin. Sprinkle with the garlic, parsley, salt and pepper and the remaining olive oil. Bake for 2 to 2½ hours. A rich, dark crust will form during cooking.

Acorn Squash Stuffed with Pear and Plantain

The fruit stuffing for this winter squash dish is caramelized with chunks of Chinese rock sugar and dark soy sauce. It would make a perfect accompaniment to a holiday dinner of turkey or goose.

Serves 4 as a side dish

1 acorn squash
1 ripe plantain (the skin should be brown) or banana
2 teaspoons butter
1 medium pear
2 teaspoons grated fresh ginger
1 tablespoon crushed Chinese rock sugar (available in Chinese groceries) or brown sugar
1 tablespoon dark soy sauce
1 teaspoon five-spices (available in Chinese groceries)

Preheat the oven to 400°.

Cut the acorn squash in half lengthwise. Scoop out the seeds and some of the pulp if the cavity is small.

Peel the plantain. Cut it in half lengthwise, then in ½-inch slices. Melt the butter in a small sauté pan or skillet, and sauté the plantain until soft.

Peel and core the pear and cut it into ½-inch cubes. In a bowl, mix the pear, plantain, ginger, sugar, soy, and five-spices. Spoon into the 2 squash halves.

Wrap each half with aluminum foil and seal tightly. Place on a baking sheet and bake for 1 hour. Wrapped in foil, the squash will stay hot for 20 minutes after removing from the oven.

Breaded Winter Squash with Emmenthaler Cheese

This is a Northern Italian dish that has been adapted to American kitchens.

Serves 4 as a side dish

1 large meaty winter squash,
    such as Hubbard or Tahitian
Salt and pepper to taste
2 cups dry bread crumbs
2 eggs, beaten
¼ cup butter
¼ pound thinly sliced Emmen-
    thaler cheese

Peel the squash. Cut it in half lengthwise and remove the seeds and strings. Cut the squash into ¼-inch slices crosswise. Add the salt and pepper to the bread crumbs. Dip each slice of squash first into the beaten eggs, then into the bread crumbs, coating the slices evenly on both sides. Melt the butter in a large sauté pan or skillet and brown the squash over medium heat. Drain on paper towels. Arrange the squash in an ovenproof dish in a single layer and top each with a slice of cheese. Broil just until the cheese bubbles. Be sure not to overcook or the cheese will toughen.

Sweet Dumpling Squash with Honey-Mustard Sauce

This small squash has a rich, nutty flavor that is enhanced by the honey-mustard sauce. Other small winter squashes can be substituted.

Serves 6 as a side dish

2 Sweet Dumpling squash
2 tablespoons sage honey or
    other dark honey
2 tablespoons Dijon mustard
2 tablespoons softened butter
¼ cup pomegranate seeds
½ cup shelled and skinned
    pistachios, partially crushed

Preheat the oven to 350°.

Cut the squash in half lengthwise and remove the seeds. Make a paste of the honey, mustard, and butter. Divide the paste among the 4 halves, filling the squash cavities. Place in a shallow baking dish and bake covered for 45 minutes to 1 hour, or until the squash is soft, but the skin still holds its shape.

Pour the sauce from the squash centers into a small serving pitcher. Cut each half into 3 crescent-shaped pieces. Sprinkle with the pomegranate seeds and the crushed pistachios. Serve the sauce separately.

Pumpkin Pasta with Baby Mustard Greens and Pecans

This "Southern"style pasta dish combines many traditional ingredients, with a surprising result.

Serves 6 to 8 as a first course, 4 as a main course

PASTA

½ cup cooked and puréed
    pumpkin
4 to 5 cups unbleached all-
    purpose flour
1 teaspoon salt
2 egg yolks

½ cup pecans
2 tablespoons butter
8 to 10 baby mustard plants, or
    1 pound mustard leaves,
    chopped
1 gallon salted water
1 cup finely slivered Smithfield
    ham (about 6 ounces)

Combine the pasta ingredients, mixing with a wooden spoon or in a food processor. Knead the dough until it is smooth and elastic, about 5 minutes for hand-mixed dough, 1 to 2 minutes for processed. Flatten into fairly thick sheets. Dry and then cut into ¼-inch-wide noodles.

Preheat the oven to 325 °. Toast the pecans on a baking sheet until browned, about 10 minutes. Melt the butter in a sauté pan or skillet. Add the mustard greens and sauté until wilted. Meanwhile, cook the pasta in the boiling salted water until *al dente*. Drain. Transfer the pasta to a heated serving dish. With a slotted spoon, remove the greens from the pan and add to the pasta. Quickly heat the pecans and ham in the butter in the same pan. Toss the greens and pasta together. Add more butter if necessary. Place the strips of ham and pecans across the top of the pasta. Serve on warmed plates.

WINTER MELON, WAX GOURD, FUZZY MELON

Benincasa hispida

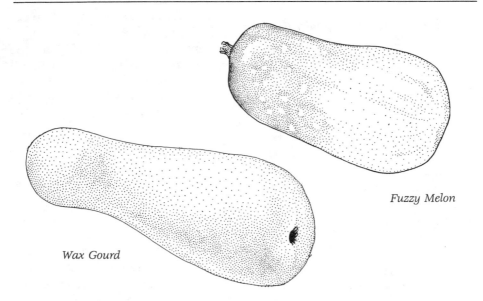

Fuzzy Melon

Wax Gourd

How grown: From seed.

Availability: Late summer and fall.

Peak of freshness: Skins that are firm and not blemished.

To prepare: Wash and cut open. Remove seeds and pulp. Use whole or peel the skin.

A confusing array of cucurbits have evolved from a single species of melon or gourd (the name varies, depending on whom you talk to), the main difference between them being their shape and the absence or presence of wax or hairs on their skins. Thus fuzzy melons, wax gourds, and winter melons are variations on the same theme.

Fuzzy melons and wax gourds look like swollen green cucumbers and may weigh up to two pounds. The wax gourd is hairy when young, but at maturity it is covered with a waxy bloom. On the other hand, the fuzzy melon, which is more tapered than the wax gourd, is covered with hair. Winter melon is the largest and may look like a green pumpkin with a heavy white bloom on its ridged skin.

All of these vegetables require a great deal of water. They grow on vines that spread over trellises either in fertile fields or on the edges of ponds. The fruits of the benincasas are rather bland, with a high water content.

The winter melon is sometimes ornately carved and used as a container for soup on special occasions. The wax gourd may be stuffed with mushrooms, duck, ginger, and garlic or a mixture of vegetables and shrimp and then baked. All the benincasas may be added to soups as well. In Asian markets you may find any of these vegetables cut and sold in sections.

Winter Melon Soup

This is a variation on a traditional Cantonese soup. The wild mushrooms provide a nice counterpoint to the other key ingredient—smoked ham.

Serves 4 as a first course

1 pound winter melon, yielding
   about 3 cups of meat
3 cups chicken stock
2 thin slices Smithfield ham, cut
   into strips ⅛ inch wide and 2
   inches long
¼ pound wild mushrooms such
   as shiitake or matsutake,
   stemmed and cut into thin
   slices
2 tablespoons medium soy sauce
   or to taste

Cut the winter melon from the rind and slice it into 1-inch cubes. Steam the melon in a basket until just tender, not mushy. In a large saucepan, heat the stock to a simmer and add the winter melon, ham, and mushrooms. Cook for 3 minutes, add the soy sauce, and serve in warm bowls.

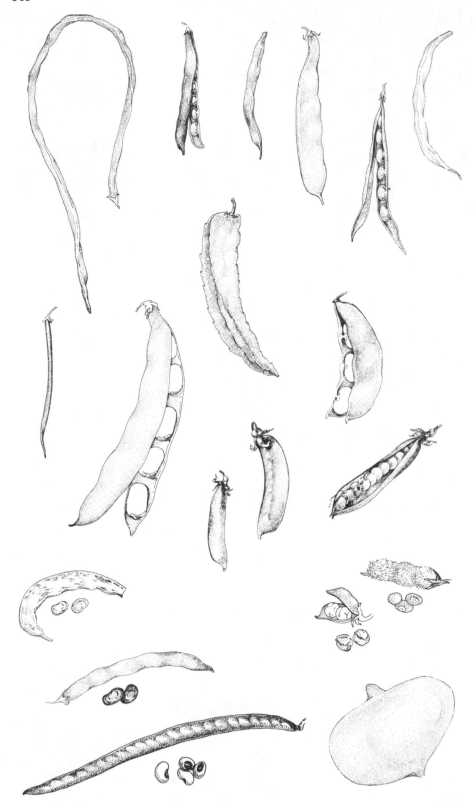

Legume Family

Leguminoseae: Beans, Chick-pea, Cowpea, Jícama, Pea, Soybean

The large, diverse group of plants called the legume family is one of the world's most important food groups. Members of this family are found in tropical, subtropical, and temperate regions of the world in the so-called Bean Belt, where they are cultivated not only as sources of protein for humans and animals, but also for soil improvement.

The legumes are so well established that certain kinds have become synonymous with the cultures and cuisines of particular areas. China is renowned for its soy products and edible-podded peas; England for its green shelling peas and runner beans; the Americas for their kidney and lima beans; Africa for cowpeas; and India for its lentils and chick-peas.

Legumes have been cultivated for thousands of years. Broad beans have been found in prehistoric European ruins; peas have been unearthed from the tombs of the pharaohs; and the cultivation of the kidney bean in Central America dates back at least to 5000 B.C.

Most legumes have a single-section pod, and each pod contains one row of seeds. As the pods mature, they dry along both seam sides. The blossoms of legume plants range from scarlet to yellow, with all shades of pink, white, and purple in between. In the garden many of the sprawling legumes need staking. They make an invaluable contribution to soil quality by combining with bacteria to fixate nitrogen, an essential element in healthy soil.

Today nearly all the world's legumes are available in American markets, and their popularity grows with the increased interest in vegetarian cookery.

BEANS

For centuries necklaces of colorful beans, interspersed with seashells and fruit pods, adorned the aristocracy of Central America. The genus *Phaseolus* evolved there, and its importance can be measured by the fact that this staple food was valued as a sign of power.

Today beans are grown all over the world. When beans were carried back to Europe by the Spanish conquistadors, Europeans quickly added them to their diet, which already included favas. The runner bean, which might seem to be native to England, comes from the mountainous slopes of Central America, and it is still possible to find indigenous lines of *Phaseolus* there. Romanos, *haricots verts*, and *flageolets* are also native to the Americas, though we invariably associate them with the Mediterranean region.

BEAN TERMS

Flageolet: Both a general and specific French term. Generally *flageolet* means shelling bean. Specifically it refers to a group of French shelling-bean varieties characterized by pale-green or thin white kidney-shaped beans used both fresh and dried. The seed is longer and narrower than our white Northern bean, which it somewhat resembles.

Haricot vert: A French bean with an edible pod. It is extremely fine and thin.

Kidney bean: Any member of the species *Phaseolus vulgaris* (named for their kidney shape); also a name given to the large dry red bean commonly found in supermarkets and health food stores. *Haricots verts* and other snap beans as well as shelling beans are all *Phaseolus vulgaris*, but cowpeas, long beans, runner beans, lima beans, and winged beans are not.

Shelling bean: Any bean grown primarily for the edible seed inside. The pod is not usually eaten, because it is tough and stringy.

Snap, string, green bean: *Phaseolus vulgaris* with edible pods. The runner bean resembles a snap bean, but requires different culinary treatment.

Beans are also an essential part of the Asian diet, which includes soybeans, winged beans, and long beans. The heavily vegetarian Indian diet has been based on long beans, lentils, and chick-peas for thousands of years. They were spread to China and subtropical Asia by caravans early on.

Today beans are available wherever there is a three-month or longer growing season. They are particularly attractive as garden plants, with bright-green leaves and white, pink, purple, yellow or scarlet flowers.

In the market, look for beans that are less familiar than the green-podded snaps. There are literally hundreds—some used for fresh shelling, others for edible pods, and some only for their dried bean seeds.

Many people have heard their older relatives relate stories of the delicious beans they used to raise and eat. It is likely that many of these were bean types that did not survive competition in the modern market. Fortunately, in the United States and Europe there are individuals and groups who act as seed banks for the purpose of maintaining heirloom varieties that are no longer commercially available. Nonprofit groups such as the Seed Saver's Exchange distribute seeds of varieties that could otherwise be lost.

CHINESE LONG BEAN

Vigna unguiculata Subsp. *sesquipedalis*

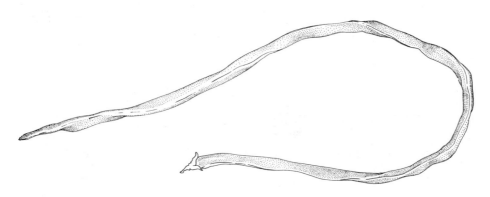

Other names: Yard-long bean, asparagus bean.

How grown: From seed.

Availability: Late summer and fall.

Peak of freshness: Select pods that are firm, not spongy. Choose beans less than ⅜ inch in diameter.

To prepare: Wash. Trim off the ends.

Chinese long beans are a staple in Asia, where they are used when young for stir-fries, while mature vegetables yield seeds that are eaten as shelling beans. Long beans are actually cowpeas rather than beans, and they are a close relative to black-eyed peas, whose seeds theirs resemble. The pods can reach 20 to 30 inches long. The plant is a trailing vine that is prolific when grown in hot, wet weather; it can take over a garden if not cut back. In the Philippines where okra is also a favorite, the bean seeds are planted after the okra seedlings are up a foot or more so the beans can use the okra plants as supports. In the United States the beans are grown on trellises or poles. There are at least two types of long beans: one is red-seeded, the other black. Since the pod is best when immature, it is difficult to tell which variety you are buying.

You can substitute long beans in almost any snap bean recipe, but they are different—blander and not so succulent. Long beans can develop an almost spongy texture, especially when they have stayed on the vines too long.

Spicy Fried Long Beans with Coconut

The slightly chewy fresh coconut is a good contrast to the fine texture of these long beans. Green beans can also be used in this dish.

Serves 4 as a side dish

2 tablespoons peanut oil
1½-inch piece fresh turmeric, peeled and chopped, or 1½ teaspoons dried turmeric
4 small fresh hot green peppers, seeded and chopped
2 curry leaves
2 teaspoons black mustard seeds
1 pound long beans, cut into 1-inch lengths
½ cup water
½ cup fresh-grated coconut
Salt to taste

Heat the oil in a wok or skillet. Add the turmeric, peppers, curry leaves, and black mustard seeds. Sauté for 2 minutes. Add the beans and sauté for 2 minutes. Add the water, coconut, and salt and cook until the beans are tender, about 5 minutes.

Dry-fried Long Beans with Pork and Preserved Vegetable

Bruce Cost is a cook, caterer, and teacher of Asian cooking classes. In his work he encourages respect for authentic techniques and ingredients. This is one of his recipes.

Serves 4 as a main course

1½ cups peanut oil
2 pounds long beans, cut into
*   3-inch pieces*
6 or more small dried hot pep-
*   pers, ground roughly or*
*   chopped*
½ pound ground pork
1 tablespoon dark soy sauce
¼ minced Sichuan preserved
*   vegetable*
1 tablespoon minced fresh ginger
1 tablespoon shao hsing or dry
*   sherry mixed with*
1 teaspoon sugar
1 teaspoon Asian sesame oil

Heat the oil in a wok or skillet until nearly smoking and fry the beans until wrinkled, about 5 minutes. Drain in a colander.

Remove all but 2 tablespoons of oil from the pan. Heat until hot and add the peppers. When they smoke, add the pork. Separate the meat with a spatula or wooden spoon. Stir-fry for 2 minutes. Add the soy sauce, preserved vegetable, and ginger and stir-fry for 1 minute. Add the beans and then the wine-sugar mixture and stir until thoroughly heated. Serve immediately, topped with the sesame oil.

PREPARING FRESH-GRATED COCONUT

Select a coconut that feels full of liquid. Firmly tap on the entire shell with a hammer to loosen the meat from the shell. Push a screwdriver through the "eyes" at one end of the coconut to drain the liquid. Split the coconut open with a hammer. The meat should pry away from the shell easily with a knife. Peel the brown skin from the meat with a sharp paring knife. Grate by hand on the large holes of a grater or in a food processor.

FAVA BEAN
Vicia faba

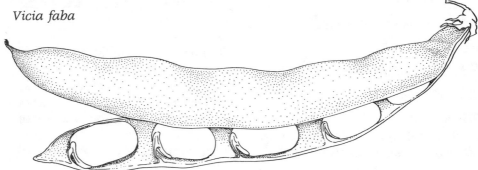

Other names: Broad bean, horse bean.

How grown: From seed.

Availability: Spring and summer.

Peak of freshness: The pods should be a shiny, bright green, with the beans inside showing an even development.

To prepare: Open the pod and remove the bean. To double-shell the beans, remove the outer skin from each bean by slitting it with your thumbnail or the tip of a knife, then peeling it off. Some people prefer the double-shelling method, as they find the outer skin bitter; others do not.

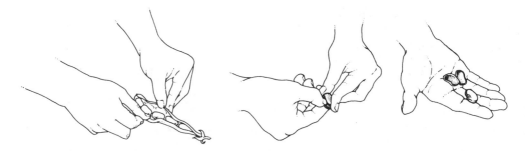

Remnants of fava beans have been found in the Swiss Lake Dwelling archeological sites, providing evidence that this vegetable was one of the earliest cultivated by Europeans. Medieval peasants made a purée of favas seasoned with a bit of salt pork, which, no doubt, kept many families alive during the cold winter. Today favas are still a favored vegetable in Europe, partially because their appearance nearly always marks the onset of spring. The plants grow to 4 feet tall, with black-throated white flowers.

The English enjoy the fava bean nearly as much as Mediterraneans. There it makes its appearance somewhat later in the year. American markets are beginning to stock favas now, and the demand for them will surely increase.

Favas have an archetypal bean taste that is both meaty and "green" at the same time. Young favas can be eaten raw and are a favorite snack in Spain. They can be steamed, used in soups, or puréed, and they are complemented by fresh herbs in sautés or baked dishes. Favas combine well with pork and duck as well as with tomatoes. Lima beans and favas are interchangeable in the young stage, as in Lima Beans and Duck Livers (page 150).

Sautéed Favas with Garlic and Fresh Thyme Flowers

Purple thyme flowers add an elegant touch of color to this simple, hearty dish. Use fresh thyme without flowers if you can't find the blossoms.

Serves 4 as a side dish

3 garlic cloves, crushed
2 tablespoons olive oil
2 cups shelled favas (about 4
    pounds unshelled)
6 flowering thyme sprigs, each
    about 3 inches long
Salt and pepper to taste
Additional thyme flowers for
    garnish

Sauté the garlic in the olive oil in a sauté pan or skillet until nearly tender. Add the favas, thyme, and salt and pepper. Cook until the favas are tender, about 10 minutes. Remove the thyme sprigs. Garnish with thyme flowers and serve.

Favas Baked with Whole Baby Garlic and Fresh Rosemary

This Provençal dish is hearty and complex at the same time. It would be a wonderful accompaniment to roast or grilled lamb. Baby garlic is succulent and sweet and adapts well to baking. It is available in the late spring and early summer.

Serves 3 to 4 as a side dish

6 whole baby garlic heads, or
    peeled cloves from 4 mature
    heads of garlic
2 cups shelled favas, about
    4 pounds unshelled
4 sprigs fresh rosemary, or
    1 teaspoon dried rosemary
¼ cup olive oil
Salt and pepper to taste
Olive oil

Preheat the oven to 350°.

Arrange the garlic in the bottom of a small baking dish appropriate to bring to the table. Surround with the favas and cover with the rosemary. Drizzle the olive oil evenly over the vegetables. Cover and bake for 40 minutes, or until the garlic is tender. Season with salt and pepper, moisten with additional olive oil, and serve as is.

Spicy Deep-fried Fava Won-Tons with Mint Sauce

Favas and many other vegetables (including carrots, squash, turnips, and broccoli) can be cooked, puréed, and deep-fried in won-ton wrappers with slices of pepper. The sweet-sour mint sauce is a refreshing cool contrast. It is also good with most steamed vegetables.

Makes 24 won-tons

2 cups double-shelled favas (see
    page 146), about 4 pounds
    unshelled
Salt and pepper to taste
1 package won-ton wrappers
4 fresh hot peppers such as
    jalapeños or serranos, cut
    crosswise into thin slices
2 tablespoons cornstarch mixed
    with ½ cup water
Oil for deep-frying
Mint Sauce, following

Boil the favas in salted water to cover for 10 minutes or until tender. Purée in a blender or food processor until smooth. Season with salt and pepper.

Fill each won-ton with about a tablespoon of the fava paste and a thin slice of pepper. Fold the won-ton in half to form a triangle. Fold the two tips in to the center. Seal the flaps with the paste made from cornstarch and water.

Fill a deep-fryer or Dutch oven with 4 inches of oil. Preheat the oil to 350°.

Fry the won-tons until golden brown. Remove from the oil with a slotted spoon and pat off the excess fat with paper towels. Serve the mint sauce with the won-tons as a dipping sauce.

MINT SAUCE

Makes 1 cup

1 cup mint sprigs (about 1 bunch
    or ½ pound)
2 tablespoons water
2 tablespoons sugar
2 tablespoons rice wine vinegar
    or distilled vinegar
2 small fresh hot peppers such as
    jalapeño or serrano, seeded and
    minced

Chop the mint sprigs. Purée all the ingredients in a blender. Serve at room temperature or cold.

LIMA BEAN
Phaseolus limensis, P. lunatus

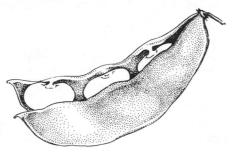

Other names: Butter beans.

How grown: From seed.

Availability: Summer.

Peak of freshness: Round types should have lumpy pods, flat types flat pods with a barely defined shape. The pods should be clear green and pliable, with no signs of drying.

To prepare: Snap the end from the pod and pull on the string, opening the pod. Remove the beans.

Lima beans have a reputation as one of the plain Janes of the vegetable world: bland, beige, and starchy are common adjectives applied to limas, which are usually sold canned or frozen. Limas don't deserve this reputation. Fresh limas are wonderfully diverse in appearance and were much favored as a food in ancient Peru, where they originated. They grow on bushes or vines with cream or pink flowers. The pods may be flat, such as those of the large pole lima, or plump and round like those of the Dixie Butterpea or the Fordhook Bush Lima. Some lima beans, such as the Christmas Pole (also called Calico) lima, are lavender when cooked, others range from creamy white to dark green. Limas also vary greatly in size, from ⅛ inch across to larger than a quarter. Size indicates varietal difference as well as maturity. The Dixie Butterpea is small when mature, the Christmas Pole quite large.

When young, lima beans are sweet and tender. They become mealy when past their prime. After shelling, limas should be quickly cooked if young; otherwise longer cooking is required. Young limas are interchangeable with favas, cowpeas, and shelling beans in all recipes.

Fresh Limas, Flageolets, and Corn

This delightful summer dish contrasts the green of fresh limas with the bright yellow of corn. You can make it with both white and yellow corn or just the yellow variety, and limas alone if flageolets *are not available.*

Serves 4 as a side dish

1½ pounds lima beans, shelled
¾ pound flageolets, shelled
1 ear white corn
1 ear yellow corn
3 tablespoons butter
Salt and pepper to taste

You should have about 1 cup of limas and ½ cup of *flageolets.* Cook the limas and *flageolets* in boiling salted water to cover for about 10 minutes or until tender. Drain. Cut the kernels from the corn. Melt the butter in a saucepan. Add the corn and cook, stirring occasionally, for about 5 minutes. Add the beans and cook until they are thoroughly heated. Add salt and pepper and serve at once.

Lima Beans and Duck Livers

White shelling beans and pork are at the heart of cassoulet, *and the same principle is at work in this dish: limas cooked with bacon and served with duck livers that have been sautéed in bacon fat.*

Serves 3 to 4 as a main course

3 pounds lima beans, shelled (about 2 cups)
2 tomatoes, peeled, seeded, and chopped
4 thick bacon slices
1 cup duck or chicken stock
A bouquet garni *made from 3 parsley sprigs and 1 sprig each thyme and oregano, tied with twine*
Salt and pepper to taste
½ pound duck livers

Preheat the oven to 400°. Place the beans, tomatoes, 2 of the bacon slices, stock, *bouquet garni,* and salt and pepper in a ovenproof casserole. Bake covered for 30 minutes, or until the beans are tender. Add more stock if necessary to keep the beans moist.

While the beans are cooking, cook the remaining 2 bacon slices in a sauté pan or skillet until they have rendered their fat. Remove the bacon and all but 2 tablespoons of the fat. Sauté the duck livers in the bacon fat. Cook the livers over a medium flame for 4 to 5 minutes, until they are browned but still pink on the inside. Remove the bacon from the cooked lima beans. Add the livers. Serve with slices of warm baguette.

RUNNER BEAN

Phaseolus coccineus

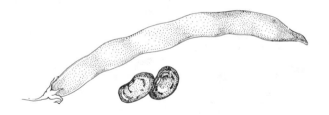

Other names: Scarlet runner bean.

How grown: From seed.

Availability: Summer and fall. The flowers do not set pods in hot weather.

Peak of freshness: Stiff, broad, flat green pods; the beans within are not visibly pronounced, and the edges of the pods are ridged.

To prepare: Cut lengthwise along both sides of the bean to remove ridges and strings. Slice the pod on the diagonal between each seed.

This long-time British favorite is not native to the Isles, but is another import from the mountainous slopes of Central America. It quickly established itself and today is found trailing up garden poles and trellises in almost every British vegetable garden.

Runner beans can be substituted for snap and long beans. Large beans can be substituted for shelling beans. The white or red runner bean blossoms are beautiful and taste just like the bean. A salad of blossoms and baby lettuces with a chervil-shallot vinaigrette is to be recommended.

SHELLING BEAN

Phaseolus vulgaris

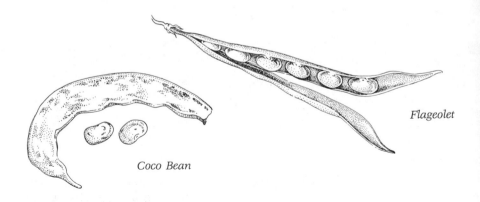

Flageolet

Coco Bean

How grown: From seed.

Availability: Summer.

Peak of freshness: Lumpy, pliable pods with the interior beans well defined. Dry pods indicate drying beans.

To prepare: Remove the beans from the pod by pulling on the tip, then peel back, opening the pod.

In July, Provençal vegetable sellers begin displaying heaps of long-podded red- and white-striped beans. In the ebullient markets of Marseille and Nice, Aix and Toulon, the *marchands* aggressively signal shoppers to their wares with cries of "Get your cocos for the *bon pistou!* Fresh cocos!" The pretty red and white beans are considered a basic for a vegetable soup laced with *pistou*: garlic, basil, and olive oil.

There are hundreds of kinds of shelling beans, including the black beans of the Southwest, the multicolored beans of Central and North America, Jacob's Cattle, Soldier's bean, and old-fashioned shelling beans with romantic names like Blue Wren and Black Valentine. Favas, limas, runner beans, and winged beans are all eaten as shelling beans, but they are treated individually in this book. Mature beans from other kinds of beans, such as Chinese long beans, can also be eaten as shelling beans.

Almost every country has a special dish using shelling beans. Black beans are the main ingredient of a Oaxacan dish that cooks in a sealed earthen pot for twelve hours; black beans are also the primary ingredient of Brazil's national dish, *feijoada.* A favorite of the United States' deep South is red beans and rice: cooked red beans flavored with a ham hock or hog jowl spooned over white rice and doused with hot sauce.

Although many dishes can use dried or fresh-shelled beans interchangeably, it is when fresh that the flavor of shelling beans is most intense.

The French shelling bean *flageolet* is so desirable fresh that a method was devised for maintaining its freshness well after harvest. It was discovered that uprooting an entire plant with its bean pods still intact and storing it upside down in a cool cellar would keep the tender, pale-green beans fresh for several months, even into the winter.

Cooked shelling beans can be made into a salad with the addition of olive oil, lemon juice, and parsley or other herbs. A delicious *pistou* soup can be made from water, beans, potatoes, tomatoes, basil, garlic, olive oil, and grated Parmesan. Shelling beans can be used in lima bean, cowpea, and fava bean recipes.

Fresh Coco Bean Purée with Red Pepper Strips

This recipe comes from a friend who lives in Salamanca, Spain. It makes a wonderful accompaniment to grilled meat or fish. Any fresh shelling bean can be used in place of coco beans.

Serves 4 as a side dish

4 pounds fresh coco beans, shelled, or 1 cup dried coco beans
Salt and pepper to taste
1 red bell pepper, cut into strips
⅓ cup virgin olive oil
1 tablespoon fresh lemon juice
1 teaspoon minced fresh thyme, or ⅓ teaspoon dried thyme
Lettuce leaves
Chopped parsley for garnish

Simmer the fresh beans in salted water to cover for 15 to 20 minutes. Drain. If using dried beans, soak overnight, then drain and simmer in salted water to cover for 30 to 40 minutes or until tender. Drain.

Purée all but 2 tablespoons of the beans with a potato masher or in a blender. Add the salt and pepper. Mince one-half of the red pepper strips. Mix these with the purée, along with the olive oil, lemon juice, and thyme. Spoon the purée onto a bed of lettuce. Surround the purée with a border of pepper strips. Garnish the mound with the whole reserved beans and parsley.

Stir-fried Shelling Beans and Ground Pork

The somewhat bland shelling bean takes well to this rich, spicy Chinese treatment.

Serves 4 as a side dish, 2 as a main course

*2 pounds shelling beans, shelled
   (about 2 cups)
3¼ cups chicken stock
½ pound ground pork
2 tablespoons oil
1 tablespoon garlic
½ cup thinly sliced celery
1 to 2 small fresh hot peppers
   such as* jalapeño, *seeded and
   chopped
1 tablespoon medium soy sauce
2 tablespoons cilantro leaves*

In a large saucepan, simmer the shelling beans in 3 cups of the chicken stock for 8 to 10 minutes or until tender. Set aside.

In a wok or heavy skillet, cook the ground pork until it loses its pink color. Remove the meat from the wok with a slotted spoon. Add the oil to the wok and, when very hot, add the garlic, celery, and peppers. Stir-fry for 1 minute, but don't brown the garlic. Add the remaining chicken stock, soy sauce, beans, and meat. Stir-fry for 1 minute. Add the cilantro leaves, stir, and serve over rice.

SNAP BEAN
Phaseolus vulgaris

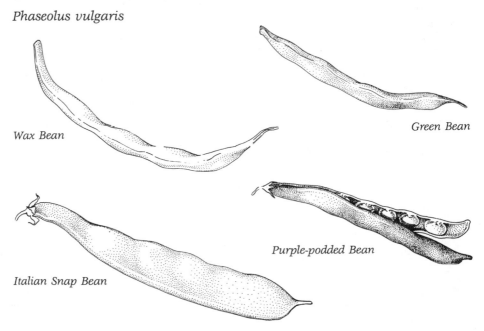

Wax Bean

Green Bean

Italian Snap Bean

Purple-podded Bean

How grown: From seed.

Availability: Summer, although some standard types are available year round.

Peak of freshness: The pods should be firm and smooth; lumpiness indicates age. The pods should not bend, but snap crisply. Strings, characteristic of some varieties, indicate mature beans.

To prepare: Wash. If necessary, remove strings. Snipping ends is optional.

Why don't green beans have strings anymore? Because seed companies, especially in the United States, have worked hard over the last thirty or forty years to develop beans without strings.

Of course, many old-fashioned beans still have strings. In French a differentiation is made between stringless *mangetout* beans and *filet* beans, with strings. No such differentiation exists in English. *Haricots verts* and Royalty Purple Podded beans will probably have strings. They have not been subjected to the intense research and selection that the stringless Contender beans and similar types have.

Many Americans believe that stringless snap beans are superior to those with strings because they are easier to prepare, but it's worth noting that some of the most flavorsome beans have strings.

Snap beans require a minimum of cooking. Steaming, sautéing, or stir-frying with garlic and olive oil or soy sauce is appropriate. Substitute in recipes for long beans (pages 144–145).

Snap Bean Varieties

ITALIAN SNAP: Also called Romanos, they are broad and rather flat. They may be either yellow or green, depending upon variety. They will need stringing.

GREEN: The most common of snap beans. Most are stringless, such as Contender. Regional favorites include Kentucky Wonder and Oregon Blue Lake. French favorites appearing in American markets now are *haricots verts*, sometimes marketed as *fin de Bagnols* or *aiguillons*.

PURPLE PODDED: Similar in flavor to garden snap beans, the pods are purple or green mottled with purple, but lose their purple color on cooking.

WAX: Popular especially in the South and the East, these yellow beans may or may not have strings.

Haricot Vert

Other names: French bean.

Peak of freshness: No more than ⅙-inch in diameter. They should snap easily. If not truly fresh, they may be tough. Shop carefully.

To prepare: Wash. Cut off the tip of any remaining stem; otherwise leave intact.

One of the most sought after of the new vegetables is the *haricot vert*. Its flavor is exquisite. Sometimes as long as 7 inches, but never more than ¼ inch in diameter, this round-podded bean is most commonly picked when only 5 or 6 inches long and ⅛ inch in diameter. The *haricot vert* usually has a tail, especially when picked very young. Most restaurants serving these beans leave the tail on—it is actually the incipient string. *Haricots verts* can be steamed, boiled, or sautéed with garlic and olive oil. Whatever the method, cook fresh *haricots verts* quickly to preserve their flavor and texture.

A Tomato Coulis (page 226) makes a delicious addition to hot or cold *haricots verts*.

Marinated Snap Beans

This simple salad is delicious on a hot summer's day.

Serves 4 as a first course

1 pound snap beans, strings removed

MARINADE

*1 garlic clove, chopped
2 scallions, cut into 2-inch lengths
½ cup virgin olive oil
⅓ cup red wine vinegar
1 tablespoon chopped fresh summer savory or thyme, or 1 teaspoon dried
Salt and pepper to taste*

Steam the beans for 5 minutes or until tender and allow to cool. Combine the marinade ingredients. Toss the beans with the marinade. Cover and refrigerate for at least 3 hours, then serve.

WINGED BEAN

Psophocarpus tetragonolobus

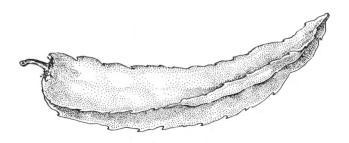

Other names: Asparagus pea, *dambala.*

How grown: From seed.

Availability: Sporadically all year.

Peak of freshness: Ridged beans that are somewhat tough. Avoid brown ones.

To prepare: Shell the beans. Or, when very young, wash the pods and slice crosswise.

The winged bean is an ancient tropical plant that is as versatile as the soybean. Americans have only discovered it in the last few years, and most of the as-yet small crop comes from southern Florida and Hawaii.

The winged bean is being extensively researched. Currently it grows as a perennial vine in the tropics and as an annual vine in temperate zones. Botanists are attempting to produce a bushy plant that will not require staking and will set fruit in temperate regions. When they succeed, the winged bean crop will probably increase dramatically.

Like the *chayote*, the entire winged bean plant, including the tuberous root, is edible. The tender green shoots can be sauteed, the seed can be crushed to produce a high-protein milk, and the beans are delicious legumes.

Winged beans can be used in lima bean, shelling bean, and cowpea recipes as well as in long-bean dishes.

CHICK-PEA

Cicer arietinum

Other names: Garbanzo bean, *cece* bean.

How grown: From seed.

Availability: Summer.

Peak of freshness: The hairy pods should be light green, with plump beans. Avoid beans that appear dry.

To prepare: Open the pod and remove the beans.

The chick-pea is not a true pea, though it is a member of the legume family. The plants are 2 to 3 feet high, with lacy leaves and white flowers, and grow best in semi-arid climates. Probably native to western Asia, the chick-pea spread from there to India in the baggage of nomads who crossed the Himalayas in caravans. Today it is a staple food in India, and 90 percent of the world's chick-peas are grown on the subcontinent.

In the Mediterranean region and the Middle East, chick-peas are an essential ingredient in soups and stews, much like our potato. No Algerian *couscous* or Moroccan vegetable *tajine* would be complete without chick-peas. The Lebanese mix mashed chick-peas with sesame oil to create *hummus*, a delicious dip to scoop up with *pita* bread. The Syrians roast chick-peas, then serve them as hors d' ouevres. The Indians make chick-peas into a flour for sweets and savories. In Southern France workers eat a crêpelike snack made from chick-pea flour, olive oil, and salt, baked in wood-burning ovens and washed down with red wine. Americans have adopted chick-peas, and most bean salads feature them. Chick-peas are usually used in their dried form, but fresh chick-peas are occasionally available. Very fresh chick-peas are sweet and can be eaten raw in salads. Chick-peas may be substituted in cowpea recipes.

Chick-pea Fritters

This dish is based on a traditional Hopi recipe that features deep-fried corn fritters served on a bed of wild greens. Chicory, mustard greens, or spinach can be substituted for the chard.

Serves 6 to 8 as a first course, 4 as a main course

2 cups fresh chick-peas, or 1 cup dried chick-peas
1 bunch chard (about 1½ pounds)
1 teaspoon salt
2 small eggs
2 tablespoons chopped scallions
½ cup fine dry bread crumbs
3 cups oil
Red wine vinegar

Simmer the fresh chick-peas in salted water to cover for 15 to 20 minutes or until tender. Drain. If using dried chick-peas, soak overnight, then simmer in salted water to cover for 30 to 40 minutes or until tender. Drain.

Cut the stems from the chard and reserve for another use. Chop enough leaves to make 1 cup; reserve the remaining leaves. Purée the chick-peas, salt, and eggs in a blender or a food processor until smooth. Add the chopped chard and scallions and mix in the blender or processor. Form the mixture into small balls, about 1 inch in diameter. Roll each fritter in the bread crumbs until completely coated.

Heat the oil to 350° in a wok or deep-fryer. Fry the balls, 10 at a time, for 30 to 40 seconds or until golden brown. Remove with a slotted spoon and drain on paper towels. Keep the fritters warm in the oven until you have cooked them all. Serve the fritters on a bed of chard leaves. Pass a bowl of wine vinegar and, if you like, Mint Sauce (page 148), to pour over the fritters.

COWPEA
Vigna unguiculata Subsp. *unguiculata*

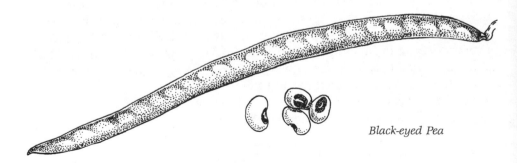

Black-eyed Pea

Other names: Crowder pea, pea, bean.

How grown: From seed.

Availability: Summer.

Peak of freshness: Lumpy pods with no evidence of drying. If too mature, the peas will pop out of the pod when opened; if too immature, they will stick in the pod as if glued. When just right they will slip easily from the pod.

To prepare: Open the pod and remove the beans.

Neither a standard pea nor a bean, the cowpea belongs to a subtropical group of legumes characterized by upright bushes that bear beautiful lilac or white blossoms. In the early morning the plants are fresh and bright, but the flowers wither quickly in the heat of the day.

Cowpeas, along with peanuts, were introduced to the Southern states during the period of the slave trade. Looked down on by the Southern aristocracy, they were christened with the name of *cowpea* because they were thought fit only for animal fodder. By the end of the nineteenth century, cowpeas had become a regional favorite. Black-eyed peas (a type of cowpea) stewed with ham hocks start the new year in many a Southern home.

Cowpeas thrive in moist, warm climates, and, surprisingly, more black-eyed peas are grown in California than in the South. If you visit a farmer's market, look for jars or bags of fresh-shelled cowpeas. Cowpeas are usually green when fresh. When dry they can be pale brown, green, or lilac, and there are even "pink eyes" along with the familiar black-eyed variety.

In the South cowpeas are usually called peas, while in other areas of the country they are called beans. Cowpeas can be substituted for shelled beans or peas in any recipe, though they have a stronger taste.

Macedoine

This hearty midsummer salad makes an unusual alternative to potato salad as an accompaniment to grilled foods.

Serves 4 as a first course

3 medium carrots, peeled and
    cut into ½-inch cubes
1 medium red potato, peeled and
    cut into ½-inch cubes
1 pound fresh black-eyed peas,
    shelled (about ¾ cup)
1 large or 2 small ears of corn
½ cup Basic Mayonnaise,
    following
6 to 8 chopped basil leaves
Lettuce leaves

Simmer the carrots and potato separately in salted water to cover until just tender, about 20 to 30 minutes. Simmer the black-eyed peas in salted water to cover until tender, 10 to 15 minutes. Steam the corn for 5 minutes; cut off the kernels. Place the mayonnaise and basil in a blender or food processor and purée. Cool all the vegetables to room temperature and toss with the mayonnaise. Serve on a bed of lettuce.

BASIC MAYONNAISE

Makes 1 cup

1 egg
1 teaspoon fresh lemon juice
¼ teaspoon salt
¼ teaspoon white pepper
¼ teaspoon paprika
¼ teaspoon dry mustard

3 tablespoons olive oil
½ cup oil
1 teaspoon sherry vinegar, red
    wine vinegar, or 1 teaspoon
    fresh lemon juice

Beat the egg in a mixing bowl with a whisk or in a blender. Add the lemon juice, salt, and spices, then add the olive oil a tablespoon at a time, whisking all the while. Add the ½ cup oil a tablespoon at a time until the mayonnaise is stiff. Continue whisking and add the 1 teaspoon vinegar or lemon juice. Mayonnaise can be kept refrigerated for 3 to 4 days.

PEPPERY MAYONNAISE

This makes a fairly mild mayonnaise. If you want a very hot mayonnaise you can double the amounts of pepper.

3 dried peppers such as ancho or
    pasilla
1 small hot fresh pepper such as
    serrano or jalapeño, seeded
    and minced
1 recipe Basic Mayonnaise,
    above, made without mustard

Simmer the dried peppers in water in a saucepan for 10 minutes and then turn off the heat. Submerge the peppers in the saucepan with a plate and let stand for 30 minutes. Rinse in cold water. Slit open the dried peppers and remove the seeds. Pull the skins off the peppers and discard. Blend or whisk all the peppers into the mayonnaise. Peppery mayonnaise becomes overly hot and bitter if kept too long. Plan to use this the same day you make it.

Black-eyed Peas with Spicy Sausage and Tomato Coulis

This dish is something of a Louis-iana-Provençal hybrid, featuring a Southern legume and sausage mixed with a French tomato sauce.

Serves 4 as a side dish, 2 as a main course

*1½ pounds black-eyed peas,
  shelled (2 cups)
3 cups water
1 pound spicy pork sausage
1 cup Tomato Coulis, page 226
Salt and cayenne to taste*

Cook the black-eyed peas in the water for 15 to 20 minutes, or until tender. Drain the peas, reserving ½ cup of the cooking liquid.

Poke a few holes in the sausage with a fork. In a sauté pan or skillet, sauté the sausage over medium heat, turning it to brown evenly. Remove the sausage from the pan when it is browned but not yet completely cooked. Save 1 tablespoon of the fat. Slice the sausage into bite-sized pieces.

Add the sausage, the fat, the tomato *coulis* and salt and cayenne to the peas. Simmer for 10 minutes. Serve with rice.

JICAMA
Pachyrhizus erosus

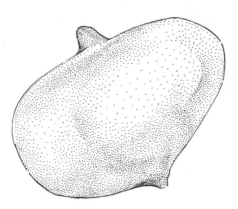

How grown: From seed or from tubers. The seeds are poisonous.

Availability: All year.

Peak of freshness: Firm to the touch, with no dark blotches.

To prepare: Wash. Peel the brown outer skin. Store in acidulated water or ice water.

Jícama is a legume that grows underground as a tuber. It is an increasingly popular vegetable. Its thick brown outer skin covers a delicious, slightly sweet, very crunchy flesh.

Many cooks are using *jícama* in Southwestern-style salads with ingredients such as tomatoes, avocados, olives, and cheeses. Its flavor is also enhanced by lime juice and hot peppers. The texture and taste of *jícama* is very similar to that of the water chestnut. Like the water chestnut, it takes well to stir-frying. *Jícama* can be grated and substituted for *daikon* on a sushi plate.

Three-Crunch Salad

This textural delight for those who love crunchy vegetables features water chestnuts, jícama, and Jerusalem artichokes. It is a variation of three-bean salad, an American staple. Serve this salad as a cooler with spicy food. It can also be dressed with the Thai dressing on page 98.

Serves 4 as a first course

1 small jícama
½ pound each fresh water
   chestnuts and Jerusalem
   artichokes
¼ cup peanut oil
3 tablespoons fresh lime juice
1 tablespoon chopped fresh
   cilantro
Salt to taste

Peel the vegetables, placing each one in acidulated water after peeling. Cut the water chestnuts and Jerusalem artichokes into thin slices. Cut the *jícama* into ½-inch cubes.

Combine the peanut oil, lime juice, and cilantro and toss with the vegetables. Refrigerate for 30 minutes to 1 hour. Season with salt and serve cold.

PEA
Pisum sativum

Peas are probably native to Central Asia, but they were quickly taken up by many early cultures including the Greeks, Romans, and Abyssinians. In the sixteenth century, European aristocrats began eating fresh immature peas, which were considered a delicacy. Two hundred years later, New World explorers brought peas to America and the Indians took to them immediately.

Peas are divided into two categories: shelling and edible-podded. The sweet British (also called sweet American) and the French *petits pois* make up the shelling category. Edible-podded peas include Asian snow peas and sugar snaps. Sugar snaps are a recent development, a cross between the shelling pea and the edible-podded pea.

Sadly, good fresh peas are hard to find. Fifty years ago countless varieties were available, each with special qualities. In the United States today most peas are grown for processing rather than for the fresh market, and unimproved strains not suitable for mass canning and freezing are being phased out. The tiny *petits pois*, in particular, are almost impossible to locate. If you find them, buy them.

Edible-podded peas can be steamed or grilled; stir-fried as in Bitter Melon with Beef and Black Beans (page 119); added to Stir-fried Water Chestnuts and Carrots (page 294); added to soups such as Spicy Soup (page 185); and sautéed and eaten raw in salads or with dips. Because of their crunchy texture, it is best to cook them as little as possible. Fresh young shelling peas should be used alone or in combination with ingredients that need little cooking. Their marvelous sweet flavor should not be overpowered by strong tastes and heavy sauces. Older shelling peas are best used in soups or purées where flavor rather than texture is important. Young sugar snaps can be used like edible-podded peas, mature ones like shelling peas.

EDIBLE-PODDED PEA

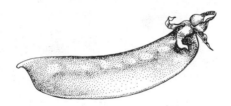

Other names: Snow pea, Chinese pea.

How grown: From seed.

Availability: Spring and fall in most markets; year round in Asian markets or in the specialty sections of some supermarkets.

Peak of freshness: Pods should be bright green, with no drying along the seam or at tips. Best when small and flat, with very immature peas.

SHELLING PEA

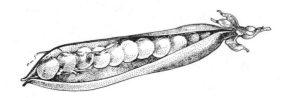

Other name: Green pea.

Availability: Spring and fall.

Peak of freshness: The peas may be large or small, depending on the variety. The pods should be ready to burst, with no dryness on the seam or at the tip.

To prepare: Open the pod and remove the peas. Leave the tiny tip or cap on the individual peas.

SUGAR SNAP PEA

Availability: Spring and fall.

Peak of freshness: The pods should be bright green. The peas should be plump but not ready to pop out, with no sign of drying at seam or tips.

To prepare: Wash. Snip off the stem end and pull off the string. Snap into bite-sized pieces.

Fresh Pea Soup with Chive Blossoms and Crème Fraiche

Chive blossoms have a wonderfully subtle onion flavor. If you prefer, you can substitute mint, chamomile, or nasturtium flowers, or chopped fresh chives. This soup is delicious cold as the first course of a brunch or light lunch. It can also be made with asparagus.

Serves 4 as a first course

2 pounds green peas, shelled
3 cups chicken stock
Salt and pepper to taste
2 tablespoons crème fraîche
2 tablespoons chive blossoms for
  garnish

In a large saucepan cook the peas in the chicken stock until tender (10 to 20 minutes, depending on size and freshness). Season with salt and pepper. Purée in a blender or food processor. Strain the liquid if you want a light broth. Serve as is if you prefer a thicker soup. Top each bowl with a bit of crème fraîche and sprinkle the chive blossoms over.

Spring Peas with Baby Bibb Lettuce

This dish would be wonderful served with risotto.

Serves 4 as a side dish

6 tablespoons butter
½ cup chopped scallions, or ¼ cup diced white onions
8 very small heads Bibb lettuce, loose outer leaves removed
3 pounds green peas, shelled
Salt to taste
½ cup chicken stock or water
1 tablespoon chopped parsley
Pepper to taste

Melt 4 tablespoons of the butter in a large, heavy saucepan. Add the scallions and sauté briefly. Add the lettuce and peas. Sprinkle with salt. Add the stock or water, cover, and cook over low heat for 20 minutes or until the peas are almost tender. Add the parsley, the remaining butter, and pepper. Cook covered another 3 minutes.

Peas with Prosciutto

Serves 4 as a side dish

6 tablespoons butter
2 garlic cloves, minced
3 pounds green peas, shelled
½ cup water
2 ounces prosciutto, finely slivered
Salt and pepper to taste

Melt the butter in a large, heavy saucepan. Add the garlic. Cook for 1 minute over moderate heat, then add the peas and water. Cover and cook slowly for 20 minutes or longer. When the peas are tender, add the prosciutto. Add salt and pepper. Let stand for 1 minute to absorb the juices.

Peas with Wild Mushrooms, Ginger, and Crème Fraiche

Serves 4 as a side dish

3 tablespoons butter
2 cups coarsely chopped chanterelles, shiitakes, or other wild mushrooms (about ½ pound whole mushrooms)
1 to 2 tablespoons minced fresh ginger
1 cup crème fraîche
1 pound green peas, shelled
Salt and pepper to taste
Cilantro leaves for garnish (optional)

Melt the butter in a heavy saucepan. Add the mushrooms and ginger and cook until the mushrooms are soft. Add the *crème fraîche* and reduce by one-half. Add the peas and cook over low heat until the peas are tender, about 20 minutes. Season to taste and garnish with cilantro leaves, if you like.

SOYBEAN

Glycine max

How grown: From seed.	**To prepare:** Remove from pods.
Availability: Summer and fall.	
Peak of freshness: Pods should be free of brown edges or spots.	

Soybeans are revered by the Chinese, who rate them as one of the five sacred foods essential to their civilization. They have been cultivated in Asia for more than five thousand years.

There are two types of soybeans: field beans used for animal fodder and green vegetable soybeans. Soybeans are the richest source of protein in the vegetable kingdom. Green vegetable soybeans have only been available in the United States since World War II. They grow in warm or cool regions and are increasingly available in American markets.

Soybeans can be dried, ground, boiled, and fermented, resulting in a number of products including tofu—fresh, dried, preserved, and deep-fried—soybean milk, soy flour, soy protein, and *miso.* Green soybeans resemble plump, round, fresh lima beans in taste and texture. They can be substituted in lima bean, winged bean, and fava bean recipes. Some chefs are using green soybeans with traditional foods such as corn and tomatoes as well as adding them to Asian stir-fries. The green soybean will probably play a substantial role in the East-West cuisine that is being developed in California and elsewhere.

Lotus Root

Nelumbus sp.

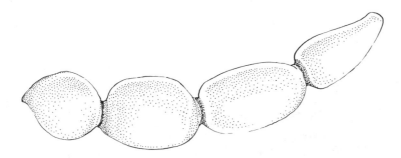

L otus root, a member of the water lily family, is a rhizome that originated in Southeast Asia. It has been cultivated as a pond plant for at least three thousand years. Both the seeds and the tuber are eaten in Asia, and the flowers are regarded as sacred by Buddhists.

Though bland, lotus root has a pleasant crunchy texture and attractive appearance. The flesh has a series of holes that form an irregular geometric design.

Lotus root is valuable both for its texture and its appearance and adds crunchiness and eye appeal to salads and stir-fries.

Other names: Water lotus, sacred lotus.

How grown: From rhizomes.

Availability: Autumn.

Peak of freshness: Firm, without soft spots or any signs of mold.

To prepare: Wash and peel. Slice crosswise.

Lotus Root Salad

Lotus root retains its crisp texture after blanching, and its bland taste takes well to spicy dressings.

Serves 4 as a first course

*2 lotus roots, weighing about 1
    pound*

DRESSING

*2 tablespoons medium soy sauce
2 tablespoons Asian sesame oil
1 tablespoon rice wine vinegar or
    distilled vinegar
1 teaspoon grated fresh ginger
½ teaspoon sugar*

*Lettuce leaves
1 tablespoon cilantro leaves for
    garnish*

Peel the lotus roots and cut into ¼-inch slices. Boil in salted water to cover for 10 minutes. Remove from the heat and plunge into cold water.

Mix the dressing ingredients together. Arrange the lotus root on a bed of lettuce. Cover with the dressing, garnish with cilantro, and serve.

Mâche

Valerianella Locusta

A ccording to one legend, *mâche*, or lamb's lettuce, got its name because European shepherds observed lambs eating the abundant green weeds growing in the grain fields and decided to try the food the sheep found so tasty. (Several hundred years ago corn was the name used for all grains, thus the origin of another of *mâche's* aliases: corn salad.) Obviously, *mâche* was a hit. A member of the valerian family, it grows best in cool, wet weather, and is especially popular in cold regions, where less hardy greens cannot survive. *Mâche* grows through frost and even snow, and it is one of the first greens available in the spring.

Mâche is a small, flat-growing plant with pale- to dark-green leaves. Some varieties of *mâche* have a spoon- or cup-shaped leaf, while others have a flat round leaf. A very bland salad green, *mâche* is frequently used to provide a balance for bitter-tasting chicories or peppery rocket. For some palates, a salad consisting only of *mâche* is *gourmand* heaven.

Other names: Corn salad, lamb's lettuce, *feldsalat.*

How grown: From seed.

Availability: Spring, fall, winter.

Peak of freshness: Succulent, unblemished leaves.

To prepare: Wash. Trim roots and discard any yellowish leaves.

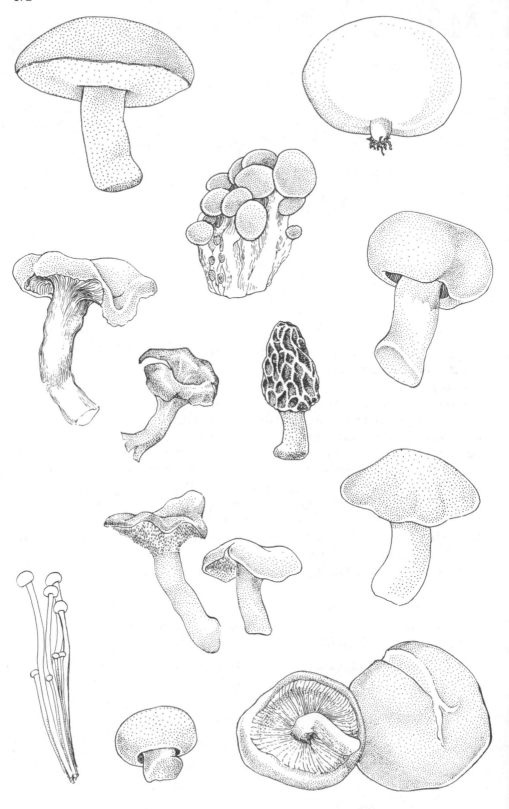

Mushrooms

Mushrooms are members of the broad division of simple plants called fungi. They are not vegetables in the strictest sense, as they reproduce by spores, single-cell organisms that are scattered by the wind. For many years eating a mushroom meant eating the cultivated mushroom. The industry began in the 1920s, when the technology that had been developed thirty years earlier in France was perfected by American researchers.

Today, Americans can choose from several types of cultivated mushrooms, as well as number of wild mushrooms that are brought to our markets by independent collectors who forage the countryside. The wild-mushroom market is growing rapidly, though consumers may find the scene a bit confusing. Many kinds of mushrooms are spread around the globe, as the spores easily enter the stratosphere and are carried huge distances. Thus a number of mushrooms are international but have a different name in each country. For example, Chinese tree-ear mushrooms can be found in England under the name *wood ear.* Given the huge variety of wild mushrooms and their minute differences, it is not surprising to find them mislabeled in the market. And supplies vary greatly even during the prime season, because a good rain is necessary for growth.

Our discussion of mushrooms includes only those varieties that are commonly sold in produce and specialty shops.

A CAUTION ON FORAGING FOR WILD MUSHROOMS

It is not safe to forage for wild mushrooms unless you are accompanied by someone who is experienced at identifying them. A few mushrooms that grow in the United States are deadly; some varieties are not lethal but can cause severe stomach distress. Learning how to select truly edible mushrooms should be learned by apprenticeship and not simply by comparing specimens with pictures in a field guide.

CEPE

Boletus edulis

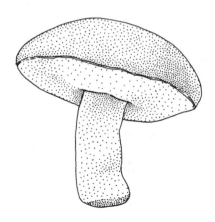

Other names: Cep, porcini, king boletus.

How grown: Wild.

Availability: Widely available in fall, sporadically the rest of the year.

Peak of freshness: *Cèpes* are very perishable. They should be firm.

To prepare: Brush dirt off or wipe with a towel. Trim stem ends. Some people remove the spore-bearing body under the cap, as it can develop an unpleasant texture after cooking.

The *cèpe* is the most prized mushroom in Europe and one of the most delicious of all fungi. Both the cap and the bulbous stalk are edible. *Cèpes* range in color from whitish to dark red. They are wonderful raw, but some people find them hard to digest, and, to be cautious, *cèpes* should be cooked.

Cèpes are very versatile and can be sautéed in olive oil, grilled, stewed, cooked in sauces, or marinated after being quickly blanched.

CHANTERELLE
Cantharellus

Black Chanterelle   *Yellow Chanterelle*

Other names: *Girolle*, egg mushroom.

How grown: Wild.

Availability: Mainly fall and winter.

Peak of freshness: The stem, when cut, should be white and dry.

To prepare: Any dirt can be brushed off, or the mushrooms can be carefully wiped with a towel. Trim the ends of the stems.

There are a number of chanterelles in the market. The most common species is the yellow chanterelle (*cibarius*), which resembles a beautifully shaped curving trumpet. It is sold fresh, dried, brined, or canned. It smells of apricot and has a wonderfully delicate flavor. Less widely available is the white chanterelle (*subalbidus*); the mildly flavored pig ear (*Gomphus clavatus*); the black chanterelle (*Craterellus cinereus*), which is actually dark blue; and the highly prized horn of plenty (*Craterellus cornucopoides*), also called the trumpet of death because of its appearance, not its after-effects.

   Chanterelles are generally prepared simply, so that their wonderful flavor is not masked. They can be sautéed in butter with shallots and garlic, scrambled with eggs, served in a cream sauce over pasta, or grilled.

COMMERCIAL MUSHROOM

Agaricus bisporus

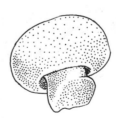

Other name: Mushroom.

How grown: Cultivated in hothouses.

Availability: All year.

Peak of freshness: Look for white mushrooms without discoloration and with the cap firmly attached to the stem. At their freshest, the gills will not be visible.

To prepare: Brush with a soft brush or wipe with a towel. Trim the stem ends.

This is *the* mushroom, the generic variety sold throughout the United States. It is cultivated in hothouses, grown in beds of sterilized organic material in the dark. Mushrooms are generally sold in small, medium, and large sizes, the largest being the most expensive. The cultivated mushroom has a fairly bland taste but is reasonably priced compared to wild mushrooms. It can be sautéed, grilled, stewed, baked, added to soups, or served raw in a marinade.

ENOKI MUSHROOM

Flammulina velutipes

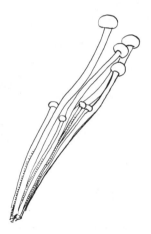

Other names: *Enoki-dake,* snow puff mushroom.	***Peak of freshness:*** *Enokis* should be white, with no discoloration.
How grown: Cultivated in sterilized organic material.	***To prepare:*** Cut off the bottom root cluster. It is not necessary to clean *enokis*.
Availability: All year, though sporadically in the summer.	

The cultivated *enoki* bears little resemblance to the velvet-foot mushroom from which it is derived. Currently, *enokis* are grown in Japan, in Malaysia, and in California. The exact conditions under which they are raised is a trade secret, though it is commonly known that they are very slow-growing. The *enoki* resembles a bean sprout. It is snow white, with a long stem and a tiny cap. *Enokis* are very delicate and require little cooking. They can be shown off well by being added to a simple broth and are often eaten raw as a garnish or mixed in salads.

FIELD MUSHROOM
Agaricus campestris

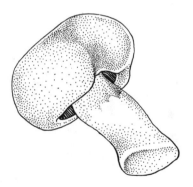

Other names: Pink bottom, *champignon*, meadow mushroom.

How grown: Wild.

Availability: Mostly fall and early winter months.

Peak of freshness: The button stage is the freshest (when the gills are not visible). If older, the bottom gills should be pink.

To prepare: Brush dirt off or wipe with a towel. Trim the ends of the stems.

The field mushroom is the most commonly picked wild mushroom in the English-speaking world. It resembles the commercial mushroom in appearance, though it can be a bit darker and is far superior in taste— richer and more complex. Use as you would commercial mushrooms.

HEDGEHOG

Dentinum repandum, D. umbilicatum

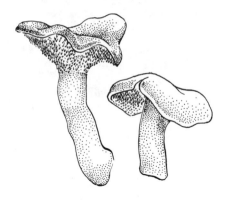

Other names: Sweet tooth.

How grown: Wild.

Availability: Winter and spring.

Peak of freshness: No brown discoloration.

To prepare: Brush or wipe clean with a towel. Trim the stem ends.

Versatile mushrooms that are becoming increasingly popular with chefs, the dentinums come in two sizes. The *umbilicatum* is the smaller, the *repandum* the larger. The cap varies in color from orange-brown to white, with all colors in between. Dentinums can be substituted in most recipes calling for chanterelles.

MATSUTAKE

Armillaria ponderosa

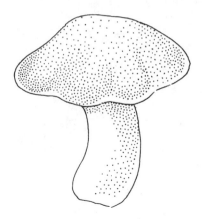

How grown: Wild.

Availability: Sporadically all year.

Peak of freshness: Best when in the button stage, with the veil intact covering the gills. The stem becomes tough with age.

To prepare: Generally picked with a damp cap, which may be sponged clean. Trim stem ends.

The *matsutake* gets its name from the pine tree (*matsu* in Japanese). Until recently, whatever *matsutakes* were harvested here were shipped off to Japan. A few were exported back in dried form. Today some of the American harvest is sold fresh in our markets. The *matuskake* is very aromatic. It can be tough, and it benefits from long slow cooking. In Japan *matsutakes* are used in soups and stews and are highly prized.

MOREL

Morchella conica, M. esculenta

Other name: Sponge mushrooms.	***To prepare:*** Brush clean or wipe with a towel. Trim stem ends.
How grown: Wild.	Morels should be eaten cooked, as some people may have a reac-
Availability: Sporadically all year, but mainly in the spring.	tion to raw ones. Because soil can get inside the cap, it is easiest to cut them in half to
Peak of freshness: The morel should be heavy for its size. It will dry out quickly, and the col- or fades with age. It should be moist and spongy to the touch.	clean them, though this precludes stuffing.

The morel is the best-known wild mushroom in North America. There are many species of morel, and they are all delicious. The *esculenta* is yellow to brown in color, while the *conica* is black. The black morel is nearly always found in burnt-over areas and is extremely hard to see among the charred wood. At one time French farmers were so enamored of the morel that they burned part of their fields to encourage them to grow there. Canned and dried morels are imported from France and they are quite good, but nothing surpasses a fresh morel. Morels can be sautéed, stuffed, brais- ed, added to an omelet, or cooked in a light cream sauce.

OYSTER MUSHROOM

Pleurotus ostreatus

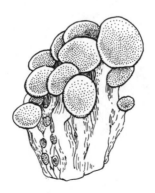

Other names: Tree oyster, *shemeji.*

How grown: Cultivated on a straw and wood base.

Availability: All year.

Peak of freshness: White oyster mushrooms should be a pure cream-white color. The caps should be slightly curled under. The size of a half dollar is optimum.

To prepare: Brush or wipe clean if necessary. Trim the stem ends.

The oyster mushroom gets its name from its sealike taste and its smooth, fishlike texture. It grows wild on the sides of trees and is also cultivated, the commercial crop being almost entirely farmed. Oyster mushrooms are grown on sterilized straw and wood fiber products as well as on cross-sections of tulip trees. At least two different strains are cultivated: one creamy white, the other almost black and called the walnut oyster. Oysters can be grilled, sautéed, fried in a batter, or used in stuffings.

PUFFBALL MUSHROOM

Calvatia gigantea, C. booniana

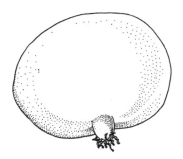

How grown: Wild.

Availability: Spring and fall.

Peak of freshness: The interior should be white. Discard any soft areas.

To prepare: Trim the stem end. Peel the skin and slice the mushroom thinly.

The giant, or smooth, puffball is one of the largest of the fungi, sometimes reaching fifty pounds or more. It is said that the puffball, which often grows in open pastures, is sometimes mistaken from a distance for a herd of grazing sheep. Size does not always indicate maturity; large mushrooms may be quite young. Puffballs are usually sliced, then breaded and quickly sautéed.

SHIITAKE

Lentinus edodes

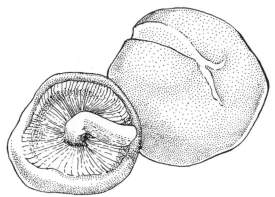

Other names: Black forest mushroom, *tung ku.*

How grown: From spores injected into logs.

Availability: All year.

Peak of freshness: Firm and dry, with caps not too far open. They should have a woody odor and should not be too pungent.

To prepare: Brush or wipe clean; trim ends.

Until very recently *shiitakes* were available only in dried form, imported from Japan and China. Today they are cultivated by a number of growers. There are some who claim that the best *shiitakes* are the dried ones sold in Asian markets, but fresh *shiitakes* are a wonderful treat.

Commercially, *shiitakes* are grown by injecting oak or composite logs with spores. The mushrooms grown on oak logs take a year to bear fruit, but the resulting mushrooms are meatier and more flavorful than those raised more quickly on composite wood. To distinguish the two varieties, look at the bottom of the stem. The oak-raised mushroom will be torn, the composite variety neatly cut.

Shiitakes are delicious in soups or simply sautéed. They can be used to flavor steamed fish and are delicious marinated in olive oil and grilled or served uncooked after marinating.

Spicy Soup

This delicately flavored and textured Thai soup features slender enoki mushrooms and the exotic flavors of galangal, a Southeast Asian rhizome, and lemon grass.

Serves 4 as a first course

STOCK

4 cups water
2 chicken wings and a neck
1 medium yellow onion
5 thin slices galangal or fresh ginger
2 tablespoons chopped fresh lemon grass, or 1 tablespoon dried lemon grass
1 fresh hot pepper such as Thai or jalapeño

2 tablespoons fish sauce
¾ cup enoki mushrooms
¼ cup unsweetened coconut milk
2 tablespoons chopped scallion
2 tablespoons cilantro leaves

Combine the stock ingredients in a large pot and simmer uncovered for 1 hour. Strain and return the liquid to the soup pot.

Return the stock to a simmer and add the fish sauce and mushrooms. Simmer for 2 minutes. Heat the coconut milk in a small saucepan and add to the soup. Add more fish sauce, if necessary, to adjust saltiness. Serve in heated soup bowls, garnished with the scallions and cilantro.

Wild Mushroom Stew

Choose large meaty mushrooms for this winter dish, which is as robust as any beef stew.

Serves 6 as a first course, 2 to 3 as a main course

1 pound mixed wild mushrooms such as chanterelles, shiitakes, or morels

VEGETABLE STOCK

4 carrots
2 large leeks
2 onions, cut in half
1 celery stalk
5 whole cloves
2 quarts water
Reserved mushroom stems

2 tablespoons butter
2 tablespoons unbleached all-purpose flour
Salt and pepper to taste
¼ medium yellow onion, minced
1 cup burgundy or beaujolais wine

Remove the stems from the mushrooms and reserve. Combine the stock ingredients in a large pot and cook, covered, for 35 minutes. Strain the stock and reserve the liquid. Slice the carrots into ¼-inch-thick pieces and discard the rest of the vegetables.

Melt the butter in a large saucepan. Remove from the heat and add the flour a teaspoon at a time, whisking as you go. Add the salt and pepper. Return the saucepan to the heat and cook the roux until it begins to brown. Add the onion and sliced carrots. Add the wine slowly, stirring with the whisk. When the wine is blended, reduce the heat and simmer for 30 minutes. In another saucepan, heat 3 cups of the stock and add the mushrooms. Cook for 10 minutes over medium heat. Add the stock-mushroom mixture to the wine mixture and simmer for 20 minutes. Serve over rice or noodles with a salad of bitter greens.

Oyster Mushroom Moo-Shoo Crêpes

This vegetarian version of moo shoo pork highlights the delicate flavor of wild mushrooms. If you prefer, you can fill flour tortillas or chapatis with the same ingredients.

Serves 8 as a main course

CREPES

*1½ cups unbleached all-purpose
   flour
3 eggs, beaten
2 tablespoons melted butter
1½ cups milk
¼ teaspoon salt*

*Oil
6 tablespoons butter
1 pound oyster mushroom, stems
   removed, cut lengthwise into
   thin slices
8 eggs, beaten
Chinese plum sauce (available in
   Chinese markets)
8 scallions, cut into 3-inch
   lengths and shredded
1 cup peeled and sliced fresh
   water chestnuts*

To make the crêpes, sift the flour into a mixing bowl. Add the eggs and mix with a wooden spoon. Gently stir in the butter, milk, and salt until the batter is smooth. Refrigerate for 1 to 2 hours. (Any extra batter can be kept for 2 or 3 days in the refrigerator.)

Heat a medium-sized (9- to 10-inch) crêpe pan over medium heat. Add a little oil if the pan is not well seasoned. Pour in just enough batter to thinly coat the bottom of the pan. Quickly swirl the pan so the bottom is evenly coated. Cook the crêpe until the bottom is browned and the top dry. Turn the pan upside down over a cutting board. The crêpe should drop out. After it cools, cover each crêpe with a piece of waxed paper. Repeat the procedure until you have made 16 crêpes. Add oil to the pan as needed.

To make the filling, melt the butter in a sauté pan or skillet and sauté the mushrooms over medium heat for 5 minutes. Pour the eggs in and scramble. Smear each crêpe with plum sauce and the egg-mushroom mixture, and top with scallions and water chestnuts. Roll up the crêpes and serve them immediately, seam side down.

Spinach Pasta Tossed with Morels, Squash Blossoms, and Cream

You can use any wild mushrooms you like in this dish. The bright color and sharp taste of the squash blossoms contrast nicely with the mushrooms and cream.

Serves 6 as a first course, 4 as a main course

3 tablespoons butter
8 medium morels, cut into thin
   strips lengthwise
½ cup fresh green peas (about ½
   pound unshelled)
¾ cup heavy cream
4 squash blossoms, slivered
1 gallon water
Salt to taste
1 pound spinach linguine or
   other pasta, preferably fresh
Fresh thyme sprigs

Melt the butter in a sauté pan or skillet large enough to hold the cooked pasta. Sauté the mushrooms until they are soft, then add the peas, cream, and squash blossoms. Slowly reduce the mushroom sauce by one-half.

Meanwhile, bring the water to boil in a large pot, add the salt, and cook the pasta until *al dente*; drain. Remove the sauce from the heat. Thoroughly toss the pasta with the sauce. Serve immediately on warmed plates, garnished with sprigs of thyme.

Braised Pheasant with Chanterelles on a Bed of Chinese Cabbage

In China and Europe cabbage and game are frequently paired. The rather bland cabbage absorbs some of the strong flavors of the game.

Serves 4 as a main course

Two 2-pound pheasants or
  Cornish hens
8 bacon slices
4 garlic cloves
2 cups dry white wine
4 celery stalks
6 fresh thyme sprigs, or 2 tea-
  spoons dried thyme
2 fresh marjoram sprigs, or 1
  teaspoon dried marjoram
Salt and pepper to taste
2 pounds fresh chestnuts
1 pound chanterelles or other
  wild mushrooms
6 tablespoons butter
Salt and pepper to taste
1 large head nappa cabbage
Salt
1 cup dry white wine
½ cup water

Preheat the oven to 350°.

Combine the pheasants or hens and the next 7 ingredients in a roasting pan and cover. Cook until tender, 1½ to 2 hours, depending on the age of the birds. Check the liquid as the birds cook, adding a little more wine or water if necessary.

Cut an "x" in the flat side of each chestnut, place in a shallow baking dish, and roast at 350° for 30 minutes. Cool and peel the shells and skins of the chestnuts. Cut into ½-inch cubes. In a sauté pan or skillet slowly sauté the chanterelles in 4 tablespoons of the butter for 10 minutes. Add the chestnuts and the remaining 2 tablespoons of butter and cook over low heat for 3 minutes. Season and set aside.

Cut the cabbage into ½-inch slices crosswise. Salt to taste. Steam until translucent, about 5 minutes.

Remove the birds from the oven. Slice the breast meat and cut off the legs. Keep the birds warm while you prepare the sauce. Discard the bacon and vegetables, then add the wine and water to the roasting juices in the pan. Reduce the liquid to 1 cup over high heat. Layer a warm platter with cabbage, cover with the mushroom-chestnut mixture, and top with the breast meat and legs. Pour the sauce over everything.

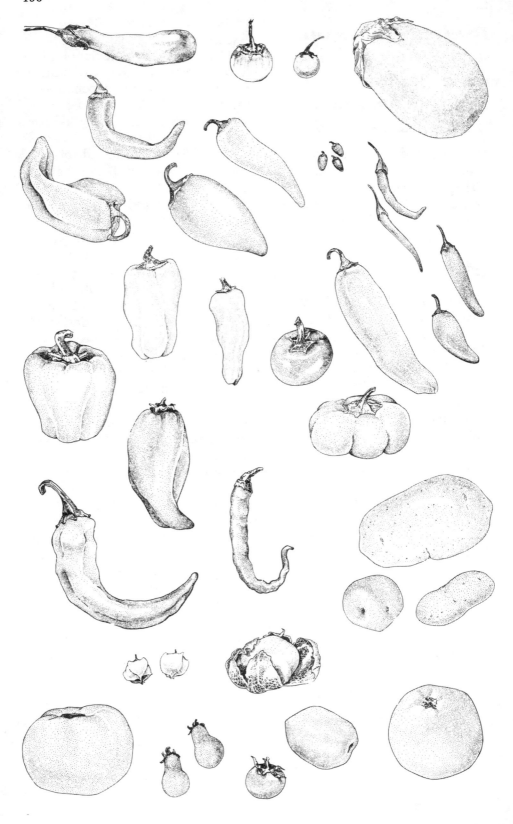

Nightshade Family

Solanaceae: Eggplant, Ground Cherry, Pepper, Potato, Tomatillo, Tomato

Many vegetable favorites, such as tomatoes, eggplants, peppers, and potatoes, belong to the nightshade family, along with some poisonous plants. Most members, whether poisonous or edible, have flowers with yellow centers and star-pointed petals reflexed from the center.

When tomatoes and potatoes were carried from the New World to the Old, Europeans were afraid to eat these strange vegetables, even though explorers and scientists had seen Central Americans consuming them. However, when eggplant traveled to Southeast Asia from India, where it originated, it gained immediate acceptance.

EGGPLANT

Solanum melongena

Other names: Aubergine.

How grown: From seed.

Availability: Year round, but best in summer.

Peak of freshness: Globular types should be firm to the touch and unblemished and unwrinkled. Long thin types should be soft and somewhat wrinkled, as they are less bitter at this stage.

To prepare: Wash if to be used unpeeled. Trim stem end. To de-bitter eggplant, peel and slice the eggplant, sprinkle the slices with salt, and weight the slices with a heavy plate on paper towels for 30 minutes.

The Victorians loved the exotic, and looking at the shading and shapes of eggplants, it is easy to understand why they grew eggplants in conservatories, then displayed them on drawing-room tables with other objects such as elephant tusks and teak carvings. Deep purple, pale cream, or lavender, long and thinly curving or globular and pear-shaped, the shiny eggplant presents a smooth, perfect surface, almost like that of polished semiprecious stone. The English gave the name *eggplant* to this exotic fruit, because one white variety is the size and shape of a large egg.

The Asians have developed long thin types of eggplants—sometimes up to 2 feet long—as well as small round varieties, in a wide range of colors. Africans, Europeans, and Americans favor the globular fruits, and Europeans and Americans choose purple eggplants almost exclusively.

Eggplants lend themselves to a number of preparations, both hot and cold. *Moussaka,* the Greek classic, consists of layered eggplant and lamb with an egg-enriched bechamel sauce. Indians use eggplants in a number of different ways including salads, and curries, often with coconut milk. Asians pickle baby eggplants and eat them with fish and rice dishes. Even the Alaskans have their eggplant favorites, mixing it with game such as caribou and moose. Eggplant can be grilled as well.

Some find that the seeds or skin of the eggplant produces a puckering sensation or bitterness that increases with age, and they debitter it with salt. Since the skin is so pretty, many choose to leave it on, and, for some dishes, such as stuffed eggplant, the skin is essential.

ASIAN EGGPLANTS

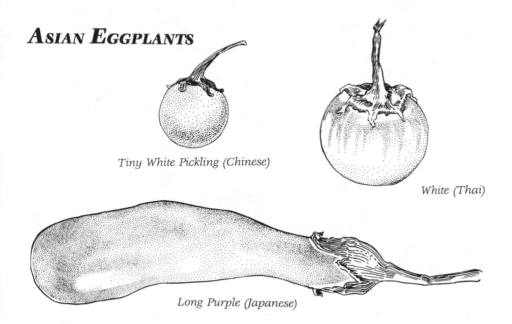

Tiny White Pickling (Chinese)

White (Thai)

Long Purple (Japanese)

BITTER ORANGE EGGPLANT: Looks like a small flattened pepper. Very bitter and good for sweet spicy soups and stews.

GREEN: May be short or long. Treated the same way as lavender and purple eggplants.

LONG LAVENDER: Delicate and fragile.

LONG PURPLE: Very tender, with a delicate flavor. Does not keep well.

SHORT PURPLE: Cylindrical and about 2 inches long. Serve whole, as the skin is tender.

TINY WHITE PICKLING: Has a tough skin and is full of seeds. Bitter; used for pickling with peppers.

WHITE: Larger than the tiny white. It may be streaked with purple, especially near the stem. Cooked or eaten raw, especially by Southeast Asians. Fewer seeds than the more bitter types.

WESTERN EGGPLANTS

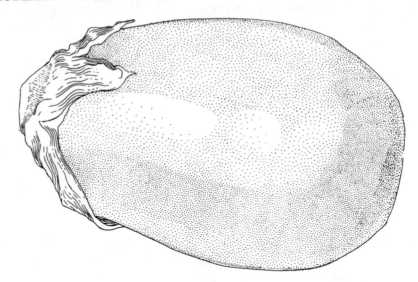

These are generally globular in shape, but they may also be round or long and cylindrical. The color ranges from lavender to purple-black. Their skins are tender, but not as tender as the long, fragile Asian types.

Caponata

A Sicilian eggplant dish, caponata may be served cold as an appetizer or as a salad on a bed of lettuce. Caponata, like many eggplant dishes, improves with age. You may wish to make it a day in advance.

Serves 4 as an appetizer or first course

¼ cup olive oil
1 large eggplant, peeled and cut into ½-inch cubes
4 tomatoes, peeled, seeded, and cut into ½-inch cubes
1 sweet onion, chopped
2 tablespoons minced celery leaves
2 hard-cooked eggs, chopped
¼ cup capers, drained
Salt and cayenne pepper to taste
1 to 2 tablespoons red wine vinegar
12 pitted green olives
Lettuce leaves

Heat the oil in a large skillet with a cover. Add the eggplant, stir thoroughly, and cook covered for about 15 minutes or until very soft. Add the tomatoes and cook 3 minutes. Spoon the eggplant-tomato mixture into a large bowl and allow to cool. Add the onion, celery leaves, eggs, capers, salt, cayenne, and vinegar. Slice 7 of the olives and add them to eggplant mixture. Chill the *caponata*. When you are ready to serve it, mound the eggplant on a bed of lettuce and stud the perimeter with the remaining olives.

Eggplant Flan

This dish is surprisingly simple to prepare, and it travels well.

Serves 8 as a first course, 6 as a main course

2 large eggplants, or 5 Asian
   eggplants
¼ cup olive oil
3 shallots, minced
2 teaspoons fresh minced thyme,
   or 1 teaspoon dried thyme
2 bay leaves
½ cup heavy cream
½ cup half and half
6 large eggs, beaten
Salt and pepper to taste
Tomato Coulis, page 226

Preheat the oven to 350°.

Peel the eggplants and cut them lengthwise in slices ¼ inch thick. Pour the olive oil into a large, heavy skillet. Cook and stir the eggplants, shallots, thyme, and bay leaves over medium heat until the eggplant is soft. Cool. Remove the bay leaves. Purée in a blender or food processor until thick but not soupy.

Add the heavy cream and half and half to the eggs and mix thoroughly. Blend the egg mixture into the eggplant. Butter a baking dish and pour the eggplant into it, and season with salt and pepper. Place the filled baking dish into a second larger dish and add hot water three-fourths of the way up. Bake for 1½ hours or until a toothpick inserted in the center comes out clean. Serve hot or at room temperature, with Tomato Coulis.

Indonesian Curried Eggplant

Coconut milk and eggplant are a popular combination throughout Southeast Asia and much of India.

Serves 8 as a side dish, 4 as a main course

½ duck, cut into serving pieces
4 tablespoons oil
1 tablespoon chopped garlic
2 shallots, chopped
1 tablespoon fresh lemon grass,
   or 1 teaspoon dried lemon
   grass
2 small fresh hot peppers such as
   Thai or serrano, seeded and
   chopped
1 teaspoon fresh-ground
   coriander
1 teaspoon ground turmeric
2 teaspoons tamarind paste
   dissolved in
2 tablespoons cold water
1 pound round Thai eggplants,
   stemmed and cut in quarters
1½ cups unsweetened coconut
   milk
½ cup chicken stock
2 tablespoons cilantro leaves

In a large skillet, brown the duck pieces over medium heat in 2 tablespoons of the oil; remove and set aside. Add the rest of the oil and sauté the garlic and shallots until the shallots are translucent. Add the lemon grass, peppers, coriander, and turmeric and sauté for 1 minute. Add the tamarind liquid, eggplants, coconut milk, chicken stock, and duck and simmer for 20 minutes. Garnish with cilantro and serve over rice.

Ratatouille Nice Style

There are as many variations of this dish as there are Provençal cooks. This one comes from Nice, where it has been handed down through at least three generations. Each vegetable is cooked separately in olive oil just long enough to bring out its flavor, then everything is tossed quickly with the tomato sauce and served.

Serves 8 to 10 as a side dish

2 pounds eggplant, cut into
    ½-inch slices
2 pounds zucchini, cut into
    ½-inch slices
Flour
1 cup olive oil
2 pounds green bell peppers,
    halved, seeded, deribbed, and
    julienned
1 pound yellow onions, coarsely
    chopped

TOMATO SAUCE

2 tablespoons olive oil
3 tablespoons chopped garlic
3½ pounds ripe tomatoes,
    peeled, seeded, and coarsely
    chopped
20 basil leaves
2 teaspoons minced fresh thyme,
    or 1 teaspoon dry thyme
3 tablespoons chopped fresh
    Italian parsley
Salt and pepper to taste

Dust the eggplant and zucchini with flour. Cook separately in 4 tablespoons of the olive oil until just tender. Remove from the pan with a slotted spoon and set aside. Sauté the green peppers in 4 tablespoons of the olive oil until soft. Remove from the pan with a slotted spoon and set aside. Cook the onions in 4 tablespoons of the oil until translucent. Remove from the pan with a slotted spoon and set aside.

To make the sauce, heat the 2 tablespoons of olive oil in a large saucepan. Cook the garlic 2 or 3 minutes over medium heat, then add the tomatoes, basil, thyme, and parsley. Cook and stir for about 10 minutes until the sauce thickens. Season to taste.

Combine all the vegetables and the tomato sauce in a large heatproof casserole and turn thoroughly over low heat until everything is hot. *Ratatouille* can be served hot, or at room temperature. It keeps well, and many prefer it the next day.

Louisiana-style Eggplant and Sausage Stew

One of the classic dishes of New Orleans is eggplant stuffed with pork sausage. This recipe features eggplant sautéed with spicy sausage.

Serves 4 as a main course

1 pound spicy pork sausage such
    as andouille or chaurice
3 tablespoons oil
2 tablespoons chopped garlic

1 large or 3 Asian eggplants, cut
  into pieces ½ inch thick, 1
  inch wide, and 3 inches long
2 cups fresh tomatoes, peeled
  and chopped (about 1½
  pounds)
2 teaspoons minced fresh
  oregano, or 1 teaspoon dried
  oregano
Salt and pepper to taste

Prick each sausage with a fork in 5 or 6 places. Brown the sausages in a skillet large enough to hold all the ingredients. Remove from the pan with a slotted spoon and set aside. In the same pan, in the sausage fat and 1 tablespoon of the oil, cook the garlic until translucent. Remove the garlic from the pan with a slotted spoon. Add the remaining 2 table-spoons of oil and sauté the eggplant until nearly soft, about 10 minutes. Cut each sausage into quarters. Add the sausage, tomatoes, oregano, and salt and pepper to the eggplant. Simmer for 10 minutes. Serve over rice, accompanied with Tabasco sauce and Dill-pickled Okra, page 235.

Layered Omelets

This is a Provençal dish that is very versatile. It is substantial enough to serve as a main course at a summer dinner, and in smaller portions makes a wonderful addition to a picnic buffet. You can use almost anything as a filling. Everything should be at room temperature when you begin.

Serves 4 to 6 as a main course

15 eggs
5 tablespoons butter
½ cup Ratatouille, page 196
½ cup Tomato Coulis, page 226
½ cup sour cream or crème
  fraîche, mixed with 5 or 6
  minced basil leaves
¼ cup Tapenade, page 126
Chopped basil leaves for garnish

To make one omelet, beat 3 eggs lightly, then heat 1 tablespoon of the butter in a 9-inch skillet. When the butter is quite hot, add the eggs. Quickly turn and tip the pan so the eggs evenly coat the bottom of the pan. Cook over medium heat until the eggs are almost set. Turn the pan over above a large plate or cutting board and gently tap one edge of the skillet if the omelet sticks. When the omelet has cooled slightly, cover it with a piece of waxed paper to prevent the omelets from sticking. Repeat this procedure until you have cooked all the eggs.

Cover the first omelet with the *ratatouille.* Lay an omelet on top and spread with the tomato *coulis.* Add another omelet and cover with the sour cream or crème fraîche and basil. Place the fourth omelet on top and spread on the *tapenade.* Cover with the last omelet. Garnish the center of the omelet with a few basil leaves. Serve at room temperature, cut into wedges.

GROUND CHERRY

Physalis pruinosa

Other names: Husk cherry, strawberry tomato, husk tomato.

How grown: By seed.

Availability: Summer and fall.

Peak of freshness: The cherry should be yellow and the papery shell just beginning to split open.

To prepare: Remove the husk. Wash.

Despite the name, the ground cherry is not a cherry but a member of the nightshade family. It grows inside a husk like the *tomatillo*. The plant grows low to the ground—the bushes are a foot or so high and twice as wide. The ground cherry is a native of Central America. Smaller than a *tomatillo* and golden when ripe, it is sweet, attractive, and easy to use, and may well become more popular in the near future. Ground cherries are used like tomatoes, though they are sweeter and smaller. They may be eaten raw in salads or cooked. A traditional American recipe is ground cherry jam.

PEPPER

Capsicum annum Capsicum sp.

Christopher Columbus named this group *peppers* when he arrived in the West Indies. Columbus thought he had sailed to India, which is the homeland of the pepper tree, the source of black pepper. Since the heat of the capsicums is reminiscent of black pepper, the name stuck. In the United States it is common to find capsicums labeled variously as sweet peppers, hot peppers, or chilies. The name *capsicum* is a derivative of the Latin work *capsa,* or "box," which refers to the shape of some peppers. There are two categories of peppers: sweet and hot.

SWEET PEPPERS

Other names: Capsicum.

How grown: From seed.

Peak of freshness: Firm, unblemished fruit. Wrinkles are not necessarily a sign of age.

To prepare: Fresh pepper skins are tough and many recipes call for roasted and skinned peppers; see the box on page 203.

Sweet peppers became popular with those Europeans and North Americans who could not tolerate hot peppers. Originally sweet peppers were smaller, more tubular, and certainly more wrinkled than the peppers we have today. Horticulturists, seeing the popularity of the sweet pepper, began intensive breeding and produced the large, puffy, thick-walled fruit now commonly available. Today in the United States the agricultural community seems to have settled on the bell pepper as the standard. You'll find it in green, red, and yellow. The Dutch have recently developed a violet bell pepper, which is now available in the United States. The violet pepper is green inside, and the skin becomes green when cooked.

Peppers grow in great abundance in all the warm climates of the world. Size, shape, and color vary greatly. White, green, salmon, red, and chocolate peppers come in shapes ranging from the long tapering bull's horn of Europe and South America to the slender, wrinkled Japanese *fushimi.* Pepper shrubs have many upright branches with white flowers and shiny heart-shaped or pointed dark-green leaves.

It is hard to generalize about taste with peppers, though there are a few constants. Thin-skinned peppers taste a bit more green and peppery, while thick-skinned varieties are sweeter and often tougher. Red peppers are the sweetest, as they are the most mature. Most green peppers turn red with age, thus red peppers aren't found in the market until late summer and early fall, unless they have been imported from Mexico or South America.

Sweet peppers are popular in Eastern and Western cuisines. Stuffed peppers are traditional in Eastern Europe, the United States and China. Roasted peppers are used in salads and sautés throughout the Mediterranean region. Peppers are grilled, often with lamb, in the Middle East. They combine well in sautés with most other summer vegetables, and in Spain peppers sautéed in garlic with olive oil is a regional favorite in Galicia. Stir-fried peppers with beef or shrimp and ginger is a classic Cantonese dish. And raw bell peppers add a firm texture to tossed salads.

BELL PEPPER

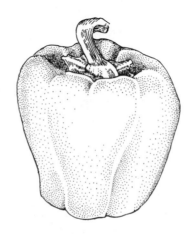

Availability: Green bells are available year round. Yellow, purple, and red are most frequently available in summer and fall, though imports from Holland and from Mexico are showing up year round.

Peak of freshness: Shiny, unblemished skin.

BULL'S HORN

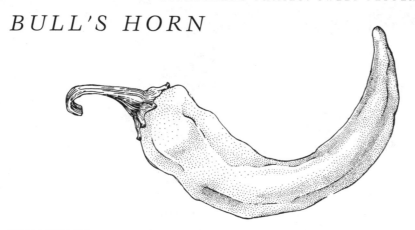

> **Other name:** *Corno di toro.*   **Availability:** Late summer and fall.

Long and curving like the horn of a bull, this sweet pepper holds its shape well after roasting. In Italy it is traditionally found layered in jars with olive oil. Bull's horn is a favorite in France and Spain and is beginning to appear in our markets. It grows well in the southern United States, and supplies should increase. Take advantage of its shape by using it whole rather than sliced.

CUBANELLE

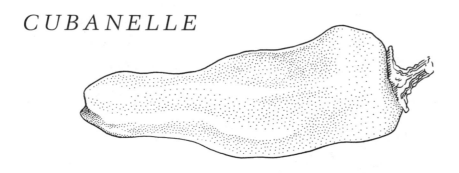

> **Other name:** Cuban.   **Availability:** Sporadic.

This is a bright-yellow or red thick-walled pepper related to the Sweet Hungarian. Many people prefer it to the bell.

JAPANESE GREEN

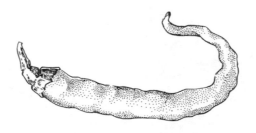

Other names: *Fushimi* green, long Asian.

Availability: All year.

Long, wrinkled, and green, this pepper has a very thin skin and a distinct taste. It is excellent in stir-fries or in sweet-sour pickle mixtures. Halfway between a sweet and a hot pepper, it has the tang without the heat. Use it as a sweet pepper or, if hot peppers are not for you, in place of hot peppers. You'll get some of the effect without the consequences.

LAMUYO

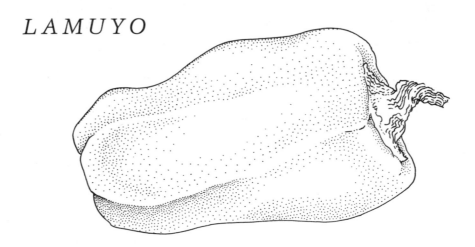

Other names: European sweet pepper, *rouge royal.*

Availability: Late summer and early fall.

Recently another European pepper, the *lamuyo,* was introduced in our markets. It is longer and much larger than the bell, but more slender in overall appearance, with tapered ends. The *lamuyo* has very thick flesh, comes in a full range of colors, and, most important, is delicious.

PIMIENTO

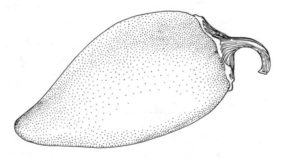

Other name: Pimento.   ***Availability:*** Late summer and fall.

We've become so used to thinking of pimientos as the little blotches of bright orange stuck into green olives that we've forgotten that they are available fresh. Fortunately, pimientos are making a comeback, and the deliciously sweet, dark-red heart-shaped peppers are now generally available. They are about the size of a small orange. The pimiento has very thick meat, which makes it a good choice for roasting.

ROASTING AND PEELING PEPPERS

The most effective way to roast peppers is over hot coals or a gas burner. They may also be roasted under a broiler. Leave the stems on so they can be used as handles for holding the peppers while removing the skins. Let the peppers roast until the skin is completely charred and blistered. Handle with tongs, not a fork.

Remove the peppers from the fire and plunge immediately into a pan of cold water. When the peppers are cool enough to handle, remove from the water. The skin of a well-charred pepper will come off easily when scraped gently with a paring knife. Hold the pepper by the stem and scrape gently away from you until the skin is off. Rinse it under running water. An alternate method to the cold-water dip is to let the roasted peppers sweat in a sealed plastic bag 10 to 20 minutes, then scrape the skin and rinse.

Hot Peppers

Other names: Chiles, chilies, chillis.

How grown: From seed.

To prepare: Wash; trim stem end. Remove seeds and ribs for milder dishes.

With the exception of the Tabasco pepper, commercial hot peppers in the United States belong to the same species as the sweet pepper— *Capsicum annum.* These peppers, which originated in the New World, are treated by farmers and gardeners as annuals, though in equatorial regions the hot types flourish as shrubs on rocky hills and ledges year after year. There, tiny little *pequin* peppers or the longer *chile de arbol* is gathered and laid in the sun to dry for future use in soups, stews, and salsas.

Asia produces another group of hot peppers. The taxonomy is somewhat complicated because they appear to be of American origin. Southeast Asians incorporate their slender peppers in sauces, relishes, soups, and stews to such an extent that some of them are now grown in this country and called Thai or Burmese peppers.

ANAHEIM

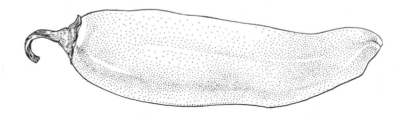

Other names: New Mexico pepper, Rio Grande pepper, California pepper.

Availability: Year round in some locations.

Peak of freshness: Firm, with a good green color. May be slightly lumpy or smooth, depending on variety.

One of the very mildest of the hot peppers, this is one of the preferred peppers for making *chiles rellenos*, the stuffed, batter-dipped, deep-fried peppers so popular throughout the Southwest United States and Mexico. Usually 6 to 8 inches long with medium thick flesh and somewhat tough skin, it is almost always used cooked.

ANCHO

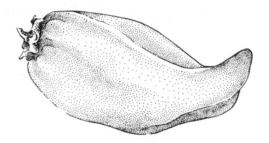

Other names: *Poblano, pasilla.*	**Peak of freshness:** Fresh *anchos* should be shiny green and unwrinkled.
Availability: All year.	

This is both a specific pepper and a pepper type. In and around the Valley of Puebla where it is grown it is also called *chile poblano* and is sometimes marketed in the United States under the name *poblano. Ancho* is the correct name for either fresh or dried; *poblano* refers only to the fresh pepper. The *ancho* is probably the most-used fresh pepper in Mexico, and it is frequently stuffed. It has a wonderful, rich taste that makes it very special. Dried, the *ancho* is essential to many *mole* dishes.

Fresh *anchos* are graded according to size, shape, and color. They vary from 2½ to 6 inches and from dark green to almost black with red splotches. Their shape ranges from a gentle taper to a sharp taper with a truncated point. To the unpracticed eye it may seem that two or three different peppers are being labeled *anchos*! To make things even more confusing, it may also be labeled as a *pasilla* pepper, as this is the name commonly given to it in Baja, California, the source of many U.S. *anchos.*

Fresh *anchos* can be used interchangeably with sweet peppers. They are the traditional peppers for *chiles rellenos.*

CAUTION: HANDLING HOT PEPPERS

When handling any hot peppers, use caution. We recommend using rubber gloves when working with peppers. It's not just biting into a pepper that can produce heat; handling the skin and then licking your fingers will burn your tongue almost as much as a bite of the pepper itself. Also be careful not to rub your eyes after handling peppers.

CAYENNE, CHILE DE ARBOL, HOT ASIAN, OR THAI PEPPER

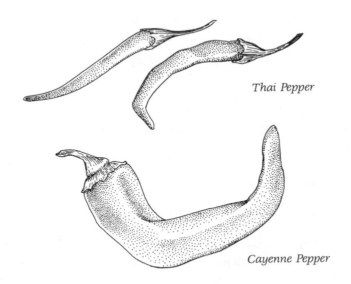

Thai Pepper

Cayenne Pepper

Other name: Bird pepper.

Availability: All year.

Peak of freshness: Shiny and firm. May be wrinkled.

The cayenne, an extremely pungent, long thin cigarette-shaped pepper, is found growing in the woodlands and mountains of Mexico and Guatemala. It is very similar to the *chile de arbol*, from the same area, and to a hot Asian, or Thai, pepper of Southeast Asia, and we have grouped them together. In both regions it is used to flavor soups, stews, and vegetable dishes. The long, thin fruits are used fresh in either the green or red stages (the red stage being the hottest). Frequently they are dried. Either way they are known to bring tears and yelps to the unaccustomed palate. Green cayennes may be used as a substitute for *jalapeños* or *serranos*.

Mash a few dried red cayenne-type peppers and soak them in vinegar and salt for a few days. The liquid can be poured over deep-fried seafood or stir-fried green vegetables. Mexicans eat the fresh-sliced pepper with fish, lime, cilantro, and a slice or two of tomato.

CHIMAYO

Availability: Late summer and fall.	**Peak of freshness:** Shiny and firm.

The *chimayo* is a hot little pepper with a sight curve that looks like the Thai pepper except that it has broader shoulders. It is just as spicy as the Thai variety and can be used in stews, soups, and salsas. It has been a favorite of North Americans for centuries.

JALAPEÑO

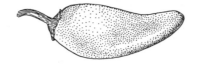

Availability: All year. **Peak of freshness:** Firm, un-wrinkled, with shiny skin. Usually green, but sometimes	red. Dry lines or striations are not a blemish, but a sign of hotness.

One of the favorite foods in Mexico and the Southwest, *jalapeños* are among the hottest peppers available. They are small, usually no more than 2 inches long, pointed, and smooth-skinned. Recent research has created strains of *jalapeños* that are not as hot, and they are used dried in foods where the flavor is needed but not the heat. *Jalapeños* can be eaten raw in salsas, simmered in stews, or added to sautés and stir-fries. Substitute for carrots in, or add to, Pickled Carrots (page 85).

MULATO

Other name: Sometimes called *ancho.*

Availability: Sporadic.

Peak of freshness: Firm and shiny. Heavy to hold. Blackish-green or reddish-brown.

An *ancho*-type pepper that is very similar to the *ancho* when green. Most *mulatos* end up dried. When dried the *mulato* is dark brown, the *ancho* a deep red. The dried *mulato* is used for *moles,* and approximately 90 percent of *mulato* peppers are dried.

PAPRIKA

Availability: Late summer and fall.

Peak of freshness: Firm and shiny red or green.

Few people pay attention to the fruit of the paprika pepper, as it is the seeds that yield ground paprika. But the pepper itself is delicious. Most paprikas are shaped like little boxes, with a thick, tasty flesh that makes them ideal for stuffing. Though classified as hot peppers, they are only a little hotter than sweet peppers.

PASILLA

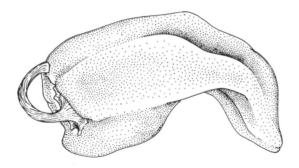

Other names: *Chile chilaca, chile negro.*

Availability: Almost year round.

Peak of freshness: Shiny and firm.

A true *pasilla* pepper is long and narrow, quite different from the *ancho*-type peppers. When fresh the *pasilla* is dark green, almost black; when dried it is chocolate brown. Most of the *pasillas* produced are used dried and are especially flavorful in *moles.* Fresh *pasillas* are a little hotter than Anaheim or sweet peppers. In some areas of Mexico they are called *chiles chilacas* when fresh. In Baja, California, the *pasilla* is also called *chile negro.* However, as mentioned above under *ancho,* many peppers marketed here in the United States as *pasillas* are in fact *anchos* or *poblanos.*

WHY PEPPERS ARE HOT

The flesh of a pepper is not hot. The heat comes from *capsaicin,* which is present in the seeds and in the ribs that hold the seeds. If you remove the seeds and ribs, the pepper's intensity will be markedly reduced.

PEQUIN

Availability: Sporadically year round.

Peak of freshness: No wrinkl-ing or drying. Dry surface veining is evidence of a hot, dry climate, not lack of freshness.

A widely used pepper in Mexico that is now appearing in the United States. It is tiny and comes in all shades of red, green, yellow, and orange when fresh. When dried it is red. Generally no more than ¾ inch long and ¼ to ½ inch wide, this very hot pepper is said to be digestible by everyone because it doesn't produce stomach acidity. Use in salsas.

SERRANO

Availability: Summer and fall.

Peak of freshness: No wrinkl-ing or drying. Dry surface veining is evidence of a hot, dry climate.

A very hot pepper, most often used for making salsas and pickles, but found in any number of dishes from *moles* to salsas. It gives cream sauces a little heat and a slightly exotic flavor. The *serrano* is grown in a wide range of shapes and sizes. They vary in length from 1 to 2 inches and in width from ½ to 1 inch. Some taper to a very distinct, almost sharp point, while others are rounded at the tip. The color varies from dark orange to dark green. All are *serranos* and all are hot.

Roasted Pepper and Seafood Salad

This spicy pepper salad features the strong flavors of cumin and ginger along with mackerel, a delicious and underrated fish that is usually quite inexpensive.

Serves 4 as a first course

5 bell peppers of assorted colors
1 to 5 medium-hot and hot fresh peppers such as jalapeño, serrano, *and Anaheim*
One ½-pound mackerel, tuna, or swordfish fillet
1 small bunch romaine, destemmed and torn into small pieces (about 2 cups)
½ cup small pitted black olives

DRESSING

4 tablespoons olive oil
2 teaspoons red vine vinegar
1 teaspoon grated fresh ginger
½ teaspoon ground cumin

Light a charcoal fire in an open grill. Roast and peel the peppers following the procedure on page 203. Roast the hot peppers until the skins are charred and remove the seeds. Cut the bell and hot peppers into thin strips.

When the charcoal is covered with gray ash, grill the fish until just done, about 2 minutes per side. (Mackerel becomes strong-tasting when overcooked.) A wooden skewer should easily pierce the thickest section of the fillet.

On a large serving plate make a bed of the romaine lettuce. Place the fish in the center. Outline it with the various peppers. Sprinkle the olives over the salad. Mix the dressing, pour it over the salad, and serve.

Grilled Pepper Soup

This fragrant coral soup can be served hot or cold. It can form part of a light summer meal of soup and salad, or introduce a rich, flavorful meat dish.

Serves 4 as a first course

4 to 5 red bell peppers (1 pound) yielding ¾ cup purée
1½ cups duck or chicken stock
½ cup heavy cream
1 teaspoon minced fresh thyme, or ½ teaspoon dried thyme
Salt and pepper to taste

Roast and peel the bell peppers following the procedure on page 203. Remove the seeds and ribs. Cut the peppers into thin strips. Reserve a dozen strips to garnish the soup. Steam the pepper strips in a steamer until very soft. Purée the peppers and a little of the stock in a blender or food processor until smooth.

In a large, heavy saucepan combine the pepper purée, cream, duck or chicken stock, thyme, and salt and pepper. Simmer over very low heat for 10 minutes. Serve the soup in warmed bowls garnished with pepper slices and accompanied with toasted slices of baguette.

Roasted Pepper, Almond, and Olive Salad

Serves 4 as a first course

2 large red bell peppers
2 tablespoons olive oil
4 thyme sprigs, or ½ teaspoon
    dried thyme
Salt and pepper to taste
1 head escarole
½ cup black niçoise olives
½ cup whole small green olives
1 cup slivered blanched almonds
4 anchovy fillets
½ cup vinaigrette, page 94

An hour before roasting them, put the peppers in a ceramic or glass bowl with the olive oil, thyme, and salt and pepper. Turn the peppers every 15 minutes so they will be evenly coated with oil.

Roast and peel the peppers (see page 203). Cut the peppers in half lengthwise and remove the seeds and ribs.

Remove the pale inner leaves from the head of escarole. Steam them in a basket until just wilted. Fill each pepper half with one-quarter of the black and green olives and the almonds. Top each serving with an anchovy fillet. Make a bed of the escarole on warmed salad plates. Arrange the peppers on top of the escarole. Drizzle with the vinaigrette and serve.

Roasted Peppers Stuffed with Goat Cheese and Garlic

Serves 8 as an appetizer, 4 as a main course

12 heads of garlic
4 tablespoons olive oil
4 tablespoons melted butter
Salt to taste
4 bell peppers (2 yellow and 2
    red)
2 fresh 4-ounce goat cheeses
2 teaspoons fresh minced thyme,
    or 1 teaspoon dried thyme

Preheat the oven to 275°.

Remove the outermost papery skin of the garlic. Place the unpeeled garlic heads in a shallow pan. Sprinkle with the olive oil, butter, and salt. Bake uncovered for 45 minutes or until the garlic is easily pierced with a knife. Separate the cloves and cut off the tops of each one. Squeeze out the garlic. (This time-consuming procedure can be done the night before.)

Cut the peppers in half lengthwise, leaving the stems and tips intact. Remove the ribs and seeds. Roast over a gas burner or under a grill until the peppers are soft, but still retain their shape (the skins of the peppers will become somewhat charred as they cook).

In a mixing bowl, with the back of a wooden spoon mash the roasted garlic and goat cheese along with the thyme. Spoon one-eighth of the filling into each pepper half. Heat the stuffed peppers in the oven or on a grill. Serve immediately.

Pepper Pasta with Crab

Jalapeño and ancho *peppers flavor a pasta topped with pieces of crab and a sauce made from crab butter.*

Serves 6 as a first course, 4 as a main course

PASTA

1 recipe pasta from Beet Pasta, page 104
3 ancho *and 3 or more* jalapeño *peppers, roasted, seeded, and chopped*

1 live crab, weighing 2 to 2½ pounds

SAUCE

1 tablespoon chopped garlic
2 tablespoons olive oil
3 medium tomatoes, peeled, seeded and chopped
2 cups chicken stock
Reserved crab butter

1 gallon water
Salt to taste
Cilantro leaves for garnish

Prepare the pasta, substituting the peppers for beets, and adding another egg, if necessary, to moisten the pasta. Set aside.

Refrigerate the crab for 1 hour to slow its movements. Place it on a cutting board, turn it shell side down, and with one quick motion cut through the center of the crab lengthwise with a heavy cleaver. Pull off the shell and discard it. Remove and discard the gills (the spongy finger-shaped appendages). Scoop out the dark-yellow crab butter from the body cavity and save it. Stand each half of the crab on its side with the legs and claw pointing up. With a cleaver or chef's knife, cut down between each leg and through the body. You will be left with 10 pieces consisting of leg and body. Crack the crab with a mallet, sharpening steel, or the back of a heavy cleaver, hitting sharply on each section of legs and claws.

In a saucepan large enough to hold the sauce and the crab, sauté the garlic in olive oil over medium heat for 2 minutes. Add the tomatoes, chicken stock, and crab butter and simmer for 10 minutes. Add the crab legs and claws and cook for 5 minutes.

Place the water in a large pot, add salt, and bring it to a boil. Add the pasta and cook until *al dente,* 1 to 2 minutes. Transfer the pasta to a warm serving tray. Arrange half the crab legs down each side of the tray with the claws at the top. Spoon the sauce over the pasta and garnish the whole tray with cilantro. Bring to the table immediately and serve on warm plates.

Chinese Stuffed Peppers

The Chinese serve stuffed peppers as a dim sum. The sweet tastes of the pepper and pork blend nicely with the flavorful dipping sauce.

Serves 4 as a main course

STUFFING

¾ pound ground pork
¼ pound cooked baby shrimp
1 teaspoon grated fresh ginger
1 tablespoon medium soy sauce
¼ cup chicken stock
1 tablespoon peeled and chopped fresh water chestnut or Jerusalem artichoke
1 to 2 tablespoons cilantro leaves
1 teaspoon cornstarch

4 green, red, or yellow bell peppers, or any combination of colors

DIPPING SAUCE

2 tablespoons chicken stock
2 tablespoons medium soy sauce
1 teaspoon white sugar
2 teaspoons grated fresh ginger
1 tablespoon Asian sesame oil

In a mixing bowl or food processor combine the stuffing ingredients. Carefully cut the tops off the bell peppers. Remove the seeds and pulp. Stuff each pepper with one quarter of the pork-shrimp mixture. Fit the tops into place. Steam until the peppers are soft, 15 to 20 minutes.

While the peppers are cooking, mix the dipping sauce. Add all the ingredients except the sesame oil to a saucepan. Bring to a boil and im-mediately remove from the heat. When the sauce has cooled a bit, add the sesame oil. Pour the sauce over the peppers and serve the rice.

Green Chili Spoonbread

This recipe combines a classic Southern recipe with flavors from the Southwest. Serve it with Tomatillo Salsa (page 221) or Tomato Coulis (page 226).

Serves 8

2 bacon slices, cut into 1-inch strips
6 large Anaheim peppers or other mild fresh peppers, roasted, peeled, and seeded (page 203)
½ cup grated Monterey jack cheese
½ cup grated sharp Cheddar cheese
3 eggs, separated
2 tablespoons fine yellow cornmeal
2 tablespoons unbleached all-purpose flour
⅓ cup milk
2 tablespoons sour cream
½ teaspoon salt

Preheat the oven to 350°.

Cook the bacon until barely browned. Remove it from the pan with a slotted spoon and remove excess oil with paper towels.

Butter an 8-inch-square baking pan. Lay the peppers in the pan side by side. Cover the peppers with the cheese. Beat the egg whites until fluffy but not stiff. In another bowl mix the egg yolks, cornmeal, flour, milk, sour cream, and salt. Fold the whites gently into the yolk-flour mixture. Spoon it over the cheese and peppers. Arrange the bacon pieces on top in a symmetrical pattern. Bake for about 20 minutes or until all but the center is set.

POTATO
Solanum tuberosum

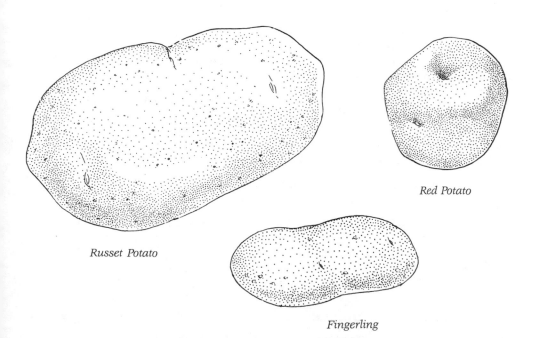

Russet Potato

Red Potato

Fingerling

How grown: From eyes cut from tubers. (One variety produces seed.) Many potatoes in the markets have been treated not to sprout, contrary to potato eyes in garden centers.

Availability: Depending on variety, all year.

Peak of freshness: Firm, unblemished skin with no soft spots or darkened areas. Potatoes should not display the small growths called eyes.

To prepare: Scrub the skin well if you will use it unpeeled.

In Europe the potato plays an important part in culinary life. The French and Belgians argue about who makes the best *pommes frites*. Across the

Channel the English plan their early summer meals around the tiny waxy new Jersey Royal potato, which makes a three-week appearance in June. In the British Isles there are still many types of potatoes available, and London markets, under the encouragement of the British Potato Marketing Board, sell them under their varietal names. An experienced British cook is familiar with at least a dozen or more varieties and the culinary qualities of each. In the United States we usually have available only three or four different kinds, though such types as Rose Fir, Finnish Yellow Wax, Blue Carib, and others are making headway in restaurants and specialty markets.

Potato Varieties

BLUE: The blue potato is increasingly sought after in this country. It has a grayish-blue skin,and the flesh is a inky blue color. Varieties include Blue Carib and All Blue.

RED: These have a very thin red skin ranging in color from pink to dark red. The flesh is usually white and crisp. Many red potatoes mature quickly. They are often dug up when small for new potatoes. Red potatoes are excellent for boiling. To bake, rub them first with olive oil. Varieties include Red Rose, Red Pontiac, Red La Soda.

RUSSET OR IDAHO: The standard baking potato. Varieties include Butte and Norgold.

WHITE OR LIGHT SKINNED: Light colored and thin skinned. They may have either yellow or white flesh, and are often found as new potatoes. Varieties include Finnish Wax, Yukon Gold (whose seed stock comes from Canada), White Rose, German Fingerling, and Kennebec. Fingerlings are small and lumpy with yellow meat.

COOKING WITH POTATOES

If at all possible, use the type of potato recommended for a particular dish. White Rose and russet potatoes deep-fry without absorbing the frying oil; waxy Finnish potatoes are easily coated with sauce and dressing and are ideal for salads. Russets are appropriate for gratins, and Blues and Rose Firs are best simply boiled and buttered because of their delicate flavor.

Gnocchi with Gorgonzola-Cream Sauce

To make good gnocchi *you need to use dry potatoes, the drier the better. Look for russets whose skins have begun to shrivel. This dish would be a fine accompaniment to roast beef or lamb.*

Serves 8 as a side dish

2½ *pounds russet potatoes*
1 *egg*
1 *cup unbleached all-purpose flour*
½ *teaspoon salt*
1 *gallon water*

GORGONZOLA CREAM SAUCE

1 *cup heavy cream*
2 *ounces Gorgonzola cheese, cut into small pieces*

Boil the potatoes until tender. Peel and grate them into a mixing bowl. Add the egg and flour, mixing well. Knead on a floured board until the dough is soft and sticky. Take 1 cup of the *gnocchi* at a time, and with the palms of your hands roll it into a cylinder a foot long. Cut it in half and roll each of the 2 pieces into a 12-inch-long cylinder. Cut into ½-inch-long pieces. Coat the *gnocchi* thoroughly with flour. Bring a gallon of salted water to a boil in a pasta pot and cook 2 dozen or so *gnocchi* at a time until they float to the surface. Remove them with a slotted spoon and keep them warm in the oven.

To make the sauce, heat the cream in a small saucepan and add the cheese, whisking until the cheese melts. Pour the sauce over the *gnocchi* and serve immediately.

Potatoes Baked with Cream, Anchovies, and Fresh Rosemary

This simple dish draws raves from lovers of assertive ingredients. A rich, flavorful sauce is created as the potatoes bake. Serve with roast meats or poultry.

Serves 4 as a side dish

6 medium Yellow Wax potatoes
2 large yellow onions
5 anchovy fillets packed in olive oil
1 tablespoon chopped fresh rosemary, or 1 teaspoon dried rosemary
1½ cups heavy cream
Olive oil from anchovies
Pepper to taste

Preheat the oven to 350°.

Peel the potatoes and cut them into finger-sized strips. Thinly slice the onions. Cut the anchovy fillets into ½-inch pieces, reserving the oil from the can. Butter a deep-dish casserole. Arrange first a layer of potatoes, then a few anchovy pieces, and next a teaspoon or so of chopped rosemary. Continue the layering, ending with potatoes. Mix half the cream with all of the oil from the anchovy tin and pour it over the potatoes. Bake, covered, for 35 minutes. Pour the rest of the cream over the potatoes, add peppers, and re-cover. Bake for another 15 minutes, or until the potatoes are tender.

Belgian Pommes Frites

For decades French and Belgian cooks have argued about who makes the best French fries. The Belgians claim to have invented the double-frying method, and for the moment we will credit them with this innovation, which ensures crisp fries. The Belgians dip their French fries in mayonnaise and wash them down with their wonderful beer.

Serves 4 as a side dish

6 large russet potatoes, peeled
Oil for deep-frying
Salt to taste

After peeling the potatoes, place them in a bowl with water to cover to prevent discoloration. Cut the potatoes into ½-inch slices, covering the slices with water as you go. Cut the slices into sticks ½ inch wide. Dry the potatoes thoroughly on paper towels.

Fill a deep-fryer or Dutch oven with 6 inches of oil. Heat the oil over high heat to 350°. (The key factor in proper deep-frying is to maintain the oil at a nearly constant temperature. If you add a large quantity of potatoes, the oil may not return to 350° for some time, and the potatoes will become soggy. If you fry too few, they may brown immediately. Experiment with your equipment to discover the right quantity. A candy/frying thermometer is very helpful if not essential in this process.) Fry the potatoes until they develop a white crust, but do not brown. Remove from the oil with a slotted spoon and spread onto paper towels. Allow the oil to return to 350° between each batch. Fry the potatoes a second time until they are golden brown. (The second frying can be done several hours after the first.) Sprinkle with salt and serve immediately.

Potatoes North African Style

This brightly colored potato dish could be served as a main course for lunch, accompanied with pita bread and Cucumber-Yogurt Salad (page 125).

Serves 6 as a side dish, 4 as a main course

2 cups dried or drained canned
   chick-peas
4 White Rose potatoes
3 tablespoons olive oil
2 red bell peppers, seeded and
   cut into thin strips
2 small fresh hot peppers such as
   jalapeño, seeded and chopped
1 tablespoon chopped garlic

If using dried chick-peas, soak overnight, then simmer in salted water to cover for 30 to 40 minutes or until tender; drain.

Boil the whole potatoes until easily pierced with a knife. Cool, peel, and cut into ½-inch cubes. Heat the olive oil in a sauté pan or skillet large enough to hold all the ingredients. Sauté the potatoes, tossing them frequently, until browned on all sides. Remove the potatoes from the pan with a slotted spoon. Add more olive oil if necessary and sauté the peppers and garlic until the peppers are soft. Add the chick-peas and potatoes and cook until the newly added ingredients are hot. Serve immediately.

TOMATILLO
Physalis ixocarpa

> **Other names:** Mexican tomato, husk tomato, green tomato.
>
> **How grown:** From seed.
>
> **Availability:** Summer, fall.
>
> **Peak of freshness:** The husk is split, showing a firm yellow-green, slightly sticky skin.
>
> **To prepare:** Remove the husk. Wash. Tomatillos are most often used whole, without skinning and seeding. If the dish is going to be eaten right away, there is no need to cook the *tomatillos*. However, if it is a dish that will be used the next day, the *tomatillos* should be cooked for 2 to 3 minutes in boiling water. An uncooked *tomatillo* will discolor after 8 to 10 hours.

Tomatillos are not tomatoes at all, but they do belong to the nightshade family. They grow on weedy plants growing up to 4 feet high. The size of a large cherry tomato, they are light green often tinged with purple when fully ripe and are covered with a parchmentlike husk. *Tomatillos* are little known outside the Southwest. They are frequently found in markets patronized by Latinos or in specialty produce markets, and in the large chain markets of the West and Southwest. *Tomatillos* were used by the Indian population of Mexico, and traveled north with the Spanish. They are an important ingredient in Southwestern cooking.

Tomatillos combine well with chicken and can be used raw in salads and in most dishes that call for green tomatoes. *Tomatillos* have a slightly acidic, lemony flavor that is a bit different from the tartness of the green tomato. A delicious *ceviche* can be made using *tomatillos*, and they can be substituted for *nopales* in Mexican Pork Stew with Nopales (page 232).

Salsa de Tomatillo

This sauce is a nice accompaniment to grilled meat. It may be kept refrigerated for five days.

Makes 3 cups

1 medium yellow onion, chopped
3 tablespoons minced blanched almonds
2 tablespoons olive oil
1 pound tomatillos
2 teaspoons minced fresh cilantro
2 teaspoons minced fresh hot pepper such as jalapeño or serrano
1 cup chicken stock

In a sauté pan or skillet, sauté the onion and almonds in the olive oil until the onion is soft. Cook the tomatillos 2 to 3 minutes in boiling salted water to cover. Mince by hand or purée in a blender. Combine the onions, almonds, tomatillos, cilantro, pepper, and stock in a heavy saucepan. Simmer for 20 minutes. Serve at room temperature.

Mole Verde

This classic Mexican dish uses tomatillos as one source of its rich green color.

Serves 6 as a main course

1 large frying chicken
6 cups water
One 1-inch piece ginger, peeled
½ medium onion
1 bay leaf
1 teaspoon minced fresh oregano, or ½ teaspoon dried oregano
1 teaspoon salt
1 teaspoon minced fresh cilantro

SALSA

¼ cup oil or lard
12 whole blanched almonds
1 tablespoon raw pumpkin seeds
2 teaspoons sesame seeds
4 cups chicken stock reserved from cooking the chicken
2 garlic cloves
¼ medium onion
1 serrano pepper, stemmed
1 bell pepper, seeded and stemmed
2 tablespoons chopped fresh parsley
6 large tomatillos, husks removed
1 tablespoon chopped fresh cilantro
Leaves from 1 head romaine lettuce, torn in pieces
1 tablespoon peanut butter
1 bread slice, torn in pieces
2 allspice berries
2 cloves
Salt to taste

In a large pot, place the chicken, water, and next 6 ingredients and bring to a boil. Reduce to a simmer, cover, and cook until tender, about 1½ hours. Let the chicken cool in the stock, then remove and strain the stock; reserve.

To make the salsa, heat the oil or lard in a sauté pan or skillet. Add the almonds and cook for 1 minute; remove with a slotted spoon and drain on paper towels. Cook the pumpkin seeds for one minute; remove and drain. Stir the sesame seeds in the pan until lightly golden; remove and drain.

In a blender or food processor, place 2 cups of the chicken stock, the almonds, pumpkin seeds, sesame seeds, and all the remaining salsa ingredients. Purée until smooth. Pour into a large saucepan and add the remaining 2 cups of chicken stock. Simmer for 15 to 20 minutes, stirring occasionally, until the fresh green color of the salsa intensifies. At this time, add the chicken to the salsa. Simmer until the chicken is heated through. Serve with corn tortillas, rice, and cold Mexican beer.

TOMATO

Lycopersicon lycopersicum

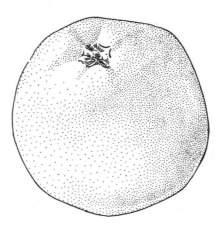

The tomato is from the New World, a native of tropical America. Most likely it originated in what is now Ecuador and Peru. Tomatoes were taken back to Europe along with silver and gold, and they were grown on the continent as a pretty curiosity. The French gave them the name *pomme d'amour,* "love apples," and the Italians called them *pomodori, "golden apples."* Some scholars think both words are derived from *pomo di Mori,* Italian for "Moorish apple," a reference to their Spanish background.

Southeast Asians were first introduced to the tomato around the middle of the seventeenth century and North Americans by the late eighteenth century, but it is only within the last one hundred years that it has become a major vegetable—it is still not well accepted in many parts of Asia.

All tomatoes taste better if vine-ripened. Unfortunately, many of the tomatoes that reach our markets have been picked when green, put into cold storage, and then allowed to ripen in warming rooms. Not suprisingly, a great deal of flavor is lost in this process.

Home gardeners have a real advantage over market shoppers when it comes to tomatoes. Not only can they grow many different varieties, but they can have fresh tomatoes well into the winter. Pulling up the entire tomato plant before the first frost, green tomatoes and all, then hanging the plant upside down in a dark place, will cause the green tomatoes to slowly ripen.

It is even more difficult for people to agree on what a "flavorful" tomato is than it is for them to agree on a "flavorful" strawberry. There is a significant range of acidity in tomatoes, and some taste buds are titillated by astringency while others cringe. Another aspect of tomato variation is structure. Look at the inside of tomatoes when you slice them. Are there lots of seeds and juice, but only a few meaty ridges? Or are there several ridges and only a few seed cavities? The irregular-shaped Roma is a meaty type, with only two or three cavities. The large European type is meaty as well, making it easy to scoop out the seeds while leaving a firm shell for stuffing. Meaty types are good for making thick sauce, and if large, the firm shells are good for stuffing. The juicier types are good for salads and in combination with other vegetables, such as Ratatouille (page 196).

Green tomatoes are unripened tomatoes, not a separate type. They are excellent used in pickles and relishes, and may be pan-fried and accompanied with caviar and sour cream. Yellow and pink tomatoes, on the other hand, are separate strains. Pink tomatoes are much like red tomatoes, except their skin is clear (red tomatoes have skin with a yellowish hue). Yellow tomatoes come in sizes ranging from pear and plum to large round ones. Try serving the pear or plum types in clusters as you would grapes, or use them whole in dishes calling for cooked tomatoes. Large yellow tomatoes are beautiful sliced in combination with red tomatoes and mozzarella cheese.

Tomatoes are a staple of summer salads alone and in combination with many other vegetables. They can be stuffed (use the filling in Stuffed Pain de Sucre on page 275), or broiled or grilled after marinating in olive oil.

There are hundreds of tomato varieties, but they all fall into a few major categories.

To Peel, Seed, and Juice a Tomato

Cut out the stems. Cut a small shallow "x" in the bottom side of the tomato. Plunge the tomatoes into boiling water just long enough for the skin to loosen, 15 to 30 seconds. Quickly transfer the tomatoes to a bowl of ice water. Peel the skin. Cut the tomatoes in half crosswise and squeeze out the seeds and juice.

CHERRY TOMATO

> **How grown:** From seed.
>
> **Availability:** Year round.
>
> **Peak of freshness:** Firm to touch. Avoid those that seem too large or have begun to split at the stem end unless you are going to eat them immediately.
>
> **To prepare:** Wash. Remove stems.

This name is commonly given to small tomatoes that are round, pear-, or plum-shaped and range from the size of a marble to that of a golf ball.

SAUCE TOMATO

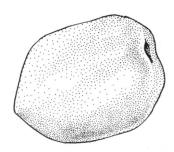

> **Other names:** Italian tomato, Roma tomato, plum tomato, paste tomato.
>
> **How grown:** From seed.
>
> **Availability:** Summer.
>
> **Peak of freshness:** Deep red; slightly soft to the touch.
>
> **To prepare:** Wash. To peel, seed, and juice, see page 223.

This tomato has lots of thick meat and very little juice. It is 2 to 3 inches long and pear or plum shaped.

SLICING TOMATO

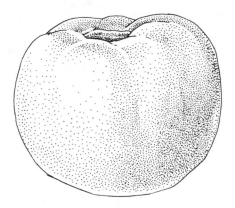

Availability: Year round, but vine-ripened only during late spring, summer, and fall.

Peak of freshness: Deep red or rosy pink. Firm to the touch.

To prepare: Wash. To peel, seed, and juice, see page 223.

YELLOW TOMATO

Availability: Summer and fall.

Peak of freshness: Firm; may show green at the stem end.

Yellow tomatoes can be used either fresh or cooked. The small yellow pear and yellow plum tomatoes are best used whole, as you would a cherry tomato. The larger ones are treated like similar-sized red tomatoes.

Tomato Coulis

This quick tomato sauce will keep 5 to 6 days in the refrigerator. Use it for pasta, pizza, vegetables—any time you want a rich, flavorful tomato sauce.

Makes 1 quart

5 to 6 pounds very ripe tomatoes, peeled, seeded, and chopped
1 tablespoon sugar
2 medium yellow onions, peeled and minced
1½ teaspoons minced garlic
5 basil leaves, finely chopped
5 parsley sprigs
½ bay leaf
2 tablespoons olive oil
Salt and pepper to taste
Cayenne to taste

Bring the tomatoes and sugar to a boil in a stockpot. Cook for 10 minutes. Drain through cheesecloth or fine strainer; reserve the juice for another use. Return the tomatoes to the stockpot and cook until nearly all the liquid is gone. In a large sauté pan or skillet slowly sauté the onions, garlic, 3 of the basil leaves, parsley, and bay leaf in the olive oil. Stir in the cooked tomatoes. Add the salt, pepper, cayenne, and the remaining basil.

This sauce will keep 5 to 6 days in the refrigerator.

Tomato Flan

This beautiful custard is the perfect appetizer for a summer buffet or picnic.

Serves 6 as a first course

10 medium tomatoes, peeled and seeded (about 3 pounds)
1 tablespoon butter
1 medium yellow onion minced
¼ teaspoon salt
5 eggs, beaten
½ cup heavy cream
Tomato Coulis

Preheat the oven to 325.°
Purée the tomatoes in a blender or food processor and set aside. Melt the butter in a sauté pan or skillet and sauté the onion until translucent. Add the salt, onion, and tomatoes to the eggs. Butter an 8-inch-round cake pan. Pour the tomato mixture into the cake pan and place it inside a larger pan. Fill the larger pan nearly full with hot water. Bake for 1¼ hours or until a wooden skewer comes out clean.

Cool for 1 hour, then refrigerate for another hour. Remove the flan from the pan by cutting around the perimeter with a knife. Turn upside down over a serving dish lined with lettuce leaves and tap the bottom of the pan. Cover the top of the flan with a thin layer of Tomato Coulis.

Tomato Tart

This open-face tart combines the sweet flavor of honey with the acidity of tomatoes. Tomatoes are sometimes combined with honey and meat in Moroccan dishes. In this dish you can use any combination of tomato colors and shapes, such as yellow and red pear tomatoes or alternating slices of green, red, and yellow tomatoes. This tart would make an intriguing appetizer, though it could also be served as a dessert.

Serves 8 as a first course, 6 as a dessert

GINGER-HONEY GLAZE

1 tablespoon minced fresh ginger
2 tablespoons water
4 tablespoons sugar
½ teaspoon grated lemon zest
1 tablespoon honey

PASTRY

¾ cup unsalted butter
1 teaspoon sugar mixed with
1 cup unbleached all-purpose
    flour
2 to 3 tablespoons water

TOMATO FILLING

1½ pounds tomatoes, sliced
2 teaspoons minced ginger,
    removed from the glaze, above
2 tablespoons slivered blanched
    almonds
1 teaspoon ground cinnamon
Ginger-Honey Glaze, above

To make the glaze, combine the ginger, water, sugar, and zest in a saucepan. Bring to a boil and simmer until thickened, 3 to 4 minutes. Strain the liquid through a sieve and save the ginger pieces for the topping. Add the honey to the syrup, mix, and set aside.

Preheat the oven to 425°. To make the pastry, work the butter into the sugar and flour in a bowl with a pastry cutter, or in a food processor using the pastry blade. Add the water until the pastry forms a ball easily. Roll the dough out on a floured cutting board or pastry cloth. Press into a two-piece tart pan.

To make the tomato filling, arrange the tomatoes evenly in the pastry shell. Sprinkle with the ginger, almonds, and cinnamon. Bake for 15 minutes. Remove the tart and drizzle with the glaze. Bake another 15 minutes at 325°. Remove from the tart pan and serve hot or at room temperature.

Golden Tomato Soup

The lovely gold color of this soup is enhanced by fresh turmeric, which has a carrotlike texture and a vivid yellow color.

Serves 4 as a first course

1 tablespoon butter
1 teaspoon chopped garlic
2 teaspoons grated fresh
    turmeric, or 1 teaspoon ground
    turmeric
1 teaspoon grated fresh ginger
5 yellow tomatoes, peeled,
    seeded, and cut into ½-inch
    cubes
2 cups chicken stock
Salt and white pepper to taste
1 red tomato, peeled, seeded, and
    cut into thin strips

In a large saucepan, melt the butter over medium heat. Add the garlic, turmeric, and ginger. Cook, stirring frequently, for 3 minutes. Add the yellow tomatoes and cook until soft. Add the chicken stock and salt and pepper and cook for 10 minutes. Ladle the soup into warmed bowls and garnish with the red tomato strips.

Green Tomatoes with Cilantro

Serve this dish with a roast of pork or chicken.

Serves 4 as a side dish

4 medium green tomatoes, cut
    into ¼-inch slices
1 cup fine-ground cornmeal
Salt and pepper to taste
3 bacon slices
½ cup heavy cream
¼ cup chopped fresh cilantro

Dry the tomato slices with paper towels. Mix the cornmeal, salt, and pepper and dredge the tomatoes in the mixture. Render 3 tablespoons of fat from the bacon in a skillet large enough to hold the tomatoes; remove the bacon. Warm the cream in a double boiler and keep warm. Fry the tomatoes in the bacon fat over medium heat for 1 minute on each side, or until the cornmeal browns. Serve immediately, sprinkled with cilantro. Pass the warm cream on the side.

Pickled Green Tomatoes

Green tomatoes are available to gardeners, and they are increasingly sold in produce markets. Green plum tomatoes look beautiful in glass jars along with green leaves, which help keep the tomatoes crunchy. A whole branch of cherry tomatoes or yellow pear tomatoes can be pickled while still green.

Makes 2 quarts

5 cups water
2 tablespoons salt
2 handfuls oak, cherry, or grape
   leaves
3 pounds small green tomatoes,
   1½ inches in diameter
4 garlic cloves, slightly crushed
4 tablespoons chopped fresh dill,
   or 1 tablespoon dried dill
1 teaspoon whole peppercorns

In a large saucepan, bring the water and salt to a boil and then let it cool; set aside. Rinse two quart-sized jars with boiling water. Line the jars with leaves, reserving a few for the top. Pack the jars with the tomatoes, adding half the garlic, dill, and peppercorns to each jar. Cover with the cooled brine, then pack the remaining leaves across the top of the jars. Cover the jars with pieces of muslin tied with string and put them in a cool, dark place for a week. Put lids on the jars and store them in the refrigerator, where they will keep for several months.

Nopales

Opuntia sp., *Nopales* sp.

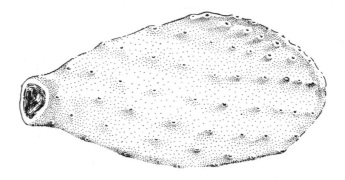

Prickly pear cactus pads yield a green vegetable known in the Southwest as *nopales*, or if cut up in small pieces, as *nopalitos*. The fruits of the prickly pear, called *tunas*, are also consumed. They appear in the markets in the fall. Although they are full of seeds, *tunas* have a sweet flavor, and they are enjoyed as a snack in Mexico City.

Cactus pads are full of water, which makes them rather mucilaginous and best suited to stews and sauce. Nopales combine well with garlic, tomatoes, and oregano.

Other names: Beavertail cactus, *nopal*, Indian fig.

How grown: From transplanted rooted pads.

Peak of freshness: The pads should be stiff, and 8 to 15 inches long. The cut ends may be oozing.

Availability: Late spring through early fall.

To prepare: Wash. (1) Hold the *nopales* with tongs and cut off the thorns with a sharp knife. (2) Peel off the skin, starting with the edges first, and then (3) the rest of the leaf. (4) Slice the pad into strips 1 inch long (5) and ¼ inch wide. Steam for 3 minutes.

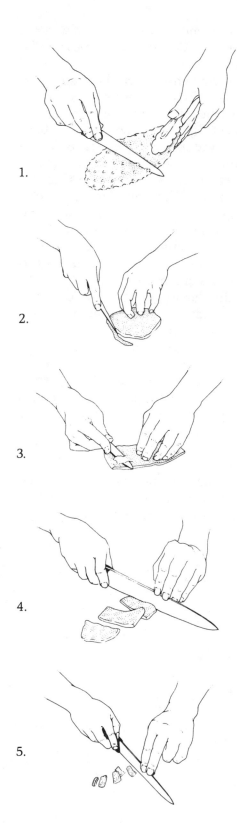

1.

2.

3.

4.

5.

Huevos Rancheros con Nopales

This spicy egg dish is served in the northern regions of Mexico. An interesting variation features bitter melon substituted for nopales. Use the same quantity of blanched bitter melon, prepared as on page 118. Serve this with warm corn tortillas and fresh tropical fruit such as papayas, mangoes, and pineapple.

Serves 4 as a main course

2 tablespoons butter
1 teaspoon chopped garlic
½ cup minced yellow onion
8 eggs, beaten
1 fresh hot pepper such as
    jalapeño *or* serrano, *peeled, seeded, and cut into thin strips (page 203)*
½ cup nopales, steamed
    (page 230)
½ cup shredded Monterey jack cheese
Salt and pepper to taste
2 tablespoons chopped fresh cilantro for garnish

In a large skillet, melt 1 tablespoon of the butter. Add the garlic and onion and sauté over medium heat until the onion is translucent. Remove the onion and garlic from the pan. Add the remaining 1 tablespoon butter and, when it melts, pour in the eggs. When the eggs begin to set, stir in the pepper, *nopales,* cheese, and salt and pepper. Turn down the heat and cook, covered, until the egg becomes firm. Cut into 4 pieces and serve garnished with fresh cilantro.

Mexican Pork Stew with Nopales

The flavor of nopales *provides a distinct accent to even the spiciest of Mexican dishes. One large* nopales *cactus pad yields about 1½ cups of vegetable.*

Serves 6 as a main course

2 pounds lean pork roast, cut
    into 2-inch cubes
4 to 6 dried pasilla peppers
1½ to 2 cups boiling water
3 fresh jalapeño peppers, chopped
1 large yellow onion, chopped
2 tablespoons chopped garlic
2 tablespoons chopped fresh
    ginger
1 teaspoon ground cinnamon
1½ pounds tomatoes, peeled,
    seeded, and chopped
About 2 cups chicken stock
1 large nopales pad
Salt and pepper to taste
Cilantro leaves for garnish

Cover the pork with salted water in a heavy pot and simmer the meat for 2 hours or until tender.

Meanwhile, toast the pasilla peppers lightly on both sides on a hot griddle, then put them in a glass bowl and cover them with the boiling water. Let them stand for 30 minutes. Remove the stems and seeds and coarsely chop. In a blender combine the *pasillas, jalapeños,* onion, garlic, ginger, cinnamon, and some of the water used to soak the peppers. Purée, adding as much of the soaking water as necessary to form a smooth sauce.

In a large pot, place the pork, pepper sauce, and tomatoes. Add chicken stock until nearly covered and simmer until tender, about 1½ to 2 hours.

While the pork is cooking, prepare the *nopales* (see page 230). When the pork is tender, add the *nopales* to the pork stew and simmer 30 minutes longer. Correct the seasoning. By now most of the liquid should have evaporated, and you should be left with a thick sauce. Serve over rice, garnished with cilantro.

Okra

Abelmoschus esculentus

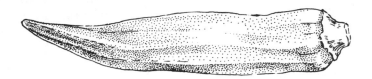

Okra is one of the staples of Southern cooking. Southern gardeners meticulously keep track of the weather so they will plant their okra seed at the right moment. Okra, a member of the mallow family, is a warm-weather plant—it originated in the Nile Valley—and it requires consistently hot weather for both germination and successful growth. It grows on an upright bush with one to three central stalks that bear beautiful yellow and maroon blossoms.

Okra is beloved by Africans, Indians, and Greeks, but other Europeans are not particularly fond of it, probably because of the texture, which some consider slimy. It arrived in America with the African slaves, who called it *gumbo*. The Louisiana French incorporated okra into their cuisine, and now gumbo with tomatoes is a star dish of the region. Okra curried with garlic, peppers, and onions is an Indian favorite. Tempura-fried okra is a natural treatment for the small pods, but the smallest okra can best be used in composed salads after a quick blanching.

Other names: Gumbo.

How grown: From seed.

Availability: Mid to late summer.

Peak of freshness: The best okra is small, 1½ to 2 inches long, but it is more commonly seen in the markets at 3 inches or longer. The ridges of the pods become fibrous when large.

To prepare: Wash okra only when ready to use it. Trim stem ends. Cut at the last moment before cooking; otherwise it will release its mucilage.

Sweet and Sour Okra

Serve this as a side dish with curries. It is also interesting as an accompaniment to traditional Southern fare such as black-eyed peas and barbecued meats. Since the pickles are hot and spicy, serve with another side dish such as Cucumber-Yogurt Salad (page 125).

Serves 4 as a side dish

8 garlic cloves, chopped
1 small fresh hot pepper such as
    jalapeño, seeded and chopped
½ teaspoon ground cumin
½ teaspoon ground coriander
1 teaspoon ground turmeric
½ cup water
1 pound okra
⅓ cup oil
½ teaspoon whole cumin seeds
½ teaspoon salt
1 teaspoon sugar
2 teaspoons fresh lemon juice
Fresh mint or cilantro sprigs for
    garnish

In a mortar or food processor make a paste of the garlic, pepper, cumin, coriander, turmeric, and 3 tablespoons of the water.

If the okra is large, cut it in half. Heat the oil in a sauté pan or skillet. Add the whole cumin, and when the seeds begin to jump, add the garlic-spice paste. Add the okra, salt, sugar, and lemon juice. Add the rest of the water and simmer until the okra is tender, about 10 minutes. Garnish with mint or cilantro.

Dill-pickled Okra

This recipe may also be used for making pickled green beans. It need only stand for a few hours, though letting it pickle overnight improves the flavor.

Makes 1 quart

1 pound young okra (no longer
   than 2 inches)
1 cup water
1 cup distilled vinegar
6 black peppercorns
1 tablespoon salt
2 heads dill
4 garlic cloves

Cut off the stem ends of the okra.

Combine the water, vinegar, peppercorns, and salt in a small saucepan. Bring to a boil. Add the okra and return to a boil. Remove the saucepan from the heat and cool the contents to room temperature. Place the dill and garlic in the bottom of a 1-quart canning jar. Pour the okra and liquid into the jar and close the lid. Pickled okra will keep for several days in the refrigerator.

Onion Family

Alliaceae: Garlic, Leek, Onion, Shallot

The members of the onion family have their own unique form of advertising. They broadcast their presence in the kitchen with a distinctive pungency. Worldwide, the response to the distinct odor and taste of the onion family is mixed, ranging from total and continuous admiration to complete rejection. Garlic is the most pungent of all, and some onions are very odoriferous as well. Less potent are shallots, leeks, and chives.

Americans think of garlic and leeks as European, though evidence points to an Asian origin. To their credit, European cooks quickly picked up on the culinary values of these alliaceous plants as soon as they became available.

Botanically related to grasses and lilies, most members of the onion family have grasslike or tubular leaves. Their flowering stalks become pithy with time. Some onion members do not set seed, and propagation is carried out by division. A few reproduce by producing tiny bulblets within flower clusters. Flowers are an important aspect of the onion family. Some onions are propagated for their ornamental value alone, producing clusters of purple, pink, blue, or white flowers atop slender stems. The onion family has wide culinary appeal because its members may be used for seasonings as well as for vegetables. Even the flowers add flavor and beauty to the kitchen: garlic and chive blossoms may be used to enliven soups and salads.

GARLIC
Allium sativum

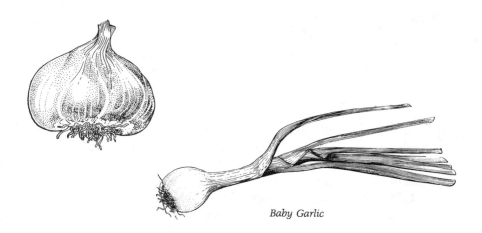

Baby Garlic

How grown: From cloves of garlic.

Availability: All year.

Peak of freshness: Garlic should be plump and firm, never sooty, discolored, or withered.

To prepare: To use the whole heads, remove the papery, outer layers of skin, leaving the cloves intact. Individual cloves may be used whole or cut up.

Garlic is grown in China, Europe, North Africa, North America, and Latin America and is an essential ingredient in most of the world's cuisines, Northern Europe being one exception.

Garlic has a long and well-documented history as a medicine in many parts of the world. It has been used as a cure for everything from hypertension to colds.

Summer is garlic season in California, where 90 percent of the nation's crop is grown. Every summer California farmers harvest thousands of tons of garlic bulbs grown from cloves planted in late fall. The fresh garlic is laid to dry in rows with the tops still on. The bulbs are pointed toward the morning sun; the straplike gray-green leaves are faced toward the hot afternoon rays. The garlic is cleaned, and most of the harvest is sent to processing plants where it comes out as salt, flakes, concentrate, or as seasoning for other processed foods. Only a small percentage is eaten fresh.

Of the three hundred known types of garlic, only two are raised on a large scale commercially in California. One is a pure white type harvested in early summer. The other, a pale-pink garlic with a sharper flavor, is dug up in August. A third kind, elephant garlic, has very large cloves that are easy to peel, though the flavor is quite mild. Mexican red garlic arrives at the market in early January. The cloves are quite small and require a little more preparation time. In March, the Mexican white garlic reaches this country just at the time when the previous year's U.S. crop has become soft, rubbery, and old-tasting.

Baby garlic is sold with the immature bulbs and stems intact. Its texture is similar to a bulb onion as it has not yet separated into cloves. Baby garlic can be used as a seasoning but is especially nice as a fresh vegetable because of its mild flavor.

Garlic may be cooked in whole heads, pressed, or peeled and used whole or chopped. Each method of preparation changes the flavor a bit (see below).

THE TASTE OF GARLIC

The more you do to garlic in preparation, the stronger the flavor will be; and the less you cook it, the stronger the characteristic garlic taste.

Preparation

1. Peeled whole cloves produce the mildest flavor when cooked.

2. Mincing and chopping release more of garlic's flavoring agents.

3. Pressing or crushing peeled or unpeeled cloves releases all of the strong sulphur compounds and a great deal of garlic flavor.

Cooking

Heat deactivates garlic. The more you cook it the milder it becomes. (Burning garlic, however, will make it very bitter.)

1. Baking produces a mild, sweet, nutty flavor.

2. Boiling yields a mild "traditional" garlic flavor.

3. Sautéing yields a moderately strong flavor with more bite than boiling but less intensity than raw chopped garlic.

Garlic Soup

This simple Galician soup becomes a whole meal when accompanied with bread and sausage.

Serves 4 as a first course

Cloves from 1 head of garlic
1 tablespoon rendered chicken
*   fat or butter*
6 bay leaves
1 quart water
4 eggs, beaten
1 cup hot milk
Salt and pepper to taste
6 French bread slices, chopped

In a large saucepan boil the garlic, chicken fat or butter, and bay leaves in the water for 20 minutes. Strain through a fine sieve. Bring the liquid to a simmer and pour in the eggs. Stir until the eggs are well mixed. Add the milk. Season to taste and serve garnished with French bread.

Garlic Oil

This rather mild oil is an excellent topping for pizza. If you want a more robust oil increase the amounts of cayenne pepper and garlic. Garlic oil can be used in salad dressing or to dress nearly any steamed vegetable —new potatoes and lima beans immediately come to mind.

Makes 1 cup

1 cup virgin olive oil
1 garlic clove, crushed
1 tablespoon black peppercorns
2 bay leaves

Combine all the ingredients in a glass bottle with a cork and let stand for 1 week. When ready to use, take out the cork and notch one side. Replace the cork and the oil will drizzle out.

LEEK
Allium Ampeloprasum

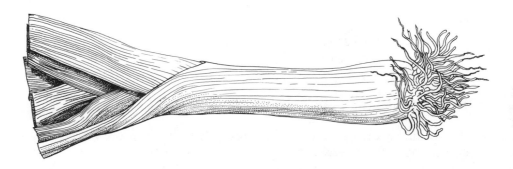

Other names: Poor man's asparagus, flag onion.

How grown: From seed.

Peak of freshness: Stiff white roots and stems. Large plants may be tough.

To prepare: The base of the leek stalk is blanched by having dirt piled up around it, so leeks must always be carefully washed. Remove the tough outer leaves. Make a slit one-third of the way down the green leaves. Spread the leaves and wash out the dirt. Cut off the root tip.

The leek has been cultivated since prehistoric times. Slowly spreading west from Asia to the Mediterranean and the British Isles, it eventually became the national plant of Wales.

In Europe, leeks have naturalized and may be found growing wild. Hence, many European recipes call for the smaller leeks that are easily found in the countryside.

In America leeks are usually sold when quite large, often a quarter pound or more. If you are fortunate enough to find small leeks (they are sometimes found in Asian markets), try steaming them as you would asparagus, or add them raw to salads. Baby leeks can be substituted in asparagus recipes. Small leeks can also be steamed or blanched and served with a vinaigrette. Leeks are often grilled after being marinated in olive oil. Large leeks frequently end up in soup, often with potatoes. They make a wonderful vegetable stock when cooked with carrots, celery, and parsley.

Leeks and Ham Baked in Filo

Serves 6 to 8 as a first course, 3 to 4 as a main course

1 pound baby leeks, trimmed to 6-inch lengths
6 to 8 sheets filo dough
2 to 3 tablespoons melted butter
1 cup coarsely chopped mild-flavored ham
¾ cup grated Gruyère cheese
½ cup sour cream

Preheat the oven to 400°.

Shred the leeks, cutting through the stems and bulbs.

Cut the *filo* into 8-inch squares. Lay the first piece in a baking dish of the same size. Brush with a light coating of butter (be careful not to use too much or the pastry will be greasy). Scatter a thin layer of leeks, ham, and cheese on top of the *filo*. Add the second piece of *filo* and brush with butter. Spread with a little sour cream and a few leeks. Cover with *filo* and repeat brushing. Layer with ham, leeks, and cheese. Repeat this pattern until the ingredients have been used up. Brush the top layer of *filo* with butter. Bake until the pastry is golden brown.

ONION
Allium Cepa

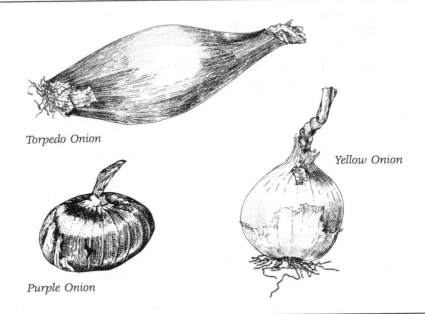

Torpedo Onion

Yellow Onion

Purple Onion

How grown: From seed or bulblets.

Availability: All year. Sweet onions are available in the summer months.

Peak of freshness: Onions should be firm and never sooty (the sign of fungus). Sweet onions do not store well, as they contain a higher moisture content. Late summer and fall onions are the best keepers.

To prepare: Trim root and stem ends, and peel the outermost layer for most dishes.

Though onions originated in Asia, they are now found worldwide, and almost every culture incorporates them into its cuisine. As onions spread they adapted themselves to different sets of soil, light, and climate conditions, and thus they vary widely. There are white, yellow, and purple bulb onions of strengths ranging from very sweet to very strong. There are tapering bulbs—the torpedos—and flat-topped Italian and Japanese types, and onions of all sizes, from small pickling varieties to monsters.

Onions can be treated as a seasoning or as a vegetable, depending on how you cut them and on the amounts used. A tablespoon of minced onions imparts a certain flavor the way a similar amount of garlic would, while pearl onions play a major role in the flavor and texture of *boeuf bourguignon*.

Small white onions are usually pickled or used as boiling onions. Medium-sized yellow and white onions are the most pungent and suited to cooking alone or stuffed with ground meat and rice or with cheese. Purple onions turn gray when cooked, though their flavor is still good. Very large white, yellow, and purple onions are usually sweet and can be eaten raw in sandwiches and salads; they may also be grilled. Caramelized onions can be added to pizza and to soups.

PEARL ONION

Allium Ampeloprasum

Other name: Pickling onion.

How grown: From seed or bulblets.

Availability: Fall and winter.

Peak of freshness: The scales are paperlike, with no sign of soot. The bulbs should be firm.

To prepare: Peel away the papery outer skin and trim both ends.

The true pearl onion is very different from the tiny pickling onion sometimes marketed as a pearl onion. The pearl is composed of a single layer of flesh, much like garlic, with the interior surrounded by paperlike scales. The pickling onion is fashioned like the slicing onion, with concentric rings. The flavor of the pearl onion is strong. It is best used in cooked dishes and for pickling. It can be used as a boiling onion.

SCALLION
Allium Cepa, A. fistulosum

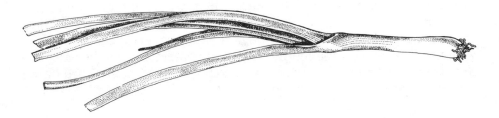

Other names: Bunching onion, green onion.

Availability: All year.

Peak of freshness: The upper leaves should not be limp; avoid slimy tips and leaves.

To prepare: Remove the outer leaves and trim both ends. Some recipes use only the white base.

Scallions are the immature green stalks of the bulb onion. Many varieties are now bred specifically for their use as scallions and are not allowed to reach maturity. Scallions vary in shape and color. Asians consider scallions with long slender white bases the finest, while Southern Europeans prefer slightly bulging white bases. The leaves may be bright green or gray-green. Scallions should be picked when young and tender, before the central stalks become pithy.

Raw scallions are a traditional ingredient in a number of salads. They are frequently used minced as a garnish for Chinese stir-fries and soups. Long cooking does not enhance the flavor of scallions, which lose their sweet quality over time. They may be used in innumerable dishes where an onion flavor but not a strong onion taste is called for.

WELSH ONION
Allium fistulosum

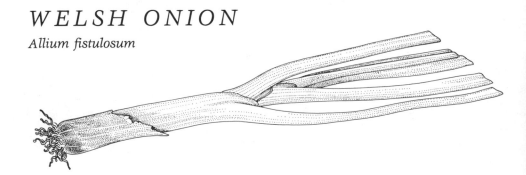

Other name: Japanese bunching onion.

How grown: From seed and from transplants.

Availability: Spring and fall.

Peak of freshness: The roots should be slender and the stems no larger than ½ inch in diameter. The leaves should not be slimy.

To prepare: Trim both ends and pull off the outer sheath with a knife.

The Welsh onion actually hails from Asia. This onion is a bunching onion like a scallion and is occasionally found in our markets. Treat it as you would a scallion.

WHY ONIONS MAKE YOU CRY

It is easier to explain why onions make you cry than to prevent it from happening. Onions contain an enzyme called alliinase, which bonds with sulphur and is activated when exposed to air. The sulfur compounds stimulate our tear ducts. Alliinase is most active at room temperature and is destroyed by cooking. To minimize crying, chill onions before slicing or run water over them while cutting. Some chefs who cook large numbers of onions use swimming masks to cover their eyes. All these techniques are only partially effective. None can stem the tide forever.

Onion Relish

This easy-to-prepare side dish is an appropriate accompaniment to sweet-flavored meats such as pork and duck.

Makes 2 cups

1½ cups chopped sweet yellow
    onions (about ½ pound)
2 tablespoons butter
½ cup dry sherry
1 teaspoon cider vinegar
½ cup sultana raisins

In a heavy skillet, sauté the onions in butter over medium heat until translucent, stirring occasionally. Add the rest of the ingredients and cook covered over low heat for 20 minutes, stirring every 5 minutes. Serve hot or warm.

English-style Pickled Onions

Pickled onions are a traditional accompaniment to the Ploughman's Lunch of bread, cheese, tomatoes, and lettuce.

Makes 2 pints

1 pound boiling onions 1½
   inches in diameter
2 cups water, mixed with
1 tablespoon salt

SPICED VINEGAR

1 teaspoon mace berries
1 teaspoon allspice berries
1 teaspoon whole cloves
1 cinnamon stick, broken into
   short pieces
6 black peppercorns
2 cups cider vinegar
2 cups water

Soak the onions in the brine for 24 hours. Drain and rinse with cold water.

To make the spiced vinegar, place the spices in a tea ball. Bring the vinegar and water to a boil in a large saucepan. Drop in the tea ball and simmer for 10 minutes. Remove the tea ball. Add the onions and bring to a boil again. Remove the saucepan from the heat. While still hot, spoon the onions into 2 sterilized pint jars and pour hot liquid over them. Store in a cool place for at least one week before using. They will keep in the refrigerator a month or more after opening, 4 to 6 months in a cool dark place before opening.

Fried Green Onion Pancakes

Serve these pancakes as an appetizer, dipped in Chinese plum sauce (available canned in Asian markets), or as a bread with Chinese dishes.

Makes 6 large pancakes

4 cups unbleached all-purpose
   flour
2 cups water
10 scallions, minced
3 tablespoons butter, cut into
   small pieces
Salt
1 cup peanut oil

Mix the flour and water in a mixing bowl. Knead by hand on a lightly floured board for 5 minutes. Let rest for 15 minutes. Divide into 6 portions. Using a rolling pin, roll each portion of dough into a round cake ¼ inch in diameter. Spread each with about 2 tablespoons of the scallions and 2 teaspoons of the butter. Sprinkle well with salt. Roll the dough up as you would a carpet. Pinch the ends closed. Twist the dough in a corkscrew motion. Stand it on end and then flatten. This action distributes the butter and scallions. Roll out the dough to a ¼-inch thickness.

Heat the peanut oil, which should be about ¼ inch deep, in a medium-sized skillet. When it is almost smoking, fry the pancakes one at a time. Brown on each side, then turn down the heat and cook for 2 minutes on the second side. Drain on paper towels and keep the pancakes hot in the oven until all 6 are cooked. To serve, cut the stack of pancakes into 6 wedges.

Green Onion Beef

Serves 4 or more as a side dish, 2 as a main course

½ pound round steak, cut into thin slices across the grain
¼ teaspoon baking soda

MARINADE

1 teaspoon medium soy sauce
½ teaspoon dry sherry
½ teaspoon sugar
½ teaspoon salt

SAUCE

2 tablespoons medium soy sauce
2 teaspoons sugar
¼ teaspoon salt
½ teaspoon peanut oil
½ teaspoon rice wine vinegar or distilled vinegar
½ teaspoon shao hsing or dry sherry
2 tablespoons chicken stock or water

1 teaspoon peanut oil
8 scallions, flattened with a knife and cut into 2-inch lengths

Place the strips of steak in a mixing bowl. Sprinkle the baking soda over the meat and mix. Combine the marinade ingredients and add to the beef, stirring. Refrigerate for 1 hour.

Mix the sauce ingredients together in a small bowl. Stir the peanut oil into the beef mixture. Heat a wok to very hot. Stir-fry the beef for 1 minute. Remove the meat from the wok with a slotted spoon. Add the sauce to the wok and cook and stir over medium-high heat for 3 minutes. Return the beef to the wok, add the scallions, and stir-fry for 30 seconds. Serve over rice.

Steamed Mussels with Sweet Onions

The sweet flavor of the onions provides a delicious contrast to the sweet-salty taste of the mussels.

Serves 4 to 6 as an appetizer

2 dozen mussels
24 shelled peas (about ¼ cup)
2 large sweet yellow onions, minced
24 pimiento strips

Select mussels that are closed or that close when tapped. Store them in the refrigerator covered with a damp cloth. Just before you are ready to use them, cut off the beards that protrude from the mussel shells. Scrub the mussels with a stiff brush and wash them thoroughly. In a large pot, steam the mussels in 1 inch of boiling water until they open. Remove them from the pan, reserving the liquid. Simmer the peas until tender (5 to 10 minutes) in the mussel juice.

Arrange the mussels in a circle on small plates. Cover each mussel with a mound of sweet onion. Connect the mussels with pieces of pimiento, forming a circle. Top each mussel with a pea and serve.

SHALLOT

Allium Aggregatum

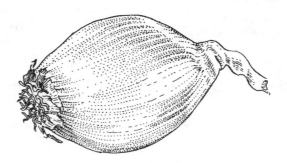

Other name: Echalote.

How grown: From bulbs.

Availability: Year round.

Peak of freshness: Papery skins and firm bulbs.

To prepare: Trim dry roots and pull off skins.

Some chefs consider the fresh shallot one of the most important ingredients for the preparation of hot and cold sauces and meat dishes. Certainly, the shallot has a rich, complex flavor. Shallots look a great deal like multiplying onions. Both grow in clumps, with one bulb planted in the spring putting off several side bulbs during the spring and summer. Shallots may be red, yellow-brown, or gray-brown. Multiplying onions are yellow-brown. The only way to be sure you have bought a shallot instead of an onion is to take it home and taste it. Shallots are mild and sweet; multiplying onions have a strong onion taste.

Shallots are the basis of a number of sauce preparations because they cook down better and thus thicken liquids more than onions do. Shallots are integral to *beurre blanc, duxelles, mirepoix, sauce bordelaise,* and *sauce marchand.* An elegant vinaigrette can be made from olive oil, champagne vinegar, and minced shallots(see page 94).

Pickled Shallots

Pickled shallots make a nice condiment for roast meat and game. They are also wonderful little tidbits for the cocktail hour.

Makes about 2 cups

¾ pound shallots
1 tablespoon salt
½ cup white wine vinegar
1 cup water
1 teaspoon sugar
1 small fresh hot pepper, such as jalapeño
5 black peppercorns

Place the shallots in a bowl, sprinkle with the salt, and allow to stand covered overnight. Drain off any liquid that has accumulated the next day. Rinse the shallots under cold water.

In a small saucepan, combine the vinegar, water, sugar, pepper, and peppercorns. Bring to a boil and add the shallots. Simmer for 30 seconds. Remove the saucepan from the heat and cool to room temperature. Pour the shallots and liquid into a jar or bowl and cover. The pickled shallots should age 48 hours before you eat them. They will keep up to 2 weeks in the refrigerator.

Sorrel

Rumex acetosa

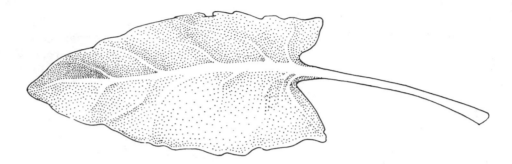

Sorrel is a member of the buckwheat family and another example of an increasingly frequent vegetable success story: an abundant and seemingly ordinary wild species gets talked about in the right circles and becomes a star. Today sorrel soups, purées, and sauces grace the menus of many fashionable restaurants, and sorrel is increasingly available in the market.

Much of the sorrel grown in the United States is raised in hothouses. Either the entire plant is picked or the leaves are cut individually. The latter method is the one favored by the market gardeners on the outskirts of Paris, because the resulting leaves are all close to the same size, and the plant, which lives 3 to 4 years, produces a larger yield. Sorrel wilts rapidly after cutting, and it is sometimes difficult to find crisp leaves in the markets, but even when wilted the sour taste of sorrel is unmistakable.

Sorrel's tartness accompanies fish well, and a sorrel sauce often accompanies salmon and trout. Sorrel and new potatoes sautéed in butter is an unusual fall dish, and cream of sorrel soup is a new American standard.

Other name: Sour grass.

How grown: From seed.

Availability: Fall, winter, and spring.

Peak of freshness: The leaves should be succulent and fully formed, showing no signs of yellowing.

To prepare: Wash well and trim the stem ends. Discard any wilted or discolored leaves.

Chicken Stuffed with Sorrel

Rabbit stuffed with sorrel is a traditional winter dish in France. Here, whole rabbit is sometimes difficult to find, and chicken is an excellent alternative.

Serves 4 to 6 as a main course

STUFFING

½ cup minced mushrooms
   (about 4 ounces)
2 medium shallots, chopped
2 tablespoons butter
1½ pounds sorrel (approximately
   3 bunches)
Salt and pepper to taste

One 3- to 3½-pound roasting
   chicken
6 garlic cloves, smashed
6 thyme sprigs, or 1 teaspoon
   dried thyme
1 cup dry white wine
Sorrel Purée, following

Preheat the oven to 350°.

Stem the mushrooms and save the stems for stock. In a small pan or skillet sauté the mushrooms and shallots in butter over medium heat until the shallots are translucent. Combine the sorrel with the shallot-mushroom mixture. Sprinkle with salt and pepper. Allow to cool to room temperature.

Stuff the chicken with the sorrel mixture. Truss the bird closed and place it in a Dutch oven or clay pot. Scatter the garlic and thyme around the chicken. Pour in the wine and cover the casserole. Bake for 1 hour and 15 minutes or until the chicken is done. The joints should still have a trace of pink and the meat should be juicy.

Mound the stuffing in the center of a serving tray. Cut the chicken into serving pieces and arrange them around the sorrel. Moisten the chicken with some of the pan juices. Serve with the following sorrel purée.

SORREL PURÉE

This purée adds another dimension to Chicken Stuffed with Sorrel. It can be served with roast beef or lamb as well as with fish.

Makes 3 cups

STOCK

1 pound chicken giblets and/or
   wings
1 cup mushroom stems
2 shallots, cut in half
Salt and pepper to taste
3 cups water

1 pound sorrel (approximately 2
   bunches)
1 cup chicken stock
½ cup heavy cream

Combine all the stock ingredients in a large saucepan and simmer for at least 2 hours. Strain and discard the vegetables and chicken.

Destem the sorrel. Mince the sorrel in a blender or food processor, adding ½ cup of the stock to form a thick purée. Transfer the sorrel paste to a saucepan. Add the rest of the stock and the cream. Simmer to the consistency of a thick purée. Serve on the same plate with the chicken and sorrel stuffing.

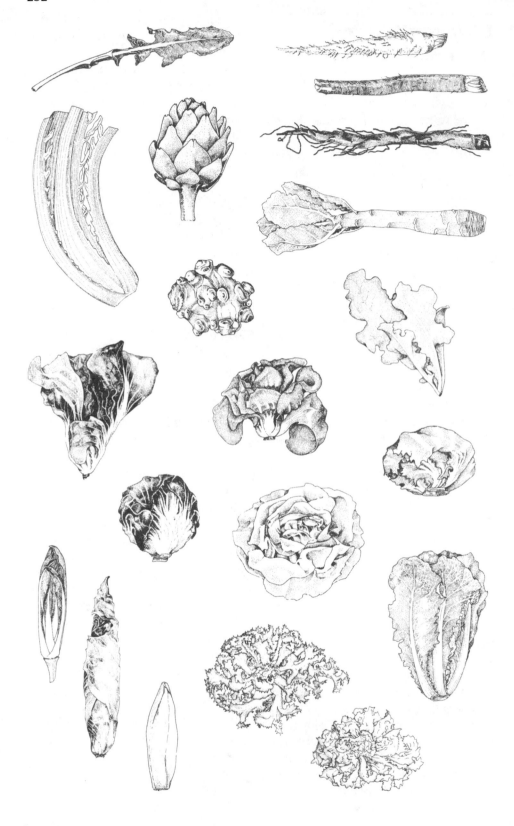

Sunflower Family

Compositae: Artichoke, Burdock, Cardoon, Chicory, Dandelion, Jerusalem Artichoke, Lettuce, Salsify, Scorzonera

The sunflower family is one of the largest botanical families. The chief distinguishing characteristic of this diverse group is that its blossoms are made up of two kinds of flowers: disc and ray. The roughly textured flowers in the center of the head of a sunflower are the disc flowers. These are not as brightly colored and are often smaller than the ray flowers, which surround the head. Other members of this family show varying configurations of this arrangement. Some members of the family, such as lettuce and salsify, contain a milky juice called latex.

ARTICHOKE
Cynara scolymus

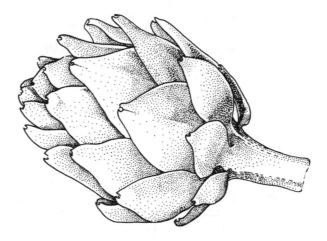

Other names: Globe artichoke, Mediterranean thistle.

How grown: From seed and plant division.

Availability: Generally all year, but the peak time is spring and fall.

Peak of freshness: Firm, tidy globes with leaves curving inward. Open heads indicate poor quality. The stem ends may be brown when cut, but avoid heads with brown tips or bases.

To prepare: Soak the heads in water. Carefully push open the leaves with your fingers to remove insects or dirt. Wash thoroughly. To prepare whole artichokes and hearts, see below.

The artichoke dramatically illustrates the frequently strong polarization between Southern and Northern European cuisines. It has been cherished by peoples of the Mediterranean region for centuries. Many Northern Europeans, however, consider this thistle to be nothing more than a weed, a simple pest to be uprooted.

Italian immigrants brought the artichoke to America in the last century, and it has thrived on the coast of California, which now produces most of the American crop. Artichokes do well in semiarid regions protected from frost. Such a place is Castroville, the self-proclaimed artichoke capital of the world, a tiny town south of San Francisco just inland from the Pacific.

The soft-looking, gray-green fernlike stalks of the artichoke have notched edges and pointed leaves and are attached to a central base. The heads are immature flowers. If allowed to flower the heads will turn to bright purple thistles. Some European varieties have purple heads, but these lose their color when cooked.

Some Americans find the artichoke a bit intimidating, but the French have no such problems. They serve the uncooked leaves of small artichokes (less than 2 inches in diameter) as hors d'ouvres, dipped into spicy sauces. The heart is cooked separately and used in stuffings for fish and poultry, or baked whole with various cream sauces. Barely cooked artichoke hearts are blended with *crème fraîche* and spread on other vegetables or served on a bed of greens. Especially when young and tender, whole artichokes are delicious steamed and served with herbed butter or olive oil. When large and mature they are equally tasty, but the center thistles (the choke) will need to be removed for some recipes.

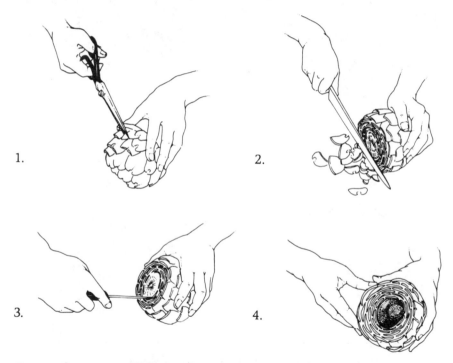

Preparing an Artichoke for Stuffing

1. Cut off the spines from the side and bottom leaves using a kitchen shears. Trim the base of the artichoke.

2. Using large, sharp chef's knife, chop off the top center leaves.

3. Scoop out the thistle inside, cutting it free with a stainless steel paring knife (carbon steel will cause discoloration).

4. Place the fresh-trimmed artichokes in acidulated water to prevent discoloration.

1.

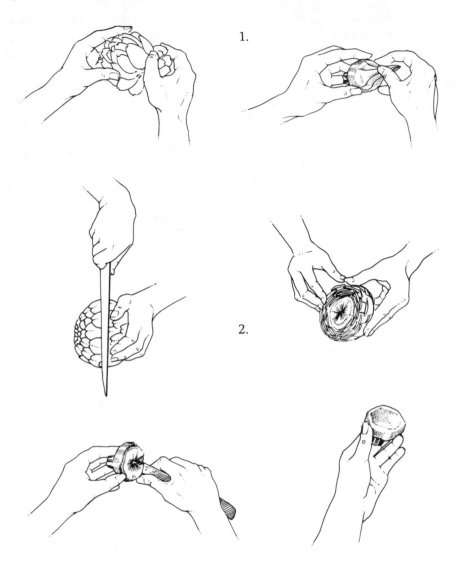

2.

PREPARING ARTICHOKE HEARTS

To obtain artichoke hearts you can either (1) cook whole artichokes, pull off the leaves, and trim away the thistle section; or (2) cut across the artichoke just above the heart, cook only the heart, then pull off the leaves and cut away the thistle.

Pickled Artichoke Hearts

Pickled artichoke hearts are delicious served as part of an antipasto or a crudité tray, or as a vegetable accompaniment for hot curries or spicy meats.

Makes 2 pints

36 to 40 artichoke hearts (see
  page 256)
2 cups fresh lemon juice mixed
  with
1 quart water
1 pint distilled vinegar
½ teaspoon salt
2 garlic cloves
4 bay leaves
½ teaspoon dried basil
½ teaspoon dried oregano
1 cup olive oil

Simmer the artichoke hearts in the lemon-water mixture, 3 minutes for small hearts, 5 minutes for mature hearts. Drain the artichokes and divide between 2 sterilized pint canning jars. Add 1 cup of the vinegar and ¼ teaspoon of the salt to each pint jar. Let stand overnight. Drain, then cover with an additional 1 cup of vinegar per jar. Allow to stand for another 4 hours. Drain. Add 1 garlic clove, 2 bay leaves, and ¼ teaspoon each basil and oregano to each jar, then fill each with ½ cup oil. Close the lids tightly.

Place the jars in a large pot and cover with water. Boil vigorously for 30 minutes. Cool to room temperature. Pickled artichokes will keep up to 1 year on the pantry shelf and for several months in the refrigerator once opened, though they will probably be gone long before then.

Deep-fried Artichokes Stuffed with Goat Cheese

Artichokes can be stuffed with a number of ingredients. Deluxe foods such as scallops or goat cheese are good company for the aristocratic artichoke.

Serves 6 as a first course

12 small artichokes
Three 4-ounce goat cheeses
2 eggs, beaten
Salt to taste, mixed with
1 cup unbleached all-purpose
  flour
Oil for deep-frying
Peppery Mayonnaise, page 161

Pull off the outer leaves of the artichokes and discard. Soak the artichokes in acidulated water for 30 minutes. Steam the artichokes for 5 to 7 minutes, until they can be pierced with a fork. Plunge them in cold water to halt cooking. Cut through the leaves parallel to the surface of the cup and ½ inch above it. Scoop out the thistle. Repeat for the other artichokes.

Cut each goat cheese into 4 pieces or pieces small enough to fit into the cups. Separately dip each artichoke and each piece of cheese in the eggs. Put a piece of cheese into each artichoke cup and coat all over with the seasoned flour.

In a deep-fryer or Dutch oven heat 4 inches of oil to 350°. Fry the artichokes until golden brown, about 2 to 3 minutes. Serve with Peppery Mayonnaise.

Artichoke Heart Pizza

This is a traditional pizza dish prepared in early spring when the first artichokes arrive at the markets in Northern Italy. It is delicious with or without tomato sauce.

Makes two 12-inch pizzas

Pizza Dough

1 package (1 tablespoon) active
    dry yeast
1 cup warm (105°) water
1 teaspoon sugar
1 teaspoon salt
3 tablespoons olive oil
3 to 4 cups unbleached all-
    purpose flour
2 tablespoons cornmeal

Tomato Sauce, following
    (optional)
1½ cups cooked artichoke hearts
    (see page 256) cut into ½-inch
    cubes
½ pound thinly sliced Italian
    Fontina cheese
½ cup freshly grated Parmesan
    or Romano cheese
Minced fresh herbs for garnish

To make the pizza dough, dissolve the yeast in the water in a small bowl. Add the sugar and let stand for 5 minutes. Combine the yeast-water mixture, salt, 2 tablespoons of the olive oil, and half the flour in a large bowl. Mix the dough with a wooden spoon. Add more flour until the dough is very stiff. Turn out onto a well-floured board and knead until the dough is elastic, about 7 minutes. Add more flour if the dough sticks to the board. Let the dough rest for 5 minutes. Place in a large oiled bowl, drizzle the top with the remaining 1 tablespoon of olive oil, and cover with a damp towel. Let the dough rise in a warm part of your kitchen until it has doubled in volume, 1½ to 2 hours.

Divide the dough in half. Flatten the dough with your hands. Holding the dough vertically with both hands, stretch and rotate it evenly. When it is about 12 inches in diameter, place it on a pizza pan that has been lightly covered with cornmeal.

Preheat the oven to 500°. Cover each pizza with a layer of tomato sauce, if you like. Layer with half of the artichoke hearts. Add half the Fontina and sprinkle with half the Parmesan or Romano. Repeat for the second pizza.

Place the pizzas on the top rack of the oven, or on a pizza stone in the bottom of the oven. Rotate them halfway through the cooking so the pizzas cook evenly. They are done when the bottom of the crust is nicely browned, about 10 minutes. Cut into 6 to 8 pieces and serve immediately, garnished with whatever fresh herb you used in the sauce.

TOMATO SAUCE

Makes about 4 cups

½ medium yellow onion, diced
2 tablespoons chopped garlic
¼ cup olive oil
1½ pounds fresh tomatoes,
    peeled, seeded, and chopped,
    or one 28-ounce can Italian
    tomatoes, drained and coarsely
    chopped
1 teaspoon minced fresh thyme,
    oregano, or marjoram
½ teaspoon sugar
Salt and pepper to taste

Sauté the onion and garlic in the olive oil in a heavy saucepan until the onion is translucent. Add the tomatoes, herb, sugar, and salt and pepper to the pan. Simmer uncovered for 45 minutes, or until the tomatoes are reduced to a paste. Stir occasionally to keep the sauce from sticking.

Spicy Artichoke Paste

This tangy spread can be served on crackers or toasted rounds of baguette.

Makes 1 cup

6 large artichokes (3 per pound)
1 tablespoon olive oil
1 fresh hot pepper such as
    jalapeño or serrano, seeded and
    minced
1 tablespoon minced garlic
2 teaspoons fresh lemon juice
1 teaspoon minced fresh oregano
    (optional)
Salt and pepper to taste

Prepare artichoke hearts as on page 256. Purée the artichoke hearts in a blender or food processor. Add the other ingredients and blend thoroughly.

BURDOCK
Arctium lappa

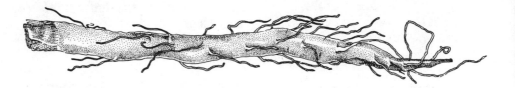

Other names: Great burdock, *gobo, takinogawa.*	**To prepare:** Wash. Trim ends. Scrape roots and soak in acidulated water until ready to cook. Pound flat with a cleaver at the last minute.
How grown: From seed.	
Availability: Fall and winter.	
Peak of freshness: Unblemished roots.	

Some people recognize burdock as a plant full of prickly burrs that grows wild along riverbanks, but few know that it is edible if grown under controlled conditions. Burdock is grown commercially in warm humid areas such as Hawaii and Florida.

The Japanese are fond of burdock. They sauté it with soy sauce, sometimes adding beef. Burdock has a sweet aromatic flavor and may be used in place of carrots in some recipes.

Stir-fried Burdock Root

Serve this as a side dish with meat or seafood.

Serves 4 as a side dish

½ *pound burdock root*
1 *tablespoon oil*
1 *tablespoon minced garlic*
2 *tablespoons medium soy sauce*
2 *tablespoons* shao hsing *or dry sherry*
2 *teaspoons sugar*
¼ *to* ½ *teaspoon cayenne or red pepper flakes*

Tenderize the burdock root (see "To prepare," page 260), then cut it into shavings as if you were sharpening a pencil. Cover the burdock with acidulated water and soak for 2 hours.

Drain the burdock root. Heat the oil in a wok or heavy skillet. Stir-fry the garlic for 3 minutes over medium heat. Add the burdock root and cook for 1 minute. Mix the rest of the ingredients together and pour over the burdock root. Simmer for 5 minutes, until the sauce becomes a glaze, then serve.

CARDOON
Cynara cardunculus

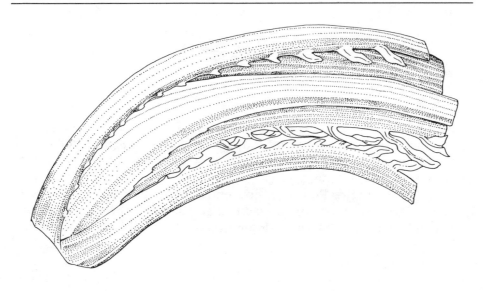

How grown: From seed and by plant division.

Availability: Winter and early spring.

Peak of freshness: Look for rigid pale-green stalks with white hearts.

To prepare: Wash. Trim ends. Remove the outer strings and fibers, stringing the stalk like celery. Cut away and discard all but 4 inches of the leaves forming the heart.

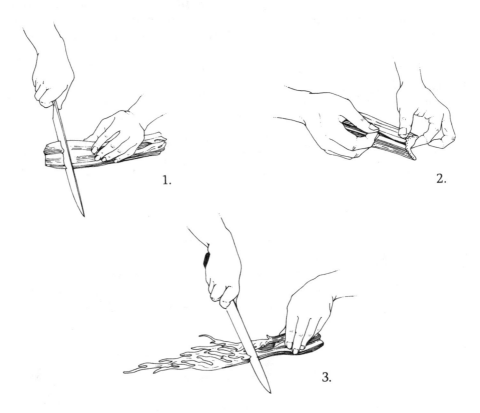

The cardoon is an exceptionally beautiful plant. It has the gray-green, deeply cut leaves of the artichoke plant, but it grows much bigger, often over 4 feet. The cardoon is often used in decorative gardening and may thus be used as edible landscaping.

No self-respecting Provençal household would have a Christmas Eve dinner without a cardoon dish. Traditionally a part of the *gros souper,* or light meal, that precedes the midnight Mass, blanched cardoon stalks are prepared in a light bechamel sauce and topped with grated Gruyère cheese. Cardoon is also delicious with sweet fennel sausage.

Many wild varieties of cardoon exist, and in the Piedmont region of Northern Italy the small tender wild cardoon is favored for dipping in *bagna cauda,* a hot anchovy and garlic sauce. Although the domesticated cardoon plant is large, it is only the blanched inner heart that is desirable; some people eat it raw, once all the strings have been removed and it is finely sliced.

Cardoon can be eaten lightly buttered and sprinkled with Parmesan cheese, or used as one would artichoke hearts or salsify.

Cardoon Niçoise Style

Serves 6 as a side dish

2 pounds cardoon, cleaned and
    cut into ½-inch slices
2½ quarts water
5 garlic cloves
2 medium yellow onions, cut in
    quarters
3 parsley sprigs
1 bay leaf
1½ teaspoons minced fresh
    thyme, or ½ teaspoon dried
    thyme
1 red bell pepper, seeded and
    julienned
4 anchovy fillets
¼ cup chopped fresh parsley
1 tablespoon olive oil
1 tablespoon flour

Place the cut cardoon in a large bowl of acidulated water to prevent discoloration.

Combine the 2½ quarts water, 2 of the garlic cloves, the onions, parsley, bay leaf, thyme, and red pepper and bring to a simmer. Cook the cardoon for 25 to 30 minutes or until tender, then drain, reserving 1 cup of the liquid.

Crush the remaining 3 cloves of garlic. Add the anchovy fillets and chopped parsley to the garlic in a mortar and crush well. In a large saucepan over low heat, blend the olive oil and the flour. Add the anchovy mixture to the oil and flour paste and gently stir. Add up to 1 cup of the cooking liquid to form a thick sauce. Reheat the cardoon in the sauce and serve.

CHICORY

The chicories are part of the new wave of formerly esoteric vegetables that are appearing in markets throughout the United States. European imports of chicories have increased dramatically, and American farmers are beginning to produce them as well.

The chicory genus is diverse and includes the curly endives, escaroles, the multitude of green Italian chicories, red *radicchios*, and the Belgian endive as well as the coffee substitute Madgeburg chicory.

BELGIAN ENDIVE

Cichorium Intybus

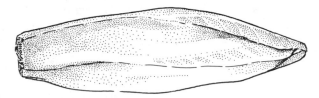

Other name: Witloof.

Availability: Late fall, winter, early spring.

How grown: From seed.

Peak of freshness: Crisp pale-yellow heads, frequently wrapped in colored paper to maintain their blanched condition.

To prepare: Wash. Remove the bitter inner core by cutting around the hard center of the base on an angle with the tip of a sharp knife. Be careful to keep leaves intact. Remove any discolored leaves.

Belgian endive, like red heading chicory, was discovered by accident. According to botanical folklore, a Belgian farmer discarded his green-leafed chicory plants at the end of summer, throwing them in the trash heap. He then covered the plants with sand from his yard. Early the following year, the gardener removed the pile of sand as he cleaned up. He noticed little pale yellow heads. He washed the endives and braised them. Obviously, the result was delicious.

Today, Belgian endive is raised in a more systematic manner. The seed is sown in a field, and the plants develop sturdy roots. The roots are dug up and placed in a dark hothouse. The plants grow out in about two weeks. Once cut, they must be protected from light until they get to the market.

Belgian endive is pale yellow, almost translucent, sweet and succulent. It is usually braised with meat juices, duck or pork being most common. It can also be grilled. Belgian endive discolors easily and should not be cooked in aluminum pans. Keep it wrapped in a paper container in the refrigerator until ready to use.

Belgian Endive, Apple, and Almond Salad

This flavorful salad is full of clean contrasting tastes that stimulate the appetite. You can serve it as a summer refresher or before a roast of pork or lamb.

Serves 4 as a first course

1 tart green apple, peeled and cut into ½-inch cubes
2 endives, thinly sliced crosswise
⅓ cup peeled and slivered blanched almonds

DRESSING

2 tablespoons walnut or almond oil
1 tablespoon fresh lemon juice
1 teaspoon minced garlic
Salt and white pepper to taste

Parsley sprigs for garnish

Mix the apple, endives, and almonds together in a bowl. Mix the dressing, pour over the salad, and toss thoroughly. Serve mounded on a plate garnished with parsley.

Endive Braised in Poultry Juices

Endive is a traditional accompaniment to roast duck or goose. The slightly bitter taste of the endive nicely complements the sweet, rich meat.

Serves 6 as a side dish

Roasting juices from goose, duck, or chicken
12 Belgian endives, quartered lengthwise

CROUTONS

2 teaspoons chopped garlic
2 to 3 tablespoons olive oil
6 slices dry French bread with crusts, cut into ½-inch cubes

Salt and pepper to taste

After the goose, duck, or chicken has cooked, remove it from the roasting pan and pour off the excess fat. Heat the roasting pan on top of the stove, adding just enough water to loosen the drippings. Add the endives and cook over medium heat until tender, 10 to 15 minutes. Turn every 5 minutes.

Meanwhile, make the croutons. In a sauté pan or skillet over medium heat, sauté the garlic in the olive oil until translucent. Remove from the pan with a slotted spoon. In the same pan cook and stir the croutons until they are uniformly browned. Return the garlic to the pan and toss thoroughly. Remove the croutons from the pan with a slotted spoon and drain on paper towels.

Season the endive with salt and pepper, top with croutons, and serve.

Belgian Endive Baked with Danish Ham and Gruyère

Serves 4 as a main course

8 large or 12 medium Belgian endives, cores removed
1 cup milk
1 cup water
1 teaspoon salt
8 thin 4-by-6-inch slices Gruyère or Emmenthaler cheese
8 thin 4-by-6-inch slices Danish ham

Arrange the endives in one layer in an enameled or stainless-steel skillet just large enough to hold them. Pour the milk and water over the endives. Add the salt and heat just until small bubbles appear on the rim of the pan; do not boil. Reduce the heat to low and cook until the endives are tender but still firm (10 to 20 minutes, depending on the size of the endives). Remove them from the skillet with tongs and put on paper towels to drain and cool. When cool enough to handle, wrap each endive with a slice of cheese and then a slice of ham. Preheat the oven to 400°. Bake uncovered until the cheese melts. Serve immediately.

CURLY ENDIVE

Cichorium endivia

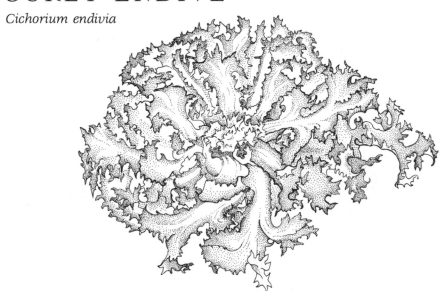

Other name: *Frisée riccia.*

How grown: From seed.

Availability: All year, although more abundant in fall and spring.

Peak of freshness: The leaves should be rigid, almost prickly.

To prepare: The dark-green outer leaves that protect the blanched center tend to be tough and bitter, and most people discard them, using only the second layer of green leaves and the pale-yellow heart. Trim the ends. To wash and store, see page 284.

The curly endive has a distinctive appearance. Its blanched yellow center is surrounded by dark-green outer leaves, which are often toothed or pointed. The heads are blanched by being tied closed with string or being covered. They range in size from 2 inches to over 1 foot in diameter. These lettucelike salad greens are often packed stem-side up to protect the tender hearts from sunlight. Depending upon the varietal type, the leaves of curly endive may be pencil thin and scraggly or broad and thick. The taste is both sweet and very slightly bitter. Frequently found in the open markets of Europe, it is harder to find in the United States because it doesn't ship well and as yet is not cultivated extensively here.

Curly endive is a welcome addition to any mixed salad and is frequently served with a warm dressing. It combines well with other strong-flavored ingredients such as duck, goat cheese, wild game, and citrus fruits. Endive also mixes well with other members of its family such as lettuce, *radicchio*, and escarole.

ESCAROLE
Cichorium endivia

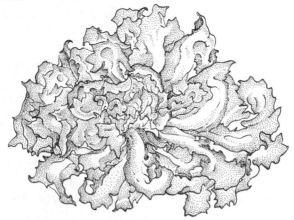

Other name: Broad-leafed escarole.

How grown: From seed or transplants.

Availability: Winter.

Peak of freshness: Crisp leaves with a creamy white heart.

To prepare: Discard the bitter outer leaves. To wash and store, see page 284.

Escarole will brighten any dull winter day with its crumpled outer leaves of green surrounding a blonde core. The spreading leafy heads are either self-blanching or tied closed to blanch the core. Used chiefly for winter salads in conjunction with other leafy greens and reds, escarole lends a slightly bitter flavor that is characteristic of the chicory family. The blonde leaves and interior heart are sweeter than the green portions.

Escarole has a sturdy, somewhat thick leaf and holds up well when cooked. Warm sauces bring out its flavor. It can be the base for salads made with strong-flavored seafood such as clams, and it can be sautéed with exotics such as sea urchin and tossed with pasta. It is often served with livers such as duck and rabbit. Escarole leaves may be used for wrapping meat and fish. It can be included in Cream of Lettuce Soup (page 285).

Escarole Salad with Chestnuts, Bacon, and Watercress

Serves 6 as a first course

15 chestnuts
6 bacon slices, cut into 1-inch strips
1 large head escarole
1 bunch watercress
1 medium purple onion, cut into thin rings

DRESSING

3 tablespoons reserved bacon fat
3 tablespoons red wine vinegar
½ teaspoon Dijon mustard

Salt and pepper to taste

Preheat the oven to 500°. With a sharp knife make an 'x' on the flat surface of each chestnut. Bake on a cookie sheet for 20 minutes. Allow to cool. Peel the chestnuts and cut off the inner brown skin. Cut each chestnut in half and set aside.

Fry the bacon until brown. Remove the bacon from the pan with a slotted spoon and drain on paper towels; reserve 3 tablespoons of the bacon fat. Tear the escarole into small pieces and arrange on a serving platter. Cover the escarole with the watercress and onion rings.

To make the dressing, heat the bacon fat. Add the vinegar and mustard to it. Stir and taste. If it is too acidic, add a tablespoon or two of hot water. Add the chestnuts and salt and pepper. Cook, stirring frequently, until the chestnuts are hot. Sprinkle the bacon bits over the salad. Pour the dressing with the chestnuts over the platter of greens and serve immediately on warmed salad plates.

ITALIAN CHICORY

Cichorium intybus

According to popular legend, an Italian farmer who had plowed his field the fall before found it filled the next spring with tight little heads of a red plant that had survived the winter's frosts. This farmer was a curious sort, and he dug some of the plants up and placed them in his home garden. They grew no more during the summer and he cut them back, discouraged. The following year new heads appeared. Thus the multibillion-lire *radicchio* industry was born.

Radicchios—the term applies primarily to the red types of chicory—are the winter-salad mainstay of Northern Europe. They are becoming very popular now in the United States. With the current culinary emphasis on color, it is easy to understand why the beautiful red *radicchio* leaves are so sought after. So far the best known is the red heading Verona, which has thick white veins running from the base of each leaf. It ranges from large Brussels sprout size to large grapefruit size, and colors may vary from magenta to maroon. There are many other strains of red heading chicory available here and in Europe, among them Palla Rosa, Chioggia, and Sottomarina, as well as some new strains being developed in Holland.

Unlike the Italians of the *radicchio*-growing region of Treviso and Venice who eat a salad composed only of red chicory and a vinaigrette, most Americans prefer to use the leaves sparingly. For some palates the bitter leaves take getting used to.

Predictably, it won't be long before more chicory types appear in our restaurants and markets. In Italy there are at least fifteen well-known kinds, ranging from the flat, dark-green rosettes of *ceriolo* to the long thin leaves of *selvatico da campo* to the variegated pink and pale green of Castelfranco chicory.

Radicchio may be grilled or served with a vinaigrette. Green chicory is served in salads and braised or steamed with meat dishes. Variegated *radicchios*, brilliant combinations of red and green, are served in salads as well.

Green Heading Chicories

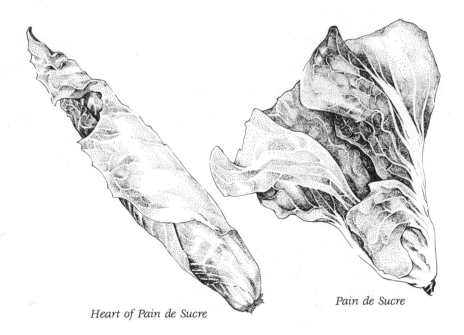

Heart of Pain de Sucre

Pain de Sucre

How grown: From seed.

Availability: Winter, spring, summer.

Peak of freshness: The inner leaves should be pale, with no signs of discoloration or wilting.

To prepare: Trim the root end. To store and wash, see page 284.

Green heading chicory includes several different varieties, but all are characterized by a loose pale-green head anywhere from 6 inches to 1 foot long and 2 to 6 inches in diameter. The plant is sometimes 1½ feet tall, with a pale-green heart and dark larger outer leaves. This group includes the sweetest of the chicories, *pain de sucre*, also called "sugar hat."

Green Loose-Leaf Chicories

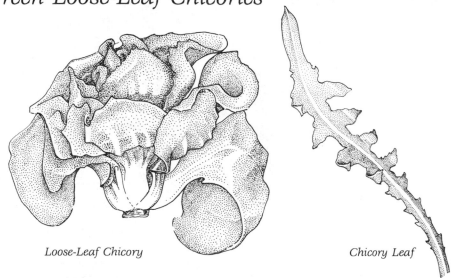

Loose-Leaf Chicory   *Chicory Leaf*

Other names: Italian chicory, green chicory, chicory, *radichetta.*

Availability: Different varieties are available all year.

Peak of freshness: Leaves should be crisp.

To prepare: Wash. Discard any discolored leaves. Trim root end.

The largest group within the chicories is the green loose-leaf type. Some have thick curly leaves, others thin flat ones. Some leaves are indented, others smooth. Some produce a second growth that closely resembles *pak choy.* This second growth is called a *puntarelle* chicory. *Puntarelle* is prepared in two ways. It may be slow-cooked like Cima di Rapa Braised with Garlic (page 63) or the stalks may be used in salads.

Red or Variegated Heading Chicories

Radicchio

Other names: Wild chicory, Italian chicory, *radicchio.*

Availability: Primarily winter and spring, but also summer and fall.

Peak of freshness: The heads and leaves are crisp. Strong bitterness develops with age.

To prepare: Wash. Remove any discolored leaves and the stout root.

Some varieties of these chicories are cut back in the fall, then forced during winter months to encourage heading. The first growth of many *radicchios* is green. The leaves may be up to 2 feet long, dark green and somewhat furry. The leaves are tough and very bitter. When cut back in the fall, if the weather is cold, the second growth will be the bright red or magenta heads we've come to know in our markets as *radicchio.*

Red Treviso Loose-Leaf Chicory

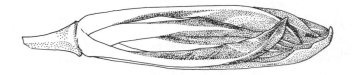

Availability: Winter and early spring.

Peak of freshness: Look for clear white color on the ribs; avoid any that show discoloration, which indicates age, toughness, and great bitterness.

The ribs should be juicy and succulent.

To prepare: Wash. Trim ends and discard any discolored leaves.

Red Treviso is a semi-heading type of chicory that is quite popular in and around Venice and is becoming available in the United States. The first growth is a large green leafy plant that is cut back in fall. The winter growth has leaves that range from 2 to 10 inches and are elongated like those of romaine lettuce. The color is generally deep magenta with a white mid-rib. It does not in any way resemble red chard, as it is the leaf, not the mid-rib, that is red.

Radicchio Salad

This salad is not for everyone, as the slightly bitter taste of radicchio dominates. It is one of the favorite dishes in the areas of Northern Italy where radicchio is grown.

Serves 4 as a first course

2 cups radicchio leaves

DRESSING

⅔ cup virgin olive oil
⅓ cup fresh lemon juice
1 tablespoon chopped fresh parsley
½ teaspoon salt

Tear the *radicchio* into bite-sized pieces. Mix the dressing and pour it over the *radicchio*. Toss and serve immediately. Serve with slices of toasted baguette or French bread.

Radicchio Cups with Curly Endive and Goat Cheese

Serves 4 as a first course

Salt and pepper to taste
2 tablespoons melted butter
1 teaspoon minced fresh summer savory, or ⅓ teaspoon dried savory
1 cup dry bread crumbs
1 fresh goat cheese, cut into 4 pieces
1 egg, beaten
2 tablespoons olive oil
1 small to medium radicchio, leaves torn
4 inner curly endive leaves
¼ cup virgin olive oil
½ teaspoon grated orange zest

Add the salt, pepper, butter, and savory to the bread crumbs. Form the goat cheese into flat patties. Dip each one into the egg and coat with the bread crumbs. Heat the olive oil in a sauté pan or skillet and brown the goat cheese over medium heat. Make beds of *radicchio* on individual salad plates. Place an endive leaf in the center of each plate and place the goat cheese on the leaf. Mix together the olive oil and the orange zest and pour over each salad.

Stuffed Pain de Sucre

This is an Italian variation of stuffed cabbage, and the slightly bitter flavor of the pain de sucre *gives this stuffed vegetable dish a panache that stuffed cabbage seems to lack. If you cannot find* pain de sucre, *use a small head of cabbage.*

Serves 3 to 4 as a main course

SAUCE

1 yellow onion, minced
1 tablespoon olive oil
6 tomatoes, peeled, seeded, and
    chopped
1 cup chicken stock

STUFFING

1 large yellow onion, chopped
¼ cup olive oil
¾ pound ground lamb
1 tablespoon grated fresh
    turmeric, or 1 teaspoon ground
    turmeric
1 cup sultana raisins
½ cup walnut halves
1 cup fresh bread crumbs, soaked
    in milk and squeezed dry
Salt and pepper
¼ cup chopped fresh mint leaves

1 head pain de sucre, *about 18
    inches long*
Walnut halves for garnish
1 tablespoon mint leaves

To make the sauce, in a large saucepan or Dutch oven sauté the onion in the olive oil until translucent. Add the tomatoes and stock. Simmer uncovered for 15 minutes.

To make the stuffing, in a sauté pan or skillet sauté the onion until translucent in 1 tablespoon of the olive oil. Remove the onion from the pan. Add the meat and cook until crumbly. Add the turmeric, raisins, walnuts, bread crumbs, salt, pepper, mint, and onion. Cook and stir for 2 minutes. Allow to cool to near room temperature.

Place the head of *pain de sucre* on its side. Open the leaves gently and spoon the stuffing into the center. Tie the head closed with cotton string. Place the *pain de sucre* in the pan with the sauce. Cover and cook for 15 minutes, or until the head is easily pierced with a fork, spooning the sauce over the vegetable every 5 minutes.

Cut the *pain de sucre* in quarters. Serve on a bed of rice, with the sauce poured over, garnished with walnut halves and mint leaves.

DANDELION
Taraxacum officinale

Availability: Early spring, winter.

Peak of freshness: The leaves should be 6 to 12 inches long, light green and crisp.

To prepare: Wash. Trim ends. Discard any discolored leaves.

This cosmopolitan weed that has spread from Eurasia to the Americas is also a vegetable. It may be used as a salad green and as an herb and made into wine. In France it is quite aptly named *pissenlit* because of its diuretic nature.

The straplike toothed green leaves arise from a central clump with a taproot. Some European strains have finely toothed, almost curly leaves. Milk sap is present in leaves and root. The leaves should be harvested before the plant flowers. Like Belgian endive, dandelion leaves may be blanched if the roots are covered in the fall and kept in complete darkness for at least six weeks. Upon blanching, the would-be bitter leaves remain sweet and crisp. The early spring crop of young dandelion leaves, light green and irregular in shape, is less bitter than mature leaves later in the year.

Dandelion is delicious in salads with other strong-flavored ingredients, and it can be eaten as a potherb.

Wilted Dandelion Salad

Serve this salad with grilled fish.

Serves 4 as a first course

6 *bacon slices*
2 *tablespoons red wine vinegar*
Salt and pepper to taste
2 *pounds dandelions*
2 *hard-cooked eggs, cut into slices*

In a sauté pan or skillet, cook the bacon until nicely browned. Remove from the pan, pat off the excess oil with a paper towel, and crumble the strips. Pour off all but 4 tablespoons of the bacon fat. Add the vinegar and salt and pepper and pour over the greens. Mix and arrange the greens on a serving tray topped with bacon bits and the hard-cooked eggs. Serve warm.

JERUSALEM ARTICHOKE
Helianthus tuberosus

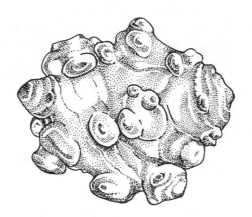

Other names: Sunchoke, sun root, *girasole*.

How grown: From tubers.

Availability: Fall and winter.

Peak of freshness: Look for large tan roots without soft spots.

To prepare: Wash and peel. Cover with acidulated water to prevent discoloration.

Jerusalem artichoke is as American as apple pie. Samuel Champlain first noticed it in 1605 as he tramped through the fields of Cape Cod. He carried it back to France, where it became food for peasants and livestock.

Today in America, Jerusalem artichokes are being used to produce alcohol for fuel, though the best use for them is probably as fuel for humans. The crunchy, starchy texture makes a pleasant winter dish. It can be substituted for water chestnut and *jicama*, which have similar textures. In the South, Jerusalem artichoke pie is made in a double crust with a cream sauce. Artichoke hearts could be added to this dish as well. A delicious purée can be made from Jerusalem artichokes, cream, butter, and a bit of cooked potato. Slices and finger-sized pieces can be deep-fried as you would potatoes. Jerusalem artichoke can also be sautéed with butter and garlic.

Jerusalem Artichoke, Cucumber, and Apple Salad

This light hot-weather salad is full of contrasting textures. It gets a special boost from the citrus flavor of lemon thyme. Use fresh mint if you can't find lemon thyme.

Serves 4 as a first course

2 to 3 Jerusalem artichokes (½ pound)
1 medium cucumber, thinly sliced crosswise
1 tart green apple, cored and thinly sliced
Whites of 3 scallions, chopped
3 tablespoons olive oil
Fresh lemon juice to taste
1 teaspoon chopped fresh lemon thyme
Salt and pepper to taste
Romaine lettuce leaves

Peel the Jerusalem artichokes and cut them into ¼-inch cubes. Cover with acidulated water until ready to use.

Arrange the cucumber slices in a circle around the outside of a large plate. Place the apple slices in a slightly smaller circle. Drain the Jerusalem artichokes, mix them with the scallions, and arrange in the center. Combine the olive oil, lemon juice, lemon thyme, and salt and pepper and pour over the salad. You may refrigerate this dish for up to 2 hours before serving. Serve on a bed of whole romaine lettuce leaves.

LETTUCE
Lactuca sativa

In the early part of the twentieth century, lettuce was known in California as "green gold." Many farmers made fortunes with the advent of refrigerated boxcars, shipping crisphead lettuce to the East Coast. The public was delighted, and soon the entire country became dependent on distant sources for their salads and other fresh vegetables.

Lettuce is thought to have originated in Asia Minor, probably from one of the wild lettuce types, of which there are more than one hundred varieties. Lettuce graced the tables of Persian kings, Roman senators, and medieval lords. It has been food for peasant and noble alike for hundreds of years. Lettuce was prized medicinally for its cooling powers and was used to tame fevers, liver inflammations, and lust.

Today there is an increasing interest in different kinds of lettuce. Colors, textures, shapes, and flavor all come into play when planning salads. Although lettuce may seem to have endless variation, there are five general types: crisphead, butterhead, romaine, loose-leaf, and stem lettuce.

BUTTERHEAD

Other names: Limestone, Boston, Bibb, Buttercrunch.

Availability: All year, but best in spring and fall.

To prepare: See page 284.

The butterheads constitute a large group that varies in size, color, and general appearance. Their leaves are soft, delicate, and almost oily. Many butterheads are grown in greenhouses, some in hydroponic solution.

Limestone lettuce is not a distinct strain, but an ordinary butterhead grown in water rich in limestone, which acts as a tenderizer. It was first grown in Kentucky, where the water is naturally high in limestone.

The soft, finely textured leaves make ideal cups for holding other foods while they are steamed or grilled. Whole heads can be gently braised in water or stock, as in Spring Peas with Baby Bibb Lettuce, 167.

CRISPHEAD

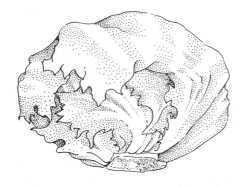

Other name: Iceberg.

Availability: All year.

Peak of freshness: The head should be firm, with leaves showing no brown tinges.

To prepare: Wash. Remove any wilted leaves. To remove the core, whack the stem end sharply on a sturdy table or cutting board. Pull the core out.

Crisphead lettuce is the firm-heading, light-green lettuce sold throughout the United States. On a case basis, more crisphead is sold than all the other lettuces combined. Consumption is on the upswing in Central America and Europe as well. Some dishes, such as tacos, are enhanced by the texture of crisphead lettuce. Like cabbage leaves, the leaves can be used to hold meat and fish for steaming.

LOOSELEAF LETTUCE

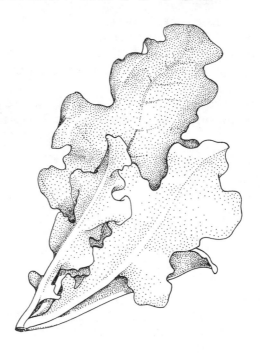

Other name: Cutting lettuce.   ***To prepare:*** See page 284.

Availability: Spring and fall.

Looseleaf lettuces are the most difficult to pack and ship because the leaves bruise easily and break when handled roughly. Until recently, many looseleaf lettuces never reached the market—they were eaten by home gardeners or sold locally. Recently, looseleaf lettuce has been showing up in produce markets, packed as cut leaves along with baby lettuce. This combination is excellent as a bed for composed salads.

ROMAINE

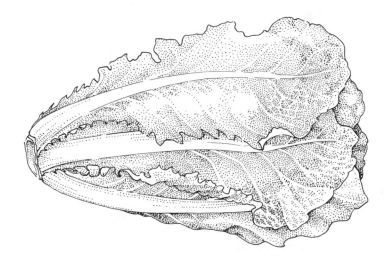

Other names: White Paris Cos, Cos.

Availability: All year, but best in fall, winter, and spring.

To prepare: See page 284.

Despite its name, this tall, heavily ribbed lettuce did not originate in Rome, but on Cos, a tiny Greek island. Romaine is eaten principally in the Mediterranean region of Europe and in the United States. It is exceptionally crisp, yet flavorsome, with upright leaves that close over an elongated heart. Colorful red romaine is appearing now in some markets.

Romaine is excellent in salads with strong dressings flavored with such ingredients as anchovies, capers, garlic, and blue cheeses.

STEM LETTUCE

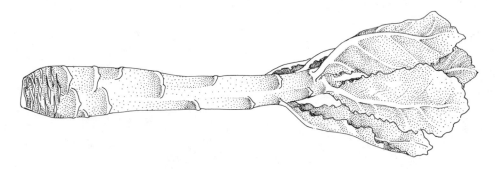

Other names: Celtuce, asparagus lettuce.

Availability: Fall, winter, and spring.

To prepare: Wash. Trim and peel the stalk.

Stem lettuce really should be called "two in one," because both the stems and leaves may be eaten. It grows as a tall stalk with pointed leaves that are ribbed and long, like romaine. The stem is the choicest part of the plant, resembling celery in flavor and texture. Stem lettuce, like many Chinese cabbages, can be stir-fried with oyster sauce or used in soups.

WASHING AND STORING LETTUCE

Lettuce is delicate and will deteriorate rapidly if handled improperly. If you are unable to wash the lettuce when you get it home, spritz it with a spray bottle before storing it in plastic. Better yet, wash it carefully and dry by spinning in a lettuce washer or shaking in a basket. Don't blot the leaves between paper towels, as this action crumples the leaves. Leaves of lettuce should be torn, not cut or chopped, unless specified in the recipe.

Cream of Lettuce Soup

This is a refreshing summer soup that also works well as a first course during winter. The color is a beautiful deep green.

Serves 8 as a first course

2 heads romaine lettuce or
  escarole, or enough endive to
  yield 8 cups of loosely packed
  leaves
1 bunch watercress, stems
  removed
¼ cup butter
1 teaspoon chopped garlic
1 teaspoon chopped fresh
  tarragon, or ½ teaspoon dried
  tarragon
1 teaspoon chopped fresh parsley
1 tablespoon minced yellow
  onion
1 red bell pepper, roasted, peeled,
  seeded, and chopped (page 203)
3 cups beef stock
Salt and pepper to taste
2 egg yolks
2 cups half and half

Shred the greens finely. In a large pot, melt the butter. Add the garlic, herbs, onion, and red pepper. Sauté for 3 minutes, then add the greens and the beef stock and cook for 15 minutes. Keep the soup warm. Just before serving remove the pot from the burner. Season to taste. Whisk the egg yolks and half and half together and add slowly to the soup. Serve in warm bowls accompanied with slices of warm baguette and butter.

Mixed Green Salad with Gruyère, Walnuts, and Warm Vinaigrette

Serves 4 as a first course

10 walnut halves
2 tablespoons peanut oil

VINAIGRETTE

¼ cup olive oil
1 garlic clove, peeled and
  crushed
1 to 2 tablespoons red wine
  vinegar
Salt and pepper to taste

2 cups mixed lettuce leaves (romaine, butterhead, curly
  endive, etc.), torn into small
  pieces
6 to 8 beet leaves
¼ cup Gruyère cheese, cut into
  ½-inch cubes

Preheat oven to 325°.

In a bowl, sprinkle the walnuts with the peanut oil. Bake on a cookie sheet for 15 minutes. Cool to room temperature.

To make the vinaigrette, heat the olive oil and garlic in a small pan until the oil is hot. Off the heat add the vinegar and salt and pepper. Allow to cool slightly.

Make a bed of the greens on a serving plate. Top with the walnuts and cheese. Drizzle the warm vinaigrette over the salad and serve.

Warm Niçoise Salad

A hearty summer salad becomes a cold-weather delight: heads of Bibb lettuce filled with anchovies, capers, and olives and braised in butter and oil.

Serves 4 as a first course

4 heads Bibb lettuce

FILLING

2 tomatoes, cut into ½-inch dice
1 tablespoon capers, drained
24 niçoise olives (about ½ cup)
8 anchovy fillets, chopped
1 tablespoon chopped fresh
   parsley

2 tablespoons butter
1 tablespoon chopped garlic

½ cup olive oil
2 teaspoons minced fresh thyme,
   or 1 teaspoon dried thyme
Salt and freshly ground pepper to
   taste

Wash the lettuce heads carefully and turn them upside down on paper towels. Blot dry carefully so as not to tear any leaves.

To make the filling, mix together the tomatoes, capers, olives, anchovies, and parsley and divide into 4 equal portions. Arrange the filling ingredients among the lettuce leaves. Melt the butter in a heatproof casserole large enough to hold the lettuces without crushing them. Add the garlic, olive oil, and thyme. Place the lettuces in the casserole. Simmer for 3 minutes to warm them through. Ladle the braising liquid over the lettuces and serve on warm salad plates. Top with salt and pepper.

SALSIFY

Tragopogon porrifolius

Other names: Vegetable oyster, oyster plant.

How grown: From seed.

Availability: Fall and winter. Frost is said to improve flavor.

Peak of freshness: Salsify should be stiff.

To prepare: Wash. Trim ends.

Salsify is a delicately flavored vegetable that is primarily grown for its long pale brown–skinned root. It has smooth grasslike green leaves, and may be found growing wild in North America and in and around villages on the Mediterranean. If allowed to flower it produces lovely lilac blossoms. Each seed has a wispy tuft that enables it to be carried by the wind, much like the seed of the dandelion. It grows with abandon anywhere it has been previously cultivated.

A properly grown salsify root may reach 10 inches long and broaden to 1¼ inches at the crown. Salsify has an oysterlike flavor, thus its aliases, above. It can be steamed or sautéed, as in Pan-Fry of Rutabaga with Parsley Sauce (page 80). A lovely warm salad can be made from steamed salsify, artichoke hearts, new potatoes, and vinaigrette or mayonnaise. A purée of salsify would include cream and butter.

SCORZONERA

Scorzonera hispanica

Other names: Black salsify, Russian salsify, Spanish salsify, black oyster plant, viper's grass.

How grown: From seed.

Availability: Winter and spring.

Peak of freshness: *Scorzonera* should be stiff.

To prepare: Wash well. Trim stem end.

Scorzonera attracts the eye more than does salsify, perhaps because its skin is black rather than brown. Yet it cooks and tastes the same as salsify. It is a native of Europe, probably Spain or Southern France. The flowers are yellow, rather than lilac like those of salsify. In Europe the first leaves from *scorzonera* are cut for salads, but since the plant is so robust, the harvesting rarely kills the plant.

The blunt roots are more slender than those of salsify, but they may reach 10 inches long. Add *scorzonera* to carrot or potato dishes. It is interchangeable with salsify.

Sweet Potato

Ipomoea batatas

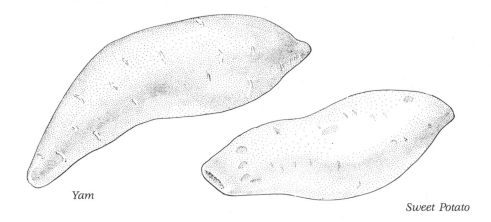

Yam

Sweet Potato

A member of the morning glory family, the sweet potato presents an archeological puzzle because it is a New World plant that somehow traveled to Polynesia long before the time of Columbus: it has been traced to Hawaii before 1250 A.D. and to New Zealand a century later. Thor Heyerdhal suggests that the root was carried two thousand miles east of Peru to Easter Island on balsa rafts, but it is not possible to substantiate that the plant grew there before the eighteenth century.

The Mayas and the Indians of Peru grew sweet potatoes along with corn and other warm-season crops. Columbus took the sweet potato back to Spain, where it flourished. There were originally a number of strains of sweet potato, some starchy, others sweet. The Spanish preferred the sweet types and discarded the stock of the starchy types, thus eliminating a number of strains.

Sweet potatoes thrive in moist, humid climates. The Chinese dry most of their large sweet potato crop, since they don't store well, preserving thin slices by first scalding them and then drying them in the sun. They use the boiled-down starch of sweet potatoes to make noodles.

The sweet potato genus also includes what Americans know as yams. This is confusing because the true yam, *Discorea*, is cultivated in Asia and is not generally found in our markets. Although sweet potatoes are sometimes called yams, American yams and sweet potatoes are distinguished by the color of their flesh—yams are a darker orange. Yams are also a little sweeter and denser than sweet potatoes.

The best-known American recipes for sweet potatoes and yams call for baking or boiling these vegetables. Although they are tasty prepared in these ways, there are a number of other approaches to consider. Sweet potatoes can be sliced and sautéed with garlic and tomatoes or puréed with honey and cinnamon. They can be substituted for kohlrabi in Lamb and Kohlrabi Tajine (page 71).

Other name: Yam.

How grown: From rooted cuttings or slips.

Availability: Late summer, fall, winter.

Peak of freshness: Look for smooth, unblemished skins.

Sweet potatoes and yams do not store well, so use them while fresh.

To prepare: Scrub well. They may be peeled before or after cooking.

Sweet Potatoes with Three Kinds of Ginger

Try this sweet potato dish as a substitute for candied yams on Thanksgiving or Christmas. Carrots can be cooked in this way as well.

Serves 4 as a side dish

4 medium sweet potatoes or
   yams, peeled and cut into
   ½-inch slices
2 teaspoons grated fresh ginger
2 teaspoons grated young ginger
   (if not available, double the
   amount of fresh ginger)
1 tablespoon chopped candied
   ginger

1 cup heavy cream
2 tablespoons soy sauce

Preheat the oven to 400°.

Cover the bottom of a small baking dish with a layer of sweet potatoes. Sprinkle with a bit of each of the three kinds of ginger. Add another layer of sweet potatoes and more ginger. Continue layering until the sweet potatoes have been used up. Mix the cream and soy sauce together and pour it over the sweet potatoes. Cover and bake for 45 minutes, or until the sweet potatoes are tender.

Deep-fried Sweet Potatoes with Cilantro Sauce

This Thai-inspired dish makes a wonderful appetizer.

Serves 4 as a first course

Oil for frying
2 sweet potatoes, peeled and cut
　　into ¼-inch slices
1 cup unsweetened coconut milk
1 cup rice flour or cornstarch

DIPPING SAUCE

3 tablespoons chopped fresh
　　cilantro
3 tablespoons distilled vinegar
½ teaspoon sugar
2 fresh jalapēnos, seeded and
　　chopped

Heat 3 inches of oil to 350° in a wok or deep-fat fryer. Dip the sweet potato slices in the coconut milk and then in the rice flour or cornstarch, coating them thoroughly. Fry 6 or 8 slices at a time until lightly browned, about 3 minutes. Remove the slices with a slotted spoon and drain on paper towels.

Combine all the ingredients for the dipping sauce. Just before you are ready to serve, reheat the oil to 375° and refry the sweet potato slices until they turn golden brown. Drain and serve immediately, along with the dipping sauce.

Taro Root

Colocasia esculenta

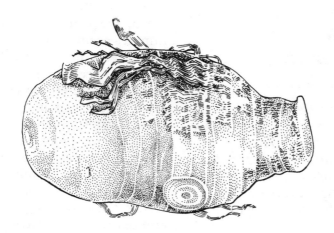

A number of bulbous roots are grown in the tropics as sources of carbohydrates. Among them are taro and a relative of taro, *yautia*, which grows wild in tropical America. Taro is native to Southeast Asia and was carried to China and Japan, where a strain called *dasheen* has been developed. *Dasheen* was taken to the West Indies by explorers in the 1500s.

Taro, and its relatives, members of the arum family, have tall elephantlike leaves and small flowers. It reproduces by its swollen corms—the edible part of the root. Taro, when boiled, yields the Hawaiian *poi* and the African *fufu*. Taro is also dried and made into flour.

Taro resembles the sweet potato in texture, though it is blander. The Chinese cook it with sweet meats such as pork and duck. It can be substituted for sweet potatoes in Sweet Potatoes with Three Kinds of Ginger (page 289).

Other names: *Dasheen, gabi, eddo,* black head.

How grown: From corms.

Availability: Year round.

Peak of freshness: Firm and plump, with no soft spots.

To prepare: Scrub well. May be peeled before or after cooking, according to the individual recipe.

Taro Root Stewed with Duck

This Cantonese dish may not replace turkey and sweet potatoes as a Thanksgiving entrée, but it bears a distinct resemblance to our American classic. The taro root absorbs all the flavors of the duck juices and the accompanying sauce.

Serves 8 as a side dish, 4 as a main course

2 pounds taro root
1 duck, cut into serving pieces
3 tablespoons oil
1 tablespoon chopped fresh
    ginger

SAUCE

1 cup shao hsing *or* dry sherry
¼ cup dark soy sauce
¼ cup Chinese rock sugar

Steam the whole taro root for 15 minutes or until just tender. Allow to cool. Peel the taro root and cut into 1-inch slices. Preheat the oven to 350°. In a skillet, brown the duck in the oil over medium heat and set aside. Cover the bottom of a clay pot or heavy ovenproof casserole with the taro root. Layer the duck on top of the taro root. Sprinkle with the ginger.

Mix the sauce ingredients and simmer them in a small saucepan for 5 minutes. Pour the liquid over the duck and taro. Bake covered for 1 hour and 15 minutes. Serve in the casserole, with rice.

Water Chestnut

Eleocharia dulcis

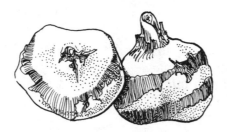

M ost fresh water chestnuts are imported from Thailand or Taiwan, although a few are cultivated in Hawaii and Florida. A member of the cyperus family, which includes the sedges, the water chestnut grows in water, but the chestnuts are really corms, which are planted much like gladiolus. After planting, the fields are filled with water and flooded to a depth of 4 to 6 inches. Within a few weeks, leaves protrude from the corms and reach above the water level. After six months the plants produce edible new chestnuts. The fresh, slightly sweet, nutlike corms are far superior to canned water chestnuts. Water chestnuts are enjoyed for their crunchy texture and are often added to stir-fries with meat and vegetables and are used in salads.

Availability: Fall and winter.

How grown: From corms.

Peak of freshness: Firm tan corms with no soft spots.

To prepare: Scrub well. Peel and soak in acidulated water to avoid discoloration.

Stir-fried Water Chestnuts and Carrots

In areas where fresh water chestnuts are not available, Jerusalem artichokes make an interesting substitute.

Serves 4 as a side dish

½ pound fresh water chestnuts,
    or 2 to 3 Jerusalem artichokes
    (½ pound), peeled and cut into
    thin slices diagonally
2 teaspoons medium soy sauce
1 to 2 tablespoons chicken stock
    or water
½ teaspoon sugar
3 tablespoons oil
1 tablespoon chopped garlic
2 teaspoons chopped fresh ginger
3 tablespoons chopped blanched
    almonds
2 large carrots, cut into thin
    slices diagonally
Cilantro leaves for garnish
    (optional)

In a glass or ceramic bowl, cover the water chestnuts with acidulated water until you are ready to use them. Combine the soy sauce, stock or water, and sugar in a small bowl. Heat the oil in a wok or heavy skillet and cook the garlic, ginger, and almonds over medium heat for 1 minute. Add the carrots and water chestnuts and stir-fry for 1 minute. Add the stock-soy sauce mixture and stir-fry until the carrots are just tender. Serve immediately, garnished with cilantro if you like.

Yuca

Manihot esculenta

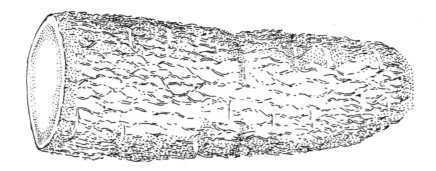

Yuca is almost unknown to most North Americans, though it is one of the world's most important vegetables. *Yuca*—not the familiar yucca native to the Western United States, but the tropical root—is a member of the milkweed family that grows in equatorial Africa and South America. It is the principal starch and sometimes the main source of nourishment in these areas.

Yuca is extremely bland. It looks like a giant sweet potato with a dark-brown barklike skin. It can be eaten boiled and puréed, shredded, dried and ground into meal, or fermented and made into an alcoholic drink. It is used as a thickener for soups and stews, much as we use flour and cornstarch, and it can be made into flat cakes and fried. Americans know one of the products of this root—tapioca—better than the root itself. Tapioca is produced by pushing pellets of *yuca* through a mesh wire and then heating them.

Yuca is not likely to become widely accepted here, but it does have an interesting texture that is quite different from more familiar starchy vegetables.

Other names: Cassava, tapioca, manioc.

How grown: From stem cuttings. Nodes similar to sweet potatoes develop below ground, while aboveground large vines are produced.

Availability: All year in some specialty markets.

Peak of freshness: Beware of yuca that exhibits black mold or greenish-black mildew, the result of prolonged storage.

To prepare: Wash and peel.

A Cook's
Vegetable
Miscellany

Part III

VEGETABLES FOR GRILLING

Many vegetables can be grilled. Some you wouldn't expect would be suitable for grilling, such as carrots or sweet potatoes, turn out to be delicious. An olive oil marinade will enhance almost any vegetable. Vegetables selected for grilling should be very fresh, as imperfections are magnified when using a simple cooking method. Be sure not to overcook whatever you grill. Generally, vegetables are done when they are just soft to the touch.

Try the following:

Cucumbers, peeled and then cut in half and seeded, with a bit of oregano, or grilled with tomatoes and purple onion and then dressed in a vinaigrette.

Baby bok choy, whole, with garlic added to an olive oil dressing.

Belgian endive, whole and cored, alone or as part of a salad with goat cheese, which can also be grilled.

Eggplant, whole or quartered. Well-cooked eggplant can be made into a purée with garlic and lemon juice to be served as a dip.

Fennel, in halves or large slices. It may be blanched first.

Greens such as *bok choy* and rocket and endive can be used as wrappings for grilled fish or meat. Wrap several layers of leaves around thin slices of fish, such as swordfish, which have been marinated in olive oil and your favorite herb. Seal the package with a toothpick. Cook just until the outer leaf begins to char. Remove the burnt leaf and serve.

Mushrooms, domestic or wild, particularly the *shiitake*, cooked whole with a little thyme.

Onions and scallions, whole, or halved for large onions. Remove the burnt outer skin.

Summer squashes, whole or quartered lengthwise.

Snow peas, cooked 15 seconds on each side. Delicious served with grilled sliced mushrooms.

Peppers, both sweet and hot. Cook whole and peel and seed after cooking. Add to grilled tomatoes and onions.

Potatoes, sweet potatoes and yams, steamed or boiled until almost done, quartered and then grilled.

MECHOUI: A SUMMER FEAST

M*echoui*—a traditional North African feast of spit-roasted lamb— is a perfect way to celebrate summer and its bounty of fresh vegetables and herbs. We were first introduced to it by friends in Southern France who did one for a Bastille Day celebration. We arrived before the thirty or so guests and helped set up long tables under the trees. We draped the tables with bright cloths, then put bottles of the local red wine and bowls of home-cured black and green olives down the center of the tables. As the herb-and-vegetable-stuffed lamb roasted over the pit of coals, we sipped aperitifs of Mauresque and Perroquet—Provençal Pernod laced with either almond or mint syrup—and took turns basting the lamb with *harissa*, a hot red-pepper sauce.

It was a memorable occasion: platters of juicy lamb, bowls of rice and vegetable stuffing, fresh garden salad, summer vegetable dishes, and lots of crusty bread shared among friends speaking a mixture of French, English, and Dutch, and everyone enjoying the warm sun and the glowing colors of the Midi. The party continued into the evening as most of us, after naps and coffee, went into the Bastille Day *fête* in the local village. After dancing, fireworks, and toasts, the day ended with onion soup at midnight, served family style in the village square.

Preparing and Cooking the Lamb

THE LAMB

Most meat markets can acquire whole lambs if given advance notice. Ask to have the innards as well as the carcass, and make sure the thin side flanks are left intact. Without them you will not be able to stuff and close the lamb. Lamb is available year round, although during February and March it may be in short supply. A 20- to 30- pound lamb (dressed weight) will serve 30 to 40 people.

THE SPIT

You will probably need to construct your own spit or have it done for you. A heavy metal rod about 6 feet long and ½ inch in diameter, such as iron plumber's pipe, works well. You will need a handle on one end, and threaded pipe fittings are perfect for this. The spit must have two crosspieces 6 inches long to hold the lamb to the spit. Ideally the crosspiece farthest from the handle should be removable so the spit can be run through the length of the carcass. The spit will be placed between two upright posts, where it will rest while being turned. The lamb should be placed about 2 to 2½ feet above the coals.

THE FIRE

The fire should be made with hardwood such as oak, hickory, ash, or mesquite, then allowed to burn down slowly, producing a 4- to 6-inch-deep bed of hot coals. Mesquite or charcoal can be added to the top of the wood. The fire may be built in a 2-by-5-foot pit or in a metal half-drum 1 to 2 feet longer than the length of the lamb.

PREPARING THE LAMB

Rub the lamb inside and out with lemon, salt, and *harissa* (page 302). Insert 20 to 30 split whole cloves of garlic into openings in the meat. Position the lamb on the spit before you stuff it. Lay the spit across the open cavity, centering the lamb between the crosspieces. Now line the backbone with branches of fresh herbs such as rosemary, thyme, and marjoram. Fill the cavity with cooked stuffing (page 302). Put a layer of fresh herbs on top of the stuffing, then cover the top of the stuffing and herb layer with a sheet of heavy-duty aluminum foil, slipping it beneath the breast and extending it inside the cavity by at least 6 inches on either side of the center. This gives added strength and support as the lamb turns on the spit. To fasten the stuffed lamb, use four lengths of plumber's tape. The flat metal bands are much more effective than either heavy twine or steel wire for closing the cavity, because they don't cut into the thin breast and stomach as the meat cooks. These modern techniques work well, although they are not traditional (traditionally the lamb is tied closed with its own intestines, which are eaten as well).

Now you are ready to secure the lamb to the spit. If this is not done correctly, the lamb will slip and cook unevenly. Fasten a piece of galvanized wire securely to the plumber's tape closest to the neck, then fasten the same wire to the closest crosspiece and back to the other side of the plumber's tape. Repeat this process at the hindquarters of the lamb. Suspend the spit with the lamb about 2 to 2½ feet above the fire. Any lower and it will burn on the outside before cooking through.

COOKING THE LAMB

Using a marinade of olive oil, *harissa* (following), garlic, and thyme, baste the lamb as it cooks, using branches of rosemary or thyme as a brush. The lamb should cook slowly so that the skin is golden brown and the meat pink. For small (20 to 30 pounds) lambs, 4 to 5 hours is about right. Larger lambs need 6 to 7 hours. The internal temperature will be 150° to 155° for medium rare.

SERVING THE LAMB

Remove the lamb, spit and all, to a carving table. Remove the plumber's tape and open the cavity. Spoon the stuffing into serving bowls and put them in the oven to keep warm. Remove the wires and plumber's tape from the rest of the lamb. The carving should be done with very sharp chef's knives. A meat saw is necessary for a large lamb. Each serving platter should get a selection of various cuts such as ribs, chops, and slices from the leg. *Harissa* should be served along with the meat and vegetables.

At a recent *michoui* we served the following side dishes:
Cucumbers Stuffed with Tapenade and Goat Cheese, page 126
Black-eyed Peas with Spicy Sausage and Tomato Coulis, page 162
Layered Omelets, page 197
Sweet and Sour Okra, page 234
Grilled Corn and Okra Served on a Bed of Onion Salad, page 99
Macedoine, page 161
Baby Squash in Marinade, page 129
Marinated Snap Beans, page 157
Roasted Peppers Stuffed with Goat Cheese and Garlic, page 212

Summer-Vegetable Stuffing for Whole Roast Lamb

This recipe makes enough stuffing for a large lamb weighing 40 to 50 pounds and serving at least 50 people. You can reduce the recipe by half for a 30-pound lamb. Make the stuffing the night before so the flavors can combine.

Serves 50

4 yellow onions, chopped
Cloves from 4 heads of garlic,
   chopped
½ cup olive oil
2 eggplants, cut into 1-inch slices
Heart, liver, and kidney of lamb,
   fat removed
6 large zucchini, cut into ½-inch
   slices
6 yellow crookneck squash, cut
   into ½-inch slices
1 cup chopped fresh parsley
3 tablespoons salt
1 tablespoon cayenne
1 teaspoon black pepper
5 pounds long-grain white rice,
   cooked

In a large sauté pan or skillet, sauté the onions and garlic in half of the olive oil until the onions are translucent. In another large pan brown the eggplants in the rest of the olive oil.

In a large pot, simmer the offal in salted water to cover until cooked, about 15 minutes. Drain, cool, and cut into bite-sized pieces. Add the onions, garlic, eggplant, zucchini, crookneck squash, offal, parsley, and spices to the rice. Mix thoroughly and taste for seasoning. The mixture should be spicy, but not overpoweringly hot. Add more salt, pepper or cayenne as your taste dictates. Refrigerate overnight.

Harissa

Makes 3 to 4 cups

12 ounces small dried red
   peppers
4 tablespoons ground cumin
8 to 10 garlic cloves
1 tablespoon salt
3 to 4 cups olive oil

Whir the peppers in a blender until they are coarsely ground. Add the cumin, garlic, salt, and enough olive oil to make a purée. (Do not overblend; the peppers should still be in small pieces.) Remove from the blender and mix in the remaining olive oil; adjust seasoning.

THE BABY VEGETABLE BOOM

*I*n the last few years, many of America's finest restaurants and a number of specialty produce markets have begun offering baby vegetables: finger-length carrots, tiny turnips, petite potatoes, even baby corn and every kind of squash imaginable, from miniscule zucchini to cute little crooknecks.

What are baby vegetables? Are they special varieties or are they just picked before they get big? Well, both. Some cooks trim and shape a large carrot, for example, to create a "baby." But other carrots are small to begin with, even when mature. When these are picked at the "baby" stage, they are still flavorful, though immature. On the other hand, the Imperator is a long, slender carrot, and if picked when only 2 inches long, at the baby stage, it will have little color or flavor. Home gardeners should look for varieties that are small at maturity. European varieties include the Dutch Minicore and the French Round and Paris Market carrots.

Squashes, regardless of mature size and shape, seem to have excellent flavor, color, and texture when quite small, from 1½ to 2 inches. Picked at the peak moment, after fertilization has occurred but before the seeds enlarge, squash do not have the watery, bland taste we associate with mature varieties but rather a sweet, intense flavor. Good choices for baby squash are yellow, pale gray-green, or green finger-length zucchinis with or without blossoms attached, golden acorns, yellow or green pattypans and scallopinis, crooknecks, and straightnecks.

Other baby vegetables to look for in the market are purple-topped, rose, or pure-white turnips with their greens attached; 2-inch-long Belgian endives; pencil-thin leeks; pearl onions; and, of course, baby lettuces. Newcomers in the baby market include cauliflower, broccoli, and even cabbage.

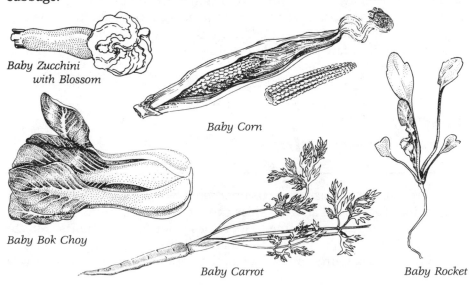

Baby Zucchini
with Blossom

Baby Corn

Baby Bok Choy

Baby Carrot

Baby Rocket

Window Box
Garden Salad

Anyone can grow that delightful mixture of tiny garden lettuces the French call *mesclun*. Spring and fall are ideal times for gardeners living in temperate climates to plant a mixture of lettuces and greens in sunny window boxes or other containers, or, of course, in garden plots.

The traditional French mixture includes at least one of each of the following lettuces and greens: a Bibb, a romaine, a curly endive, a red lettuce or chicory, rocket, and dandelion. You should select seeds from the following varieties: Looseleaf (Salad Bowl, Oak Leaf, or Black Seeded Simpson); red (Ruby or Prizehead); Bibb (Buttercrunch, Tom Thumb, Dark Green Boston); romaine (Paris White Cos); curly endive (Green Curled Ruffec, Broad Leaf Batavian).

Once you've selected the seeds, prepare the soil. It should be light and slightly sandy, if possible, not heavy with clay. If you are planting in containers, use a potting mix from a nursery. To plant your garden salad, take a few seeds from each of your packets in the proportions you want and mix them together. Sprinkle them over the soil, and cover them lightly with a layer of soil. Keep the seedbed moist until the seeds sprout. Remember that each variety may sprout at a different rate. Once they have sprouted, be sure to water them regularly. For a more conventional style of planting, do not mix your seeds before planting, but instead plant each variety separately, then mix on harvest.

For garden salads, the young greens are picked when the leaves reach 2 to 3 inches long. At this stage the flavor is at its most delicate, and the leaves are very tender. Sow more seeds every 15 days to ensure a steady supply of greens throughout the fall and spring. After harvesting your garden salad, wash the leaves gently and either spin them dry or shake in a basket to remove excess water. Toss them with a vinaigrette made from the best ingredients. Shallots are a nice addition to olive oil and vinegar. Garnish your salad with a few purple thyme flowers or blue borage blossoms.

Foraging for
Mixed Green Salads

There are culinary treasures to be uncovered by foraging for salad greens. Vacant lots, backyards, and waysides can yield many seasonal wild herbs and salad plants. The best time to look for sprouts or tiny plants is in the early spring or after a rainy period. Nearly all of these plants have distinctive flavors and textures, and in general a little of each goes a long way.

As you collect you will learn which combinations you enjoy. One of our favorites is a few dark-green bitter leaves of wild chicory mixed with escarole for a robust winter salad. Miner's lettuce, which is mild and succulent, makes a nice addition to tender Bibb or leaf lettuce salads. Miner's lettuce is one of the first greens to appear in California in early spring. Shepherd's purse, with its notched leaves and peppery flavor, spices any lettuce salad, while the strong-flavored yarrow adds soft feathery touches. The leaves of chickweed, an early spring plant, are the perfect size for salads. It, too, is an early spring plant.

If foraging appeals to you, and you are not familiar with wild plants, check with someone else who forages and knows about plants. Not all weeds are edible; in fact, some are toxic. Plants that may be used for mixed garden salads and that are not easily confused with poisonous plants include wild mustards and cresses, plantains, sow's thistle, purslane, chickweed, chicory, the inner heart of cattail, the tips of wild asparagus, and the emerging sprouts of the fiddleneck fern. There are many others as well, depending upon region, but this list is enough to get started on what can be a fascinating hobby.

Edible Flowers for Salads

Many flowers of vegetable plants are edible, and some are delicious. Try bean flowers—especially scarlet runner bean flowers—yellow cucumber blossoms, white-petaled pepper flowers, and large yellow squash blossoms. Squash blossoms are easily handled in salads when chopped into small strips.

Ornamental flowering plants and herbs also provide a full array of colors and flavors for salads. Among the most commonly used flowers are those of the nasturtium, borage, day lily, lavender, hollyhock, violet, and rose. The large flowers—the rose, hollyhock, nasturtium, and day lily—are best used as focal points. Flower buds may be used for both flavor and texture. The cornflower blue of the wild chicory is stunning if used immediately after picking, but its blossoms close up quickly on sunny afternoons.

Blossoms that develop from bulbs may be toxic. For this reason avoid lilies of the valley, tulips, and daffodils, among others.

Herb flowers, such as those of the thymes, marjoram, and oregano, summer and winter savory, rosemary, garlic, and chives are aromatic and colorful. Many of these flowers are small and shouldn't be added to tossed salads, where they will disappear. Use them to garnish composed salads or other arranged dishes. Blossoms can also be floated in bowls of soup.

THE EUROPEANIZATION OF AMERICA: RESTAURANT GARDENS

One of the great attractions for many of us who visited Europe these past years was spending a long afternoon or evening eating country-style French food at little out-of-the-way *auberges*, or country hotels. More often than not, cook and owner were one and the same, and the pâtés, *terrines, jambons*—even the olives—were made right there in the kitchen from produce and products originating on the premises. It was almost a given that the lettuce in the salad, the carrots for the *crudités*, and the sautéed squash and onions were picked that day, probably just an hour or two before serving.

Today, people are talking about the Americanization of France, the preponderance of *le fast food*, and the loss of the old leisurely ambiance so treasured by Americans abroad. At the same time, one might speak of the Europeanization of America. The *auberge*, with its made-on-the-premises *charcuterie* and its garden-grown produce, is one sign of this trend. While not ubiquitous as yet, restaurant gardens are making an appearance across the nation. Some examples: Nora's in Washington, D.C., has its own herb garden at the restaurant, as does Chez Panisse in Berkeley which also has extensive salad gardens, maintained by Andrea Crawford. The Fourth Street Grill in Berkeley is in the process of putting in a large garden. And the New Boonville Restaurant, located in the rolling hills two hours north of San Francisco, is a conscious re-creation of a French country restaurant. The chef-owners, Vernon and Charlene Rollins, have an archetypal kitchen restaurant garden where they grow tomatoes, potatoes, beans, squash, chard, peas, strawberries, apricots, and almost every kind of fruit and vegetable that can be grown in the area. After a slow, leisurely meal, one can stroll through the lush vegetable garden on walkways bordered with herbs and flower beds.

Many other restaurants, though unable to have gardens adjacent to their premises, nevertheless have gardens nearby that are directed at least in part by the chefs. Choices of varieties are made in cooperation with the gardener and chef, and the daily menu is often dictated by what the gardener announces is available in prime form. The Europeanization of American restaurants is perhaps only in a nascent stage, but it is an increasingly appealing approach that will no doubt grow rapidly in the next decade, and has already begun to influence produce buyers across the nation.

GROWING GREAT PRODUCE

A cross the nation there is an expanding network of growers, packers, brokers, air-freight expediters, receivers, and truckers who are, intentionally or not, revolutionizing produce in the United States. In Florida, New Jersey, California, Georgia, Washington—all over—growers small and large are harvesting squash, turnips, leeks, tomatoes, broccoli, even wild mushrooms. They pick the whole gamut of fruits and vegetables when they are ripe—just at the peak of flavor. In some cases, cooling units are in the fields. The temperature is kept at 40 degrees to ensure an immediate chill and to prevent limpness. The morning's harvest is then whisked off to the packing sheds, where the vegetables are carefully washed and then packed in Styrofoam or other insulated cartons, loaded into trucks, and taken to the nearest airport. From there they are air-freighted to big cities and trucked to the wholesale produce terminals. There they are delivered to the brokers who ordered them that morning, or maybe the night before. At the broker's docks, the cartons of vegetables are unloaded, in some instances repacked into smaller units, and then delivered to the restaurants and produce markets throughout the city—and to neighboring cities as well. Sometimes, vegetables picked in the early morning in Georgia are served that afternoon for lunch in Washington, D.C.

This fantastic quality and service does not come cheap. The French, having enjoyed this style of living for years, know that. They spend a large portion of their disposable income on food. Americans are just beginning to realize that fresh, top-quality food, whether in the markets or in restaurants, is not going to be available at bargain prices.

As large farming corporations begin to invest in "quality" farming— new methods of harvesting and packing to ensure freshness—the kinds of fresh fruits and vegetables that used to be available only to restaurants whose clientele could support the necessary intensive hand labor are now becoming available at many supermarket chains.

Americans have a handful of adventuresome pioneers to thank for this happy turn of events. Spawned by the need created by top-quality restaurants for fresh, flavorful food, small farmers began growing esoteric crops to restaurant specifications. Baby lettuce is a case in point. Farmers used to growing huge heads of iceberg lettuce were guided by chefs and knowledgeable produce brokers as to just when the lettuces were the right size for their restaurants, and they were willing to pay a premium price not based on weight. Special European kinds of lettuce and chicories were chosen by the chefs and brokers and then recommended to the growers. *Haricots verts* were experimented with, then grown by the acres. A new kind of produce began to appear in American restaurants and markets. The revolution had begun.

THE NEW GROWERS

More and more farmers across America are raising specialty produce and high-quality traditional fruits and vegetables on tracts of land from three to thirty-five acres. Some of their cultivation and nearly all their harvesting and packing of crops such as tiny carrots, *haricots verts*, golden zucchini blossoms, and yellow pear tomatoes is done by hand. They often endure long hours and difficult conditions so that their crops will be grown in just the right way and picked at just the right moment. Anyone who has tasted the results of their labors will tell you that the extra effort of these growers really makes a difference.

Here are brief profiles of five growers from Northern California who we feel are representative of new trends in commercial vegetable farming throughout this country.

Warren Weber's Star Route Farm is a certified organic farm, a designation of the California Department of Food and Agriculture. Star Route Farm employs six fulltime college-educated workers who are studying organic farming. Star Route's thirty-five acres are located in the coastal town of Bolinas, some forty miles north of San Francisco.

Among other crops, they tend two to three thousand lettuce plants, many of which make their way into Chez Panisse's now-famous garden salads. Two years ago Weber agreed to supply Chez Panisse with a year-round supply of a variety of baby lettuces, all picked at lengths less than 4 inches. "It's a risk to grow vegetables that are in fashion, because fashion changes," says Weber. "But I like to experiment, to take risks. I guess that's what I like best about farming."

Weber balances his experimentation with the bread-and-butter operation of selling his organic broccoli, cauliflower, and other vegetables to restaurants and organic markets.

Lucky Duck Farm in Petaluma produces some of the Bay Area's best baby and standard-size carrots on ten acres of organically farmed land. The farm gets its name from one of its means of pest control: ducks, which feed on snails and insects before the fields are seeded and after they are harvested. Italian red and Creole red garlic, summer squashes, melons, and carrots are their special love. They are currently experimenting with eight different baby carrot varieties to see which ones the chefs and markets prefer.

For the Corwins, getting their produce to market is a job they take particular care with. Most of it is picked and cooled down the evening before the trip to the city, an extra step that maintains the vegetables at their freshest. It is cooled again in Santa Rosa and then shipped with other produce to Greenleaf. Some produce is also sold at farmer's markets in Marin and Santa Rosa.

Bob Cannard farms twenty acres of Sonoma land, growing one hundred different crops a year. With such diverse production he still manages to give each vegetable special care. Cannard grows about five thousand zucchini plants, and he keeps track of the life cycle of each one so that it will be harvested at just the right time. Cannard judges the readiness of each plant by the color of the flower, which changes from golden yellow to a slightly muddy deep gold as the fruit matures. When the blossom barely begins to detach from the fruit, Cannard picks it. Just at that time the flavor changes from watery and bland to milky and delicate. If not harvested immediately, seeds develop, the texture changes, and the perfect moment is lost.

Cannard does almost all the cultivation, picking, and packing himself. He stays as close to nature as possible in his farming methods, even leaving weeds in his fields. "It's natural," he says. "The more naturally foods are grown, the better they will taste. Nettles, for example, seem to improve the taste of broccoli. I leave them there, then plow them under, back into the soil after I harvest."

Cannard supplies a number of restaurants and also sells at farmer's markets in Marin and Sonoma counties.

Lynn Brown and Pete Forni of Calistoga have quickly established a reputation as a source of some of the most varied and desirable produce around. Nearly all of their Charantais melons end up in the kitchen of St. Helena's celebrated Rose et Le Favour restaurant. They grow three kinds of *mâche*, among a number of other crops. Brown and Forni are fascinated by the microclimates of the Napa Valley, which range from frost-free regions to areas where frost may arrive as early as October. They have found more than two hundred varieties of vegetables that can be grown by matching them to the geographically dispersed tracts of land they rent, each usually totalling between fifteen and thirty-five acres.

Dale Coke grows fruits and vegetables on ten acres of land in Watsonville, south of Santa Cruz. He grows tiny squashes, rocket, and golden beets, as well as six acres of at least four kinds of strawberries. Coke delivers boxes of produce to loading docks in Watsonville, from which brokers direct shipments up and down the coast. Through his own broker he learns what the restaurants will be looking for next season. Information like this is invaluable for Coke and other growers, who are always hedging their bets in the risky world of chic produce.

FARMER'S MARKETS AND U-PICKS

*T*wo sources of so-called "exotic produce" are farmer's markets and "u-picks." At farmer's markets, fruits, vegetables, olives, honey, and other edibles are available, all of which have been grown or processed by the individual selling them. Normally a certificate must be displayed by the producer verifying that to be true.

Like produce shops and supermarkets, the quality at farmer's markets varies, and you will need to shop around. Talk with the growers. Most farmers ask a fair price for their fruits and vegetables, and many are more than willing to offer shoppers a taste of a special melon or apple. And it's fun to stand in the sun (or rain) under bright awnings, talking to the people who actually grow all the gorgeous produce. However, it is especially true of farmer's markets that the early bird gets the best buys. Wise shoppers come early, as the premium items are often sold out by 9 am, and it's not uncommon to find people queued up, waiting patiently at certain stalls known for having great tomatoes or the sweetest strawberries.

A relatively new aspect of the American farmer's market scene is the increasing participation by newly arrived Asian-Americans. Newcomers from Vietnam, Cambodia, Thailand, and Laos offer an enticing array of fruits and vegetables, many of which have been grown from seeds brought with them from their native countries. At the stalls featuring Asian produce you'll find all kinds of greens, eggplants, melons, and exotic herbs. Ask the growers about how best to use them and you'll probably acquire some fascinating new recipes.

Possibly even more fun than a farmer's market is a "u-pick." True, along with the fun comes dirt, scrapes, scratches, and sweat. But a few battle scars are worth the rewards of buckets, crates, even sacks of fruits and vegetables you know are fresh, because you picked them yourself! U-picks are farms where you are welcome to come onto the property, go out into the fields, crouch among the berry bushes, climb ladders, reach up into the peach trees, wander among the corn stalks, and generally act out your farm fantasies. Some u-picks require you to bring your own pails and baskets to put your produce in as you pick; others supply standard boxes or buckets. Call ahead to find out the details. What can you pick at a u-pick? Well, just about anything. Fresh black-eyed peas, okra, tomatoes, cucumbers— even *haricots verts.*

To find out if your area has a farmer's market, call the Agricultural Commissioner's office of your county. Lists of farmer's markets are also available from the Agricultural Department of each state. If the term "farmer's market" draws a blank at the department, ask for the Direct Marketing Association.

For u-picks, look in the classified sections of newspapers under listings for food and/or produce.

BIBLIOGRAPHY

Arora, David. *Mushrooms Demystified: A Comprehensive Guide to the Fleshy Fungi of the Central California Coast.* Berkeley, CA: Ten Speed Press, 1979.

Campbell, Mary Mason. *Kitchen Gardens.* New York: Universal Publishing, 1982.

Coyle, Patrick. *The World Encyclopedia of Food.* New York: Facts on File, 1982.

Dahlen, Martha, and Phillips, Karen. *Chinese Vegetables.* New York: Crown Publishers, 1983.

Fox, Helen Morgenthau. *Gardening with Herbs.* New York: MacMillan, 1940.

Genders, Roy. *Vegetables for the Epicure.* London: Museum Press, 1956.

Grigson, Jane. *The Mushroom Feast.* London: Penguin Books, 1978.

Halpin, Anne Moyer. *Unusual Vegetables.* Emmaus, PA: Rodale Press, 1978.

Harrington, Geri. *Grow Your Own Chinese Vegetables.* New York: MacMillan, 1978.

Hortus Third. *Hortus Third Dictionary.* New York: MacMillan, 1976.

Johnson, F. Roy. *The Peanut Story.* Murfreesboro, NC: Johnson Publishing Co., 1964.

Knott, James E., and Deanon, Jose R. *Vegetable Production in Southeast Asia.* Philippines: University of the Philippines Press, 1967.

Muenscher, Walter Conrad, and Rice, Myron Arthur. *Garden Spice and Wild Pot-herbs.* Ithaca, NY: Comstock Publishing Associates, 1955.

Organ, John. *Rare Vegetables.* London: The Garden Book Club, 1960.

Robbins, W.W., Bellue, Margaret, and Ball, Walter S. *Weeds of California.* Sacramento: California State Printing Division, 1951.

Splittstoesser, Walter E. *Vegetable Growing.* Westport, CT: AVI Publishing Co., 1984.

Talekar, N.S., and Griggs, T.D. *Chinese Cabbage.* Taiwan: AVRDC Publications, 1981.

Vilmorin-Andrieux, M.M. *The Vegetable Garden.* Berkeley, CA: Ten Speed Press, 1980.

INDEX

Roman numbers refer to the encyclopedic entries. Italic numbers indicate recipes in which the vegetable can be used as an alternative or is a major ingredient.

ABOUT THE AUTHORS
AND ILLUSTRATOR

Georgeanne Brennan is a historian who lives north of San Franciso with her husband Donald and their two children. They have lived in Provence, France, as well as in Arctic Alaska. Georgeanne contributes her home garden expertise to the specialty mail-order vegetable seed company, Le Marché Seeds International, which she co-owns with Charlotte Glenn. She and Charlotte also write weekly food and garden columns for major California newspapers and are at work on two more cookbooks.

Isaac Cronin is the author or co-author of several popular cookbooks, including *The California Seafood Cookbook* (Aris). His weekly column on seafood runs in several California newspapers. Mr. Cronin lives in Berkeley, California, with his screenwriter wife Terrel Seltzer and their two children. He is working on a new book to be published in 1986, and he travels widely to promote his cookbooks and talk about trends in food.

Charlotte Glenn is a horticulturist who lives on a small farm in California's Central Valley with her husband John and their two children. At Le Marché, she specializes in liason work with market and restaurant growers. Charlotte travels extensively pursuing her research on vegetables and their traditional uses.

Amy Pertschuk is a scientific illustrator with numerous cookbooks to her credit, including two Tastemaster Award–winners for Aris Books, *The California Seafood Cookbook* and *Ginger East to West*. When not illustrating cookbooks, Ms. Pertschuk works for the California Academy of Sciences in San Francisco, and free-lances from her home in Berkeley, California.

Good Books for Good Cooks
from Addison-Wesley

The Book of Garlic by Lloyd J. Harris. A compilation of recipes, lore, history, medicinal concoctions, and much more. *"Admirably researched and well written."* – Craig Claiborne in *The New York Times.* 286 pages, paper $11.95, ISBN 0-201-11687-1.

The International Squid Cookbook by Isaac Cronin. A charming collection of recipes and culinary information. 96 pages, paper $7.95, ISBN 0-201-19030-3.

Mythology and Meatballs: A Greek Island Diary/Cookbook by Daniel Spoerri. A marvelous, magical travel/gastronomic diary with fascinating recipes, anecdotes, and mythologies. 238 pages, cloth $16.95 (ISBN 0-201-19178-4), paper $10.95 (ISBN 0-201-19179-2).

The California Seafood Cookbook by Isaac Cronin, Jay Harlow, and Paul Johnson. The definitive recipe and reference guide to fish and shellfish of the Pacific. 288 pages, paper $13.95, ISBN 0-201-11708-8.

The Feast of the Olive by Maggie Blyth Klein. A complete recipe and reference guide to using fine olive oils and a variety of cured olives. 223 pages, cloth $16.95 (ISBN 0-201-12226-X), paper $10.95 (ISBN 0-201-12558-7).

The Art of Filo Cookbook by Marti Sousanis. International entrées, appetizers, and desserts wrapped in flaky pastry. 144 pages, paper $9.95, ISBN 0-201-10871-2.

Ginger East to West by Bruce Cost. A complete, fascinating reference guide to ginger – its mystique, history, and important role in international cuisine. Includes over 80 marvelous recipes. 192 pages, cloth $17.95 (ISBN 0-201-17343-3), paper $10.95 (ISBN 0-201-17344-1).

From a Baker's Kitchen by Gail Sher. A comprehensive guide to the art of baking. 244 pages, paper $11.95, ISBN 0-201-11539-5.

The Grilling Book by A. Cort Sinnes and Jay Harlow. A guide to the techniques, tools, and tastes of today's American grilling phenomenon. 192 pages, paper $10.95, ISBN 0-201-19037-0.

Asian Pasta by Linda Burum. Recipes and descriptions of noodles, pasta wrappers, and the delights of Asian pasta cuisine. 224 pages, paper $12.95, ISBN 0-201-10833-X.

Antipasto Feasts: Variations on an Italian Theme, with Aperitivi and Sweets by Karen Lucas and Lisa Wilson. Recipes for traditional antipasti, plus complementary aperitivi and desserts to make contemporary American feasts. 120 pages, paper $9.95, ISBN 0-201-10892-5.

Grain Gastronomy: A Cook's Guide to Great Grains from Couscous to Polenta by Janet Fletcher. Innovative recipes for polenta, risotto, hominy, and five other grains, from savory main dishes to hearty breakfast fare to simple desserts. 112 pages, paper $9.95, ISBN 0-201-17952-0.

Available at your local bookstore. Or address orders or inquiries about these or other Addison-Wesley cookbooks to: Retail Sales Group, Addison-Wesley Publishing Company, Route 128, Reading, MA 01867. Order Department or Customer Service: 1-800-447-2226.